ANGLAIS 1RE / TLE

B1-B2

Gaël Manescau
Chargé de mission d'inspection
Enseignant au Lycée Jean Monnet (78)
Auteur coordonnateur

Vincent Aufauvre
Campus scolaire de Coulommiers (77)

Annette Delbecchi
Lycée Frédéric Mistral (94)

Héliette Garcia-Fernandez
Lycée polyvalent La Saulaie (38)

Alexandra Nantet
Lycée Jean Dautet (17)

Gaël Poirion
Lycée Assomption (35)

Yasmine Trouillard
Lycée Jules Hardouin-Mansart (78)

Pages ETLV conçues en collaboration avec :

Géraldine Bazille Freymann
Enseignante en économie-gestion (STMG)
Formatrice ETLV
Lycée Frantz Fanon (972)

Frédéric Gomel
IA-IPR Sciences médico-sociales (ST2S),
Académie de Normandie (14)

Bruno Fériaut
IA-IPR Sciences et techniques industrielles (STI2D)
Académie de Normandie (14)

Chers/Chères élèves,

Soyez les bienvenu(e)s au cycle Terminal !

Hit the Road! vous propose un grand nombre de documents authentiques qui vous prépareront efficacement dans vos apprentissages, vous étonneront et vous ouvriront de **nouveaux horizons.**

Bien sûr, la réussite aux épreuves du baccalauréat est une étape importante, mais la maîtrise de l'anglais, première langue du monde de l'entreprise et des échanges internationaux, est également un atout pour votre avenir. **Au terme de ces deux années de lycée, une belle aventure vous attend, vers les études, les voyages et le monde professionnel !**

Pour assurer votre réussite, **saisissez toutes les occasions qui vous seront offertes :** communiquez en anglais, participez en classe, échangez, lisez, écoutez, regardez des films et des séries en VO, cultivez-vous, osez l'anglais !

Hit the Road to success! We know you can!

Les auteurs

MAGNARD

Direction éditoriale : **Alexia Zoulas**
Édition : **Josiane Attucci-Jan** et **Marie Chochon**
Mise en page : **Philippe Brulin** et **Nadine Aymard**
Couverture : **Primo & Primo**
Iconographie : **Marie-Laure Fior**
Droits vidéo : **Virginie Dauvet**
Droits textes : **Hana Hamrouni**
Cartes : **Légendes Cartographie**
Enregistrements : **EuroDVD**
Chef de projet numérique : **Dominique Garrigues**
Édition numérique : **Lucile Collin** et **Charlène Hugonin**
Relectures : **Lee Smart** et **Isabelle Breton**

Remerciements à l'équipe des Éditions Delagrave pour le partage d'expérience sur les programmes technologiques, ainsi qu'aux enseignants qui ont participé à des enquêtes – leurs témoignages nous ont été précieux.
Merci également à Octave, et à tous les élèves de cycle Terminal qui ont été consultés !

5, allée de la 2e D.B.
75015 Paris

www.magnard.fr

ISBN : 978-2-210-11539-2

Achevé d'imprimer en juillet 2021 en France par Imprimerie de Champagne
Numéro éditeur : MAGSI20210053 - Dépôt légal : Avril 2021

SOMMAIRE

LES PICTOGRAMMES DES ACTIVITÉS LANGAGIÈRES

Compréhension de l'oral | Compréhension de l'écrit | Expression orale en continu | Expression orale en interaction | Expression écrite | Médiation

Axe 1 : Identities & Exchanges

UNIT 1 I AM A SNEAKERHEAD

How do sneakers define our identity? P. 8

Grammaire
Le comparatif et le superlatif

Phonologie
Les consonnes muettes

YOUR PROJECTS LV

Debate: Can sneakers be exhibited in a museum as works of art? OR: Is it reasonable to spend so much money on a pair of sneakers?

ETLV STMG
Create and present your own eco-friendly brand.

ETLV STMG
Make a presentation of Nike and the elements that build its identity.

UNIT 2 CHOOSE IRELAND

What makes Ireland an attractive destination? P. 22

Grammaire
L'impératif

Phonologie
La prononciation de la lettre *h*

YOUR PROJECTS LV

As a publicity agent, design a poster to promote Ireland.

ETLV STMG
Make a promotional campaign to incite foreign companies to locate and invest in Ireland.

UNIT 3 GLOBAL BRANDING

Have American brands conquered the world? P. 34

Grammaire
Le présent simple

Phonologie
La pronociation des diphtongues

YOUR PROJECTS LV

Write an article entitled "The recipe of success" to explain why some American products succeed abroad.

ETLV STMG
As marketing experts, compare how brands adapt their strategies to foreign markets and the consequences it has.

Axe 2 : Private Space & Public Space

UNIT 4 LET'S BREAK THE GLASS CEILING!

How to empower women in the 21st century? P. 42

Grammaire
Le *present perfect*

Phonologie
La prononciation de la lettre *o*

YOUR PROJECTS LV

Nominate a woman from the English-speaking world for the "person of the year" *Time* cover.

ETLV STMG
Nominate the female role model you find the most inspiring.

ETLV ST2S
Write an article about a female scientist and her role in science.

UNIT 5 NEW WAYS OF WORKING

How are today's trends transforming jobs and workspaces? P. 54

Grammaire
Les quantifieurs
Le présent simple

Phonologie
La prononciation de la lettre *e*

YOUR PROJECTS LV

You are the CEO of an innovative workspace building in Florida. Create a commercial for potential employees.

ETLV STMG
You are the HR manager of a big American company. Present the company's new policy concerning the employees' working hours to the board of directors.

UNIT 6 THE WATER GAP

What makes toilet and water access an issue for human health? P. 66

Grammaire
L'obligation, la possibilité
Le comparatif et le superlatif

Phonologie
La prononciation du *th*

YOUR PROJECTS LV

Create this year's campaign poster for *World Toilet Day*.

ETLV ST2S
In a video, present the facts about sanitation in India for an awareness campaign.

ETLV STMG
Present your company to UNICEF to become their *#Toilets4All* partner.

Axe 3 : Art & Power

UNIT 7 BLACK ART MATTERS

How has the art world been portraying America's racial tensions? P. 76

Grammaire
La voix passive

Phonologie
Les homographes
et les mots transparents

YOUR PROJECTS LV

Choose a work of art and imagine the post of a Black Lives Matter activist, explaining why it is important to support the movement and push for change.

ETLV STMG

In teams, choose an American brand and imagine its official statement supporting the Black Lives Matter movement.

Axe 4 : Citizenship & Virtual Worlds

UNIT 8 CITIZEN GAME

How do video games create bonds between individuals? P. 88

Grammaire
Structures causatives
(« faire faire qqch à qqn »)
L'expression du futur

Phonologie
La prononciation de *ea*

YOUR PROJECTS LV

Make a commercial for a virtual world inside a video game.

ETLV STI2D

Create an infographic about A/R and V/R for *Popular Science*.

ETLV STMG

Write an article revealing the business strategies of an American video games company.

UNIT 9 THE WILD WILD WEB

Is there much privacy left in today's world? P. 102

Grammaire
Le conseil et la suggestion
La voix passive

Phonologie
La prononciation de la lettre *i*

YOUR PROJECTS LV

Create a poster to give a list of tips for a safe use of social media.

ETLV STMG

Make a video dealing with the use of personal data by potential employers. Give examples and tips.

UNIT 14 FROM THE MINE TO "IT'S MINE!"

How can we consume new technologies more ethically and responsibly? P. 162

Grammaire
La place des adjectifs
Les adverbes

Phonologie
La prononciation de la lettre *i*

YOUR PROJECTS LV

Write an article titled: "The Life and Death of Your Phone."

ETLV STMG
Prepare a report about an NGO on the issues of mining rare metals.

Axe 7 : Diversity & Inclusion

UNIT 15 HEALTHY FOOD FOR EVERYONE

How can we fight food inequalities? P. 174

Grammaire
Le conseil et l'obligation

Phonologie
L'accentuation des mots composés

YOUR PROJECTS LV

Discuss to agree on the best project to promote a healthy diet for all.

ETLV STMG
Present a brand or a shop which promotes healthy food.

ETLV ST2S
Create a tutorial to advise the population to adopt better food habits.

Axe 8 : Territory & Memory

UNIT 16 INDIGENOUS PRIDE

How can Natives fight for the preservation of their land and culture? P. 186

Grammaire
Le *present perfect*
Le prétérit

Phonologie
La prononciation de la lettre *a*

YOUR PROJECTS LV

Organise a TV show about Indigenous culture.

LV
Present your slogan T-shirts inspired by Native culture.

ETLV STMG
Write an article about conflicting viewpoints on treaties in Canada.

ANNEXES

AXE 1

UNIT 1

I AM A SNEAKERHEAD

How do sneakers define our identity?

YOUR PROJECTS

LV

Debate: Can sneakers be exhibited in a museum as works of art? OR: Is it reasonable to spend so much money on a pair of sneakers?

ETLV STMG

Create and present your own eco-friendly brand.

ETLV STMG

Make a presentation of Nike and the elements that build its identity.

Au menu de cette unité :

DÉCOUVERTES CULTURELLES

- L'histoire d'une marque américaine emblématique : Converse
- Les adolescents américains et les baskets
- Les baskets comme moyen d'expression de son identité (d'artistes américains et canadiens)
- Les baskets et l'environnement ETLV STMG
- La collaboration entre les marques et les sportifs ETLV STMG

OUTILS LINGUISTIQUES

- Le comparatif et le superlatif
- Le lexique de l'expression de son identité, de la fabrication et du commerce des baskets (vente et revente, contrefaçon) et des problèmes environnementaux
- Les consonnes muettes

GET READY!

WORD CHALLENGE

Use as many of these words as possible throughout the unit.
Tick ✓ the box when you have used the word.

- ☐ CEO (Chief Executive Officer) (n.)
- ☐ collab(oration) (n.)
- ☐ collectible (n.)
- ☐ counterfeit /'kaʊntəfɪt/ = fake (adj.)
- ☐ customise (v.)
- ☐ eco-friendly /iːkəʊ'frendli/ (adj.)
- ☐ endorsement /ɪn'dɔːsmənt/ = support (n.)
- ☐ environment /ɪn'vaɪərənmənt/ (n.)
- ☐ ethics /'eθɪks/ (n.)
- ☐ exhibition (n.)
- ☐ fabric (n.)
- ☐ icon /'aɪkɒn/ (n.)
- ☐ iconic /aɪ'kɒnɪk/ (adj.)
- ☐ kicks = sports shoes (n.)
- ☐ leather /'leðə/ (n.)
- ☐ Nike /'naɪkiː/
- ☐ retailer (n.)
- ☐ rubber /'rʌbə/ (n.)
- ☐ second-hand (adj.)
- ☐ shoe company (n.)
- ☐ sneakerhead (n.)
- ☐ sneakers (n.)
- ☐ sole (n.): *semelle* (n.)
- ☐ sustainable /sə'steɪnəbəl/ (adj.)
- ☐ trademark (n.)
- ☐ vintage /'vɪntɪdʒ/ (adj.)

BEFORE CLASS!

A. Watch the video and fill in the information.

	1st young man	2nd young man
Age	....	....
Where they live	....	....
Number of shoes	....	....

www.lienmini.fr/htr7-u101

B. Does the second man wear his shoes? Why (not)?

....

....

....

C. Match the dates with the events they correspond to.

mid 1800s •	• Black urban communities became the new sneaker market.
1917 •	• Goodyear invented the vulcanised rubber sole.
1980s •	• Converse created the first canvas top basketball sneaker.

D. Tick the correct statements.

a. ☐ Both young men are sneakerheads.

b. ☐ The sneaker culture is different from the hip-hop and streetwear culture.

c. ☐ Sneakers are sometimes like art, that is why they are exhibited in museums.

d. ☐ Owning a pair of famous sneakers is absolutely not a status symbol.

e. ☐ They estimate their total expenses on sneakers up to $50,000.

1 A Famous American Brand

How have sneakers become American icons?

1 A history of the Converse All Star

In 1908 in Malden, Massachusetts, Marquis Mills Converse founded The Converse Rubber Shoe Company. Although initially a producer of rubber-soled galoshes[1], by 1917 Converse was ready to venture into the world of basketball, and set out to create the company's first performance athletic shoe. The precursor to the "All Star", the "Non-Skids[2]" consisted of a rubber sole and a canvas upper designed specifically for athletes.

[...] The first basketball shoe was born. Four short years later, American semi-professional basketball player Charles "Chuck" Taylor joined the company as a salesman, and his impact was monumental in every aspect.

[...] Taylor understood the value of good marketing and branding, opting to incorporate the now-iconic All Star logo on a circular patch above the ankle[3]. Taylor's signature was added to the ankle patch, officially creating the "Chuck Taylor All Stars," the first athlete-endorsed signature sneaker, in 1922.

[...] Chuck Taylor All Stars transcend sneakers. Over the past century, titans of culture including Elvis Presley, James Dean and Steve McQueen all, at one time or another, strapped on All Stars. [...] The shoes prolonged influence on not only basketball, but sneaker culture as a whole remains unrivaled. Above all, All Stars have always been democratic, affordable[4] shoes worn by those with taste, talent and a sense of history. Former Chicago Bulls player Dennis Rodman said it best: "Growing up in Texas, I wore Chuck Taylors till they fell off... I was poor. I had nothing, but I felt like I had something in those shoes. They're the shoe."

1 sabots en caoutchouc • *2 anti-dérapante* • *3 cheville* • *4 abordable*

Grailed.com, June 2019

A. Read the text and highlight dates and key facts.

B. Recap orally what you have learnt about this brand.

2 The evolution of Converse

www.lienmini.fr/htr7-u102

3'35 to 5'45

A. Watch the video. Match the dates with the facts.

- **a.** 1970s •
- **b.** 1980s •
- **c.** 1990s •
- **d.** 2003 •

- • Converse became old-fashioned, but it also became a symbol of rebellion in the music industry.
- • New competitors appeared in the sneaker market.
- • Nike bought Converse for $305 million.
- • Nike and Adidas became the top brands.

B. What do all these bands have in common: The Clash; Iron Maiden; Pink Floyd?

....

C. How many pairs of sneakers did Converse sell by its 80th birthday?

☐ 60 million ☐ 600 million ☐ over 60 million

☐ over 600 million

D. Write the two reasons why Converse struggled financially for decades.

....

HELP!

Nouns
- brand
- competitor
- customer /ˈkʌstəmə/
- founder /ˈfaʊndə/
- rival /ˈraɪvl/

Adjectives
- appealing = attractive
- cheap ≠ expensive
- expensive = costly

Verbs & Expressions
- afford: *avoir les moyens*
- appeal
- compete

3 Sneakers: defining your identity

Kamala Harris's preference for non-traditional footwear was first seen last year when she was a Democratic presidential hopeful, and appeared in Converse Chuck Taylor All Stars. [...] Ever since James Dean wore his, Converse has become the go-to shoe for the rebellious and the outcasts. "Chuck Taylors have a long history of being used to convey ideas of authenticity rather than hype," says [Elizabeth Semmelhack, the author of *Sneaker X Culture: Collab*]. Fans have included Andy Warhol, the Ramones, Karl Lagerfeld and Kurt Cobain.

Nick Engvall, the founder of Sneaker History, thinks Harris's choice of sneakers rather than the traditional business attire worn by politicians on the campaign trail could mean she will "appeal to others like myself who feel it makes her more authentic or normal". Jeff Carvalho, the co-founder of streetwear website Highsnobiety, thinks they will "help her connect not only to a younger audience but also to the important Gen X[1] crowd".

Culturally, they are also "a quintessentially[2] American sneaker," says Semmelhack. But Harris's US is in contrast to Donald Trump's blindingly white one, and she is making a statement about the country she represents. A biracial woman whose parents met while protesting for civil rights in Oakland in the 60s, Harris is stepping into a political landscape where, for example, 90% of the Senate is white. As Bobbito Garcia[3] wrote in *Out of The Box*: "The progenitors of sneaker culture were predominantly... kids of colour who grew up in a depressed economic era."

1 People born between 1965 and 1980 • 2 typically • 3 An American DJ, author, streetball player

The Guardian, September 2020

A. **Read the text and tick the correct statements.**

- **a.** ☐ Rebels and people who feel rejected do not wear this brand.
- **b.** ☐ It is a typical American sneaker brand which focuses on authenticity.
- **c.** ☐ Kamala Harris wears these sneakers because they are fashionable.
- **d.** ☐ By wearing these sneakers she wants to be seen as an ordinary person.
- **e.** ☐ She wishes to be connected to young white people only.

B. **Highlight all the reasons why Kamala Harris wears Converse Chuck Taylors.**

C. **Once you have collected all the information, recap orally what you have learnt about the relationship between K. Harris and Converse sneakers.**

YOUR TURN! 4 Prepare a quiz

Test your classmates' knowledge about Converse. Use the information you collected about sneakers (creation; history and evolution; important collaborations; competitors...).

2 Generation Sneakers

How important is the teen market for sneakers?

1 Sneakers and US teens

A. Focus on the "Footwear" part of the infographic and compare the brands: Nike/ Vans – Foot Locker/Converse – Nike, other brands. Use comparative forms.

B. Are they your favourite brands too? Explain why (not). Use the following expressions:

Personally,… As far as I'm concerned….
As for me… I agree (with)/I disagree (with)…
I don't agree (with)…

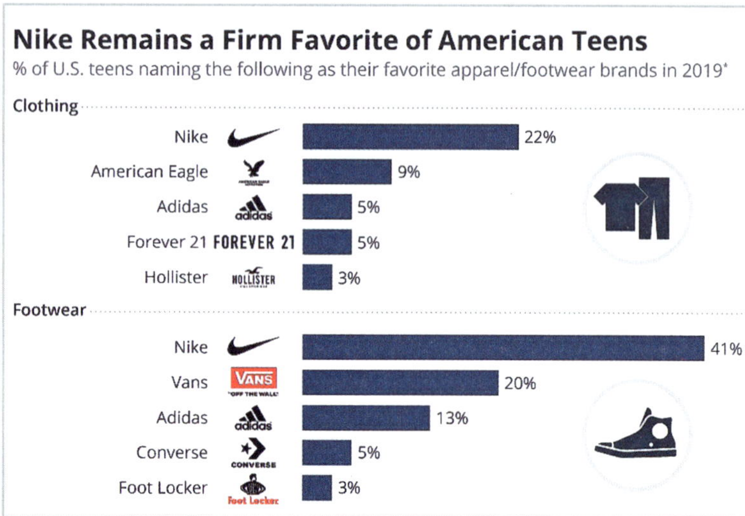

2 The resale market

Angel Melendez […], a self-proclaimed sneakerhead from Humboldt Park in Chicago's West Side, is obsessed with collecting, trading and reselling footwear. […] The deadstock, or unworn, sneakers tucked[1] inside his backpack, Nike Air Jordan's newest collaboration with rapper Travis Scott, dropped online for $175 on April 30. A week later, the resale prices skyrocketed[2] due to their immense popularity and limited stock – almost six times higher than the price Melendez paid. […]

Trading sites like eBay and StockX boost the sneaker's secondary market into a $1 billion business. The once lucrative resale market is now saturated with teenagers due to the accessibility of resale websites and apps.

Melendez has been reselling sneakers as a side hustle[3] since his freshman year[4] of high school. His first resale experience was when he spent his birthday money on Air Jordan 11 "Columbia" […] and resold it to a schoolmate for $40 more than what he originally paid for.

He used the profit to install a basketball hoop[5] in his backyard so he could "get [his] younger brothers into basketball."

Melendez has since invested in the sneaker business, constantly checking shoes' release dates and entering various online raffles. His favorite pair that he won is Nike's Air Max collab with artist Sean Wotherspoon. Melendez wanted to keep the shoes, but the "money talks" and he resold them for a $600 profit.

"It gives me a little bit of comfort with my money," Melendez said. "[The profits] can help me out financially in the next week or two." […]

With extra cash on their hands, these young sneaker-heads are not only using it to fuel their next purchases but also saving up with a goal in mind.

1 *rangés* • 2 *monter en flèche* • 3 *en parallèle* • 4 *seconde* • 5 *panier de basket*

Stitch, November 2019

A. Match words from the article with their French equivalent.

a. deadstock •	• *jamais porté*
b. trading site •	• *tirage au sort*
c. release •	• *invendu*
d. unworn •	• *sortie*
e. raffle •	• *site marchand*

B. Highlight the elements meaning that:

a. You need shoes that never got to be sold in stores or worn.

b. Buy famous collab sneakers when their price is decreasing, then, as the stock is limited, their resale price will increase.

c. Go on resale websites to check on the resale market.

C. Cross out the false statements.

a. Melendez makes pocket money by reselling famous sneaker brands.

b. Prices of sneakers drop when there is a limited stock.

c. The resale market is mostly on the Internet.

d. The resale market is very fluid at the moment.

e. Only adults have access to trading sites.

D. Recap orally what you have understood about the resale markets of sneakers.

3 Real or fake?

Two teenagers discover a secret place in Chinatown, NY, where boxes of sneakers are stored.

"Wow," Jen said. "I know." Acting on instinct, I pointed my phone and took a picture. "Wow," she repeated. I reached out, and my hand glowed in the shaft of sunlight, as if the shoes were infecting me with their magic. The texture of the panels was something I'd never felt before, as rough and pliable as canvas but with the silvery shine of metal. The laces flowed through my fingers as softly as ropes made out of silk. The eyelets[1] seemed to have tiny spokes[2] that turned when I flexed the shoe, using the same effect as those 3-D postcards that change when you look at them from different directions. But the individual flourishes weren't what made the shoes incredible. It was the way they called to me to put them on, the way I was sure I could fly if I was wearing a pair. The way I needed to buy them *now*. [...]

She was pointing at a circle of plastic set into the tongue, where the client's logo stood out bright white and proud. With my brain gradually recovering from its dazzlement[3], I saw what Jen had spotted right away. The logo – one of the world's best-known symbols, up there with the white flag of surrender[4] and the golden arches – had been cut through with a diagonal line in bright red. Like a no-smoking sign. Like a no-whatever sign. The bar sinister, a symbol of prohibition also recognized around the world. It was an anti-logo.

"Bootlegs[5]" I murmured. That was another thing that went on in the shadows of Chinatown. In rows of small, discreet shops on Canal Street you could buy watches and jeans, handbags and shirts, wallets and belts, all with the labels of famous designers sewn onto them by hand. All cheap and fake.

1 œillets • 2 rayons • 3 éblouissement • 4 capitulation • 5 produits de contrebande

So Yesterday,
by Scott Westerfeld, 2004

Canal Street, New York

A. Read the introduction and say what the extract could be about.

B. Read the text. Underline all the words or expressions showing that sneakers are like art or magic.

C. True or False? Find out about the logo of the shoes they found. Justify orally.

a. The logo looks like the McDonald's logo with a white flag on it and a red line across it.
T ☐ F ☐

b. The logo has a golden line across red arches and a white line flag.
T ☐ F ☐

c. It is a famous logo.
T ☐ F ☐

d. It is the opposite of a logo.
T ☐ F ☐

D. Can you explain the meaning of "prohibition" (l. 24)? Do you know any historical American event related to this word? Can you relate it to the word "bootlegs" (l. 26)? Do some research to find out about it.

E. Say how the characters spot counterfeit sneakers. What other fake objects can you buy on Canal Street?

HELP!

Nouns
- copy
- counterfeit /'kaʊntəfɪt/: *contrefaçon*

Adjectives
- genuine /'dʒenjuɪn/ = authentic ≠ fake
- honest /'ɒnɪst/ ≠ dishonest
- reliable /rɪ'laɪəbl/ ≠ unreliable

Verbs & Expressions
- imitate
- manufacture /mænju'fæktʃə/ = produce
- mislead: *induire en erreur*

YOUR TURN! **4 Write an article** BAC

Imagine the narrator is a reporter for his high-school newspaper. Write his article about his experience of discovering counterfeit goods in Canal Street.

3 From the Sidewalk to the Museum

Can a shoe be a work of art?

A new form of art

A. Focus on the photos and captions on both pages. Use the following prompts to describe them:

What strikes me... What I find surprising... I didn't know that... I would never have imagined that...

B. Read the texts. Find out the reasons for these artists' interest in sneakers and say how their art defines their identity.

Artists	Reason for their interest in sneakers	Defining their identity: sources of artistic inspiration
Brian Jungen		
Faith Ringgold		
Virgil Abloh		

Brian Jungen is a leading Canadian artist from Native American ancestry. His artistic expression is based on First Nations identity, on poetry, but also on inequality and consumerism. He graduated with a diploma in Visual Art in 1992, and then studied art history. He uses ordinary everyday objects to turn them into works of art and pay tribute to his Native American ancestry. He was inspired both by watching his relatives recycle objects and by his Indigenous heritage. The artist used Nike Air Jordans to make up traditional aboriginal masks. The red, white and black colours of Nike Air Jordans are the same traditional colours of the Haida, an Indigenous people of the Pacific Northwest coast, with whom Jungen shares ancestry. He has exhibited his work in art galleries and museums, both in Canada and the US.

A mask made of sliced Nike sneakers by Canadian artist Brian Jungen.

MoMA and Vans Faith Ringgold Era Sneakers, 2020

Faith Ringgold is a New York artist born in 1930 in Harlem. She grew up in an artistic environment and later on she studied art in college. She has been influenced by poetry and music. Her art is extremely varied: from painting and sculptures to children's books. She collaborated with, among other artists, the MoMA and Vans to design a sneaker collection: the Faith Ringgold Era Sneakers. Her work also highlights her experiences with racism and social injustice: "My mother said I'd have to work twice as hard to go half as far." This quote is printed on the pair of the Vans sneakers midsole.

Virgil Abloh's exhibition, "Figures of Speech", Museum of Contemporary Art Chicago, 2019

Virgil Abloh is a multifaceted American artist: a designer, artist and DJ. He is the creative director of Off-White and Louis Vuitton men's collections. He was born in 1980. He started collecting sneakers as a child and now owns about 1,500 pairs. An exhibition of Abloh's work opened at the Museum of Contemporary Art in Chicago in 2019. It shows his interests from Renaissance painting to the deconstructed Air Jordans he created for Nike, which he considered as a work of art. According to him, sneakers link you to your childhood and your parents, to your first pair. They stir[1] emotion. He also believes they are part of Black culture. He founded a scholarship[2] to make sure there is more diversity in design, and to open up doors to artistic creation.

1 *provoquer* • **2** *bourse*

HELP!

Nouns
- exhibition
- museum gallery
- work of art

Adjectives
- Native American
- poetic
- unexpected

Verbs & Expressions
- exhibit = show = display
- look like = be similar to
- turn into = transform

YOUR PROJECT

Get ready to debate on a BBC radio podcast. Prepare your arguments and counterarguments!

Choose one topic: Can sneakers be exhibited in a museum as works of art? <u>OR</u>: Is it reasonable to spend so much money on a pair of sneakers?

You will be assigned a team for or against these questions. A jury will decide which team is the most convincing.

4 Giving a Positive Brand Image

ETLV STMG

Corporate ethics and sustainability: myth or reality?

OBJECTIVES STMG

➤ Show how some management decisions meet environmental issues and are connected to CSR
➤ Explain how PLM can increase the value of a product

1 Are sneakers eco-friendly?

www.lienmini.fr/htr7-u103

0'38 to 1'23 — 2'46 to 4'25

A. Watch the video. Match the figures with the facts.

billions •	• century of the sneaker invention
19th •	• people wearing trainers in the world
3 •	• number of pairs people buy per year
23 billion •	• the production of carbon dioxide metric tonnes
313 million •	• number of sneakers produced in a year

B. Reorder the four different steps of the production process.

a. ...... The 65 different parts are shipped to one assembly plant.

b. ...... Each part is mass-produced separately because it is cheaper.

c. ...... The assembly of a typical sneaker requires more than 360 steps.

d. ...... A typical sneaker is made of 65 different parts.

C. Write down two reasons for the workers' poor working conditions.

1 ....

2 ....

D. Tick the statements that correspond to the context.

a. ☐ A pair of running shoes is worn out after six years.

b. ☐ It is easy to recycle a pair of sneakers.

c. ☐ It is impossible to recycle them.

d. ☐ The biggest part of the sneakers is thrown into landfills and will take ages to degrade.

E. At home: watch the end of the document and find out how to improve the sneaker companies' CSR.

F. Recap orally what you have learnt about the production of sneakers.

HELP!

Nouns
- abuse /ə'bjuːs/
- assembly line
- factory = plant
- labour /'leɪbə/ = work
- landfill: *décharge*
- mass production
- sweatshop /'swetʃɒp/
- eco-friendly / organic sneakers

Verbs & Expressions
- customise
- export ≠ import
- pollute /pə'luːt/
- produce
- recycle /riː'saɪkəl/
- ship: *transporter*
- wear out /'weə aʊt/: *s'user*

DEFINITIONS ETLV
- **Corporate Social Responsibility (CSR)** is a management concept that includes social and environmental concerns in business.
- **Product Lifecycle Management (PLM)** is an approach to managing a product from its design and development to its end of life.
- **A production process** is an organised system of activities that contributes to the product output.

2 A second life for your favourite kicks

Ask anyone who the king of custom sneaker design is and you'll only hear one name mentioned – Dominic Ciambrone aka The Shoe Surgeon. [...] Not content with having a wildly successful shoe customisation business, self-taught Ciambrone is keen to share all the tricks of the trade he's spent a lifetime learning with attendees of the Shoe Surgeon Shoe School workshops he regularly hosts across America.

As the fashion industry comes under scrutiny for its impact on the planet, could sneaker customisation be a way to break the cycle of environmental harm? Either way, it's clear that Dominic's wish with his Shoe Surgeon Shoe School [...] is not just to inspire the next generation of Tinker Hatfields or Steven Smiths, nor is it to help bring the next Air Jordan 1 into existence, but to just simply give everyone the tools to be creative and shape their identity in the same way he did. And that's worth much more than any sneaker will ever be.

Farfetch.com, May 2020

A. Read the text and highlight the equivalent for "shoe doctor".

B. Underline the words giving information about Dominic Ciambrone and his activities.

C. What sentence shows that customisation is a way to protect the environment?

....

....

D. Find the other marketing argument in favour of customisation.

....

....

YOUR PROJECT BAC

Groupwork. **Imagine you own a sneaker company, and you are keen on making sustainable and ethical products. What steps would you take? Write down a list of suggestions. Then prepare your presentation to a board of investors. Do not forget to focus on the importance of ethics in your project. You may use pictures to illustrate your presentation.**

5 The Iconic Nike Air Jordan

ETLV STMG

What impact has this successful sneaker had on the market?

OBJECTIVES STMG

- Analyse the ways an organisation implements its communication
- Identify the value produced by an organisation

1 The Air Jordan 1

The Air Jordan 1 is arguably the most important sneaker in the history of footwear. Not only was it Michael Jordan's first signature sneaker from Nike[1], but it was the beginning of Nike's ingenuity when it comes to storytelling. The Air Jordan 1 began as a basketball sneaker, found a second life with skateboarders in the 1980s, launched the retro crazed world that we live in today where new colorways and collaborations seem to release every week.

1 /'naɪki:/

Sneaker History, November 2019

A. Read the text and underline what Michael Jordan did for Nike.

B. Highlight the sentence telling the history of this sneaker brand.

C. Are these sneakers still produced? Why (not)?

....

....

D. Explain the link between "storytelling" and marketing.

2 Athletes and marketing

A. Read the infographic, then explain what a "signature shoe deal" means.

....

....

....

....

B. Explain the role of basketball players in the success of sneaker brands.

....

....

....

....

....

HELP!

Nouns
- advertisement /əd'vɜːtɪsmənt/ = advert = ad
- amount
- consumer /kən'sjuːmə/
- marketer

Adjectives
- appealing
- eye-catching
- outrageous = indecent /ɪn'diːsənt/

Verbs
- attract
- earn
- endorse = support
- launch = release
- promote
- succeed

DEFINITIONS ETLV

Commercial communication promotes a product whereas **corporate communication** promotes a business and its values.

3 Sneakers for auction!

Text 1

A pair of sneakers worn by basketball legend Michael Jordan in his rookie[1] season in the NBA have fetched a record $560,000 in an online auction, Sotheby's said.

The autographed Air Jordan 1s, designed for Jordan in 1985 and the first-ever signature sneakers, were expected to fetch between $100,000 to $150,000 in the auction that closed on Sunday.

Known for selling multimillion-dollar art, Sotheby's held its first auction dedicated entirely to sneakers last year and had then set a world record of $437,500 for a pair of 1972 Nike running shoes known as the "Moon Shoe".

Like most of Jordan's basketball shoes, they are a mismatched pair in a size 13 (left) and size 13.5 (right). The auction coincided with the 35th anniversary of the Air Jordan brand and the screening of the 10-part ESPN documentary *The Last Dance* about the Chicago Bulls and Jordan. [...]

The shoes were sold by collector Jordan Geller, the founder of the sneaker museum Shoezeum in Las Vegas.

1 *(ici) première*

Reuters, May 2020

Text 2

The Air Jordan 1 is credited with kick-starting the craze of sneaker culture in the NBA and turned Nike – then a small company – into a global household name. The sneaker became so popular that Nike continues to release new Jordans to this day despite the player's final NBA game having taken place over 17 years ago.

NBC, May 2020

A. Read both texts and tick the correct statements.

a. ☐ Jordan's sneakers have been sold for a fortune.

b. ☐ Jordan used to play for the San Antonio Spurs.

c. ☐ American fans competed to buy this pair.

d. ☐ The final price was higher than expected.

e. ☐ The Air Jordan 1 is at the origin of Nike's success.

B. Explain Nike's strategy to become a famous brand.

C. Recap what you have learnt about this auction.

YOUR PROJECT BAC

Make a presentation of Nike. Talk about the elements that build its identity, using what you have learnt and your own research. Your presentation will include: the history of the company; the location of its headquarters; its logo; its ethics (production in the world and working conditions of the workers); how sustainable Nike sneakers are (the impact of its products on the environment). Choose a famous American artist or athlete who endorsed the brand (explain your choice).

RULE THE GRAMMAR!

LE COMPARATIF ET LE SUPERLATIF

• **Le comparatif** permet de comparer deux éléments ou plus. L'élément de comparaison peut être omis.

Comparatif	Adjectifs courts et adjectifs de 2 syllabes en *-er*, *-y* ou *-ly*	Autres adjectifs de 2 syllabes et adjectifs de 3 syllabes et plus
Supériorité	adjectif + *-er* + *than* : *Your sneakers are nic**er** **than** mine.* *This brand is costl**ier** **than** the other.*	*more* + adjectif long + *than* : *The production of sports shoes is **more polluting than** the production of T-shirts.*
Égalité	*as* + adjectif + *as* : *My sneakers are **as comfortable as** yours.*	
Infériorité	*less* + adjectif + *than* : *Canvas sports shoes are **less expensive than** leather shoes.*	

• **Le superlatif** permet de comparer un élément par rapport à un ensemble.

	Adjectifs courts	Adjectifs longs
Superlatif	*the* + adjectif + *-est* : ***The oldest** sneakers are two centuries old.*	*the most* + adjectif : ***The most expensive** sneakers are in this museum.*

Adjectifs irréguliers : *good – better – the best* • *bad – worse – the worst* • *little – less – the least*

Remarque : pour exprimer le superlatif quand seuls deux éléments sont comparés, on utilise ***the* + comparatif**.
*Of these two pairs of sneakers these are **the prettier** ones.*

VOCABULARY

Sneakers

Identity

- **display** (v. / n.)
- exhi**bi**tion (n.)
- **i**conic /aɪ'kɒnɪk/ (adj.)
- **snea**kerhead (n.)
- **vin**tage /'vɪntɪdʒ/ (adj.)
- work of art (n.)

Your words: ......

Production

- as**sem**bly line (n.)
- **can**vas (n.)
- **fac**tory = plant (n.)
- **lea**ther /'leðə/ (n.)
- manu**fac**ture /mænju'fæktʃə/ (v. / n.)
- mass pro**duc**tion (n.)
- **rub**ber /'rʌbə/ (n.)
- ship (v.)
- soles (n.)
- **sweat**shop /swetʃɒp/ (n.)

Your words: ......

Environmental issues

- **cus**tomise /'kʌstəmaɪz/ (v.)
- eco-**frien**dly /i:kəʊ'frendli/ (adj.)
- **e**thics /'eθɪks/ (n.)
- **land**fill (n.)
- or**ga**nic (adj.)
- pol**lute** (v.)
- pol**lu**ting (adj.)
- re**cy**cle (v.)
- sus**tai**nable /sə'steɪnəbəl/ (adj.)
- **wear** out /'weə aʊt/ (v.)

Your words: ......

Sales and marketing

- **ad**vertise /'ædvətaɪz/ (v.)
- con**su**mer /kən'sju:mə/ society /sə'saɪəti/
- **co**py = **i**mitate /'ɪmɪteɪt/ (v.)
- **coun**terfeit /'kaʊntəfɪt/ (n. / v.) = fake (adj.)
- **cus**tomer /'kʌstəmə/ (n.)
- en**dor**sement = sup**port** (n.)
- **ge**nuine = au**then**tic /ɔ:'θentɪk/ (adj.)
- launch /lɔ:ntʃ/ (n. / v.)
- mis**lead** (v.)
- pro**mote** (v.)
- re**lease** (n. / v.)
- **re**sale (n.)
- **se**cond-hand (adj.)

Your words: ......

MP3
www.lienmini.fr/htr7-u104

LANGUAGE LAB

1 Match the words with their definitions.

A. sole •	• 1. not new
B. organic •	• 2. approval and support
C. counterfeit •	• 3. the bottom part of a shoe
D. second-hand •	• 4. grown in a natural way
E. endorsement •	• 5. imitation

2 Fill in the blanks with the following words.
shipped • manufacture • mass-produce • factories • assembly plants

Traditional sneaker brands .... sneakers in .... in Asia because it is cheaper to .... there. Then all the sneaker parts are .... to .... and the final product is finally exported to stores all around the world.

3 Use the superlative as shown in the example.
There is not a cheaper pair of sneakers in the world. → It is the cheapest pair of sneakers in the world.

A. There is not a more eco-friendly brand in the world. ....
....
B. There is not a more polluting factory in Asia. ....
....
C. There is not a less talented designer in the US. ....
....
D. There is not a nicer pair of trainers in the shop. ....
....

4 Compare the brands using comparatives or superlatives.

A. Nike is .... sneaker brand on the market. (> big)
B. A pair of Converse sneakers is .... a pair of Air Jordans. (< expensive)
C. The Allbirds brand is .... a traditional brand. (> eco-friendly)
D. Skaters think that Vans makes .... sneakers for their sport. (> good)
E. As far as I'm concerned, all sneaker brands are .... the others. (= polluting)

5 Unit's checkout

You are a visitor at the museum with a friend and you compare the pairs of sneakers that are exhibited. Use the comparative and the superlative.

....

OPEN YOUR EARS!

Les consonnes muettes

Il y a beaucoup de consonnes muettes en anglais. En voici des exemples :
- *l* devant *d* ou *k* : *would, could, should, walk, folk, talk…*
- *w* devant *r* et dans les pronoms interrogatifs : *write, wrong, who, whose…*
- *k* devant *n* : *knight, knee, knife, knock…*
- *b* en position finale : *bomb, climb, tomb, dumb…*
- *b* ou *p* devant un *t* : *doubt, debt, receipt…*
- *p* devant un *s* : *pseudo, psychology…*
- *h* pour les mots suivants : *honour, honest, hour, heir, vehicle*
- *w* pour les mots suivants : *two, sword, answer, whole*

Écoutez la phrase suivante MP3 N°1 **et surlignez les consonnes muettes dans les mots soulignés. Relisez cette phrase à voix haute selon le modèle.**

It is my great honour to present an artist whose effort to make sneakers artworks should be encouraged. No doubt his sneakers exhibited in museums will have the effect of a bomb.

AXE 1

UNIT 2

CHOOSE IRELAND

What makes Ireland an attractive destination?

YOUR PROJECTS

LV

As a publicity agent, design a poster to promote Ireland, and defend it to win the contract.

ETLV STMG

Make a promotional campaign to incite foreign companies to locate and invest in Ireland.

Au menu de cette unité :

DÉCOUVERTES CULTURELLES

- Des sites incontournables d'Irlande
- Dublin et Belfast
- Les légendes, l'histoire et la culture irlandaises
- La fête de la Saint-Patrick en Irlande et aux États-Unis
- Les avantages et les inconvénients du tourisme
- L'impact des films et séries sur le tourisme
- Un pays recherché par les entreprises ETLV STMG

OUTILS LINGUISTIQUES

- L'impératif
- Le lexique descriptif de l'île, du tourisme, de la culture, du monde des affaires
- La prononciation de la lettre *h*

GET READY!

WORD CHALLENGE

Use as many of these words as possible throughout the unit.
Tick ✓ the box when you have used the word.

- ☐ celebrate (v.)
- ☐ celebration (n.)
- ☐ Christianity /krɪsti'ænɪti/ (n.)
- ☐ cliff (n.): *falaise*
- ☐ culture /'kʌltʃə/ (n.)
- ☐ Eire /'eərə/ = Republic of Ireland /'aɪələnd/
- ☐ go on a trip = take a trip
- ☐ go sightseeing /'saɪtsiːɪŋ/
- ☐ invest (v.)
- ☐ Irishness /'airiʃnɪs/ (n.)
- ☐ island /'aɪlənd/ (n.)
- ☐ landscape = scenery /'siːnəri/ (n.)
- ☐ legend (n.)
- ☐ legendary /'ledʒəndəri/ (adj.)
- ☐ myth (n.)
- ☐ mythology /mɪ'θɒlədʒi/ (n.)
- ☐ overtourism = mass tourism (n.)
- ☐ parade /pə'reɪd/ (n.)
- ☐ shamrock (n.)
- ☐ soft power (n.)
- ☐ thrive /θraɪv/ (v.)
- ☐ tourism /'tʊərɪzəm/ (n.)
- ☐ tradition (n.)
- ☐ travel by plane / by car / on boat / on foot

BEFORE CLASS!

A. Watch the video and complete the chart.

Northern Ireland
Capital city: ....
1 other city: ....
3 airports: ....
2 harbours: ....
Speed limit: .... mph (miles* per hour) (around .... km/h) * 1 mile ≈ 1.6 km
Currency: ....
Republic of Ireland
Capital city: ....
5 other cities: ....
3 airports: ....
3 harbours: ....
Speed limit: .... km/h
Currency: ....

www.lienmini.fr/htr7-u201

B. Find the missing information or tick the correct answer.

- How long it is: ....
- How wide it is: ....
- Electrical plugs:
  ☐ similar to France ☐ different from France
- Languages: ....
- Weather:
  ☐ cold ☐ hot ☐ cold & hot
  ☐ can change quickly
  ☐ never too hot or too cold
- The Irish drive on: ....
- Clothes: ....
- Landscapes: ....

....

C. Get ready to share your information with the class.

1 A Symbol of Irish Culture

How did St. Patrick's Day become a symbol of Ireland?

1 St. Patrick's Day in Dublin

A. Observe the photo and describe it.

B. Highlight the elements that you think are related to St. Patrick's Day.

green clothes – sing the Irish national anthem (*hymne*) – 17th March – Christianity – sporting events – heritage and culture – tradition – tribute to the Irish soldiers – the national rugby team – Leprechauns – street parades with floats (*chars*) – Easter (*Pâques*) – official celebration

C. Watch the video and focus on:

www.lienmini.fr/htr7-u202

0'00 to 1'23

a. Saint Patrick ID card:

- Nationality: ☐ British ☐ Irish
- Birth: ☐ in the 15th century ☐ around the 5th century
- When he was 16, he ....
- He converted to:
  ☐ Protestantism ☐ Christianity
- He worked as a:
  ☐ Christian missionary ☐ Protestant priest in Ireland.
- Death: ....
- He became the patron saint of Ireland:
  ☐ at his death ☐ centuries later thanks to legends

b. The Saint Patrick myth (2 stories):

1. ....

2. ....

c. Another symbol of Ireland:

- What? ....
- When did it start? ....
- Symbolism: ....

d. Give as much information as you can. St. Patrick's celebration today: ....

D. Share your information with the class.

HELP!

Adjectives	*Verbs & Expressions*	*Useful expressions*
• colourful • fantastic • wonderful	• celebrate • have the time of one's life = have fun • participate in = take part in…	• in order to / so as to: *dans le but de / afin de*

2 Boston's St. Patrick's Day Parade

A. Watch the video and fill in the missing information about St. Patrick's Day in Boston.

a. People: ....

b. All these people come from:

☐ Boston ☐ Ireland ☐ Wales ☐ all over the world

c. What do these numbers correspond to?

- 1 million: ....
- 118: ....
- tens of thousands: ....

d. Activities: ....

www.lienmini.fr/htr7-u203

0'00 to 1'21

B. Recap orally what you have understood.

3 St. Patrick's Day worldwide

Saint Patrick's Day is unique in that it is celebrated worldwide. It is most unusual that a country has such an international celebration and is really evidence of the generational effects of emigration that has afflicted Ireland for centuries. After the 1845 to 1849 Irish Famine emigration soared with as many as a million native Irish leaving their homes in the decades after the famine to settle in places like Boston, New York, Newfoundland, Perth, Sydney and beyond. The US Census Bureau now reports that 34 million US citizens claim Irish descent. Most emigrants like to commemorate their heritage and thus the Saint Patrick's Day Parade came into being. [...]

The New York Parade is now the longest running civilian parade in the world with as many as three million spectators watching the parade of over 150,000 participants.

ireland-information.com

A. Read the text and find the equivalents of:

a. *inhabituel:* ....

b. *accablé:* ....

c. *monter en flèche:* ....

d. *s'installer:* ....

B. What happened in the 19th century in Ireland?

....

C. Explain why St. Patrick's Day is so popular in the USA.

....

YOUR TURN! 4 Promote St. Patrick's Day

You work for the Cork Tourist Information Centre. Make an oral promotional campaign for the St. Patrick's Day Parade and celebrations for tourists.

2 Irish Tourism Campaigns

How does tourism impact Ireland?

1 The "Fill your heart with Ireland" campaign

Tourism Ireland invited a real married couple from Sweden – who had never visited Ireland before – to take a trip here, wearing custom-made technology to track their physiological responses along the way. The couple was hooked up[1] to covert[2] heart monitors, which were linked to a head-mounted[3] camera that captured all of their experiences. The data provided by these heart rate monitors determined what footage[4] would feature[5] in the advertising.

The result is a campaign that proves the heart-filling effect that the island of Ireland has on our visitors.

1 *branchés sur* • 2 *cachés* • 3 *porté sur la tête* • 4 *image* • 5 *apparaître (ici)*

Tourism Ireland, December 2018

www.lienmini.fr/htr7-u204

A. Before reading: explain the meaning of the title given to the campaign. Choose the most appropriate answers.

a. ☐ Experience joy and love while visiting Ireland.
b. ☐ Fall in love with an Irish man or woman.
c. ☐ Collect and bring back home wonderful memories of Ireland.
d. ☐ Experience Irish hospitality.

B. Observe the photo. Try to guess how the campaign worked.

....

C. Read the text and check your hypotheses. Sum it up in one sentence.

....

D. Watch the video and take notes about the activities mentioned and the feelings conveyed. Get prepared to talk about it in class.

a. Activities: ....

b. Feelings: ....

E. Give your opinion about the campaign. Explain why you like it. If not, say how it can be improved.

....

HELP!

Nouns
- heartbeat /'hɑːtbiːt/: *battement de cœur*
- view

Adjectives & Adverbs
- above: *au-dessus (de)*
- amazing = fantastic
- be surrounded by: *être entouré(e) de*
- completely = totally

Verbs & Expressions
- allow sb to + BV: *permettre à qqn de faire qqch*
- admire /əd'maɪə/
- be amazed = be taken aback
- convey a feeling of...
- fill: *remplir*
- find sth extraordinary
- hug = embrace
- make one with...
- overlook: *surplomber*

2 Pros and cons of increased tourism in Ireland

While we welcome tourists with open arms and are passionate about sharing and celebrating in our culture, it is good to be aware of both the pros and cons of increased tourism in Ireland [...].

CONS

Commercialisation of culture: [...] This occurs when one takes an element of a culture, which is intrinsically linked to its native people, and exploits and exaggerates it in order to be more attractive to and make money from tourists.

Disruption or destruction of ecosystems and heritage sites: [...] as a tourist, it is important to conduct oneself as a citizen of humanity and respect local customs, rules, and the integrity and fragility of ecosystems and heritage sites. This is especially crucial in places like Ireland, where so many of our main attractions are ancient ruins or natural landscapes.

PROS

Job creation: A massive upside to tourism is job creation. In Ireland – a country that was ravaged by the Irish recession – job creation, as a direct result of demand in the tourism sector, was a huge upside to the tourism trade across the Emerald Isle.

An economy boost: Financially, tourism is always beneficial to a country. Regardless of the economic state of a country, a "boost" comes alongside tourists and the tourism sector, as visitors spend money at our shops, restaurants, bars, hotels, attractions, and entertainment venues.

Preservation of culture: Tourism and the money it brings to a country enable local governments to preserve the culture. Heritage sites, museums, and places of cultural and historical significance are often carefully preserved in order to boost tourism. This preservation is a huge benefit of the tourism sector, allowing us to continue enjoying remarkable sites for years to come.

irelandbeforeyoudie.com, August 2019

A. Before reading: choose the correct meaning of "increased tourism" (l. 4):

a. ☐ fewer tourists in Ireland
b. ☐ more tourists in Ireland
c. ☐ fewer Irish promotional campaigns
d. ☐ more Irish promotional campaigns

B. Guess what the pros and cons of increased tourism may be.

C. Read the text and check if you were right.

D. Recap what you have learnt about increased tourism. Give your opinion about this phenomenon.

HELP!

Adjectives
- beneficial /benɪˈfɪʃəl/: *bénéfique*
- detrimental (to) /detrɪˈmentəl/: *néfaste*

Verbs
- allow /əˈlaʊ/ = enable sth / sb to + BV
- benefit from: *bénéficier de*
- boost
- preserve /prɪˈzɜːv/
- risk + V-ing: *risquer de*
- take advantage from: *profiter de*

3 Films Boost Tourism

How has cinema helped tourism to develop in Ireland?

1 Ireland as seen on screen

www.lienmini.fr/htr7-u205

When we talked to *Normal People's* executive producer Ed Guiney in late February, the cast and crew had finished filming its scenes spread across Ireland [...]. "It's a slightly different view of Ireland than – I'm being really ridiculous now – the clichés and the leprechauns and the old castles in the mist. But there is this very vibrant, very unique, modern, European Ireland at play here," he says. [...] "A lot of the images of Ireland that are presented in this show are images of contemporary Ireland, which I think possibly contradict some of the slightly old-fashioned views that people have of the country. [...] We really wanted to give it a sense of the Dublin identity, but without making it look like an ad for the Irish tourist board."

CN Traveler, April 2020

A. **Watch the video**. Focus on the series / films, the places and their characteristics. Fill in the grid.

Film / Series	Places	Characteristics

B. In your opinion, why do film directors choose Ireland?

C. **Read the text** and explain what the clichés about Ireland are according to Ed Guiney and why he decided to film in Ireland and Dublin.

Normal People scene at Trinity College, Dublin.

HELP!

Nouns
- castle /ˈkɑːsəl/
- cathedral /kəˈθiːdrəl/
- cliché = preconception
- county /ˈkaʊnti/: *comté*
- in the west / east / north / south /saʊθ/ (of)
- waterfall: *chute d'eau*

Adjectives
- northern / southern /ˈsʌðən/
- old-fashioned ≠ contemporary / modern
- modern ≠ ancient /ˈeɪnʃənt/

2 Game of Thrones

At almost 90 metres in length, [the *Game of Thrones* tapestry] was created in Northern Ireland with its material sourced from one of the last surviving mills[1] in the country. Around 30 local stitchers[2] spent a total of 1,500 hours to make it.

Kathryn Thomson, the director of the National Museum of Northern Ireland, hopes the tapestry will attract younger generations to learn about the region's history and cultural traditions. Northern Ireland was also one of the main filming locations for the series.
Mark Henry, the marketing director of Tourism Ireland, said the TV series exponentially boosted tourism for the region. "Last year, 1 in 6 visitors to Northern Ireland came because they had an interest in *Game of Thrones*. They visited some of the locations spending nearly €60 million in the economy of Northern Ireland," he said. "When people think of *Lord of the Rings* they often associate it with New Zealand and the last film in that series came out 16 years ago, yet it's still driving tourism to New Zealand today. We believe *Game of Thrones* will have the exact same effect on tourism to Northern Ireland."

1 *usines* • **2** *tisserands*

Euronews, March 2020

A. Observe the picture and describe it briefly. Imagine why this work of art was made.

B. Read the text. Focus on:

a. the numbers and what they correspond to:

b. the reasons why the tapestry was made:

c. the consequences of the series on tourism in Ireland:

C. Explain why Tourism Ireland chose *Game of Thrones* to launch a touristic campaign.

D. Groupwork. Discuss the tapestry tourism strategy. Do you find it attractive, effective, original? Why (not)?

YOUR PROJECT

As a publicity agent, make a poster to promote Ireland in your agency (include touristic places and cultural facts), add a slogan and a catchphrase. Include photos. Present your poster orally to convince the travel agent.

4 Ireland, the Business Island

ETLV
STMG

Why does Ireland have a strategic role in Europe?

OBJECTIVE STMG

➤ Analyse the macro-environmental factors

1 Ireland: Europe's beating heart

www.lienmini.fr/htr7-u206

A. Observe the photo and guess why Ireland is a strategic place in Europe.

....

....

....

B. Watch the video. Focus on the reasons why Ireland is Europe's beating heart, and explain why it can be considered as an opportunity for businesses that want to set up there.

....

....

....

2 Dublin: Europe's Silicon Valley

When most people think about global startup hubs, Ireland may not be everyone's first thought. However, according to Adeo Ressi (CEO and co-founder of the Founder Institute), Ireland is ready to become a thriving center of entrepreneurial activity in Europe, even in the wake of Brexit and the effects it has on the European economy. [...]

Essentially, because Brexit has made Britain a risky region in which to incorporate a company, Ireland now has the chance to fill in the void and serve as a desirable location for start-ups from not only Europe, but also from Africa and the Middle East. With a solid capital market, a talented labor pool, and an ideal tax regime, it's only a matter of time before Ireland becomes another Silicon Valley.

Luckily, Ireland has numerous advantages that make it favorable for tech companies. For example, one of the key aspects of the Irish workforce is its collaboration and, which is essential for building a lasting business. Also worth noting is the surprising number of smart, technical workers in the region, with experience in everything from communications to health tech to artificial intelligence.

Founder Institute, April 2018

A. Read the text and explain the choice of the title "Silicon Valley". Underline examples in the text.

....

....

B. Find the equivalents of the following words.

a. *plaque tournante :* ....

b. *prospère :* ....

c. *à la suite de :* ....

d. *le vide :* ....

e. *main-d'œuvre (2 noms) :* ....

f. *durable :* ....

C. True or False? Justify orally with keywords.

a. Ireland will never be a global start-up hub.
T ☐ F ☐

b. Adeo Ressi thinks that Ireland is a land of opportunities for companies.
T ☐ F ☐

c. Ireland will benefit from Brexit.
T ☐ F ☐

d. Ireland can be seen as an ideal place for Europeans only.
T ☐ F ☐

e. Its main assets (*atouts*) are its tax regime and talented workforce.
T ☐ F ☐

3 Ireland's iconic tax

Text 1

Ireland's headline 12.5% corporate tax rate – much lower than most industrialized nations – has been key to attracting many multinationals to the country, especially among tech giants with Apple, Google and Facebook having presences in the EU nation.

CNBC, November 2020

Text 2

DUBLIN – When a top EU court ruled[1] in favor of Apple in its tax dispute with the European Commission, there was a collective sigh of relief[2] among much of Ireland's business community.

In July, the court backed Apple and Ireland in their appeal[3] against a 2016 verdict that the iPhone maker must pay 13 billion euros ($15.5 billion) in back taxes[4]. Another appeal is still possible, but a decision in the other direction could have had severe consequences for Ireland's ability to attract multinational firms.

Foreign direct investment, or FDI, has been a major cog[5] of Ireland's industrial development strategy for decades, influenced heavily by the low corporate tax rate[6] of 12.5%.

"Obviously it was a huge relief to the Irish government and definitely there was a sense of victory and triumph in terms of taking on what was regarded as an overreach[7] by the EU commission," Lucinda Creighton, a former Irish minister of state for European Affairs, told CNBC.

1 *ici, prononcer un jugement* • **2** *soulagement* • **3** *appel* • **4** taxes that are due • **5** *rouage* • **6** *taux d'imposition des entreprises* • **7** *abus de pouvoir*

CNBC, September 2020

A. Read Text 1 and highlight the reasons why multinationals settle in Ireland. In your own words explain if it has positive or negative impacts on companies.

....

....

....

....

....

B. Read Text 2 and tick the correct statements.

a. ☐ The European Commission wanted Apple to pay 13 billion euros.

b. ☐ Ireland blamed Apple for not paying its taxes.

c. ☐ The EU court supported Apple and Ireland.

d. ☐ The Irish government was relieved and considered it a victory.

e. ☐ Both foreign direct investment and the low corporate tax rate explain Ireland's industrial development.

C. Recap orally what you have learnt about corporate taxes in Ireland.

HELP!

DEFINITIONS ETLV

- The **PESTEL analysis** is a tool used to analyse and evaluate the **macro-environmental factors** (political, economic, social, technological, ecological and legal = PESTEL) that may have positive or negative impacts on an organisation's performance.
- A **tax rate** is a percentage at which a corporation is taxed.

YOUR PROJECT BAC

The Irish government is launching a promotional campaign to incite foreign companies to locate and invest in Ireland. You are in charge of the campaign.

Step 1: First, present, as an example, a famous company from the English-speaking world that is located in Ireland and explain the reason(s) why the CEO has chosen to invest there.

Step 2: Using what you have learnt about Ireland and all the information that you may have gathered on the Internet, present the advantages of doing business in Ireland.

RULE THE GRAMMAR!

L'IMPÉRATIF

• Emploi

On emploie l'impératif pour donner des consignes, des recommandations, faire des suggestions, des requêtes ou donner des ordres.

• Formation

À la 2e personne : l'impératif a une seule forme : on utilise la base verbale (le verbe sans *to*).

__Choose__ Ireland! __Come__ and __visit__ our country!

À la 1re personne du pluriel et à la 3e personne : on utilise *let* + pronom *us* / *him* / *her* / *them* + verbe.

__Let's (Let us) go__ and __see__ the Cliffs of Moher!

__Let her take__ a trip to Ireland next summer!

__Let them go__ to Saint Patrick's Day Parade.

À la forme négative :

– *Do* + *not* + BV + complément : *__Do not (Don't) forget__ to visit Belfast!*

– *Let's* + *not* + BV + complément : *__Let's not visit__ Cork today.*

VOCABULARY

Ireland

The island /'aɪlənd/

- castle (n.)
- cathedral /kə'θiːdrəl/ (n.)
- cliff (n.)
- **Eire** /'eərə/ = Republic of **I**reland /'aɪələnd/
- hill (n.)
- in the west /east /north / south /saʊθ/ (of)
- **la**ndscape = sce**n**ery /'siːnəri/ (n.)
- **nor**thern / **sou**thern /'sʌðən/ (adj.)
- **wa**terfall (n.)

Your words: ....

Business

- **be**nefit from (v.)
- **boo**ming (adj.)
- boost (v.)
- **cor**porate tax rate (n.)
- hub (n.)
- in**vest** (v.)
- soft **po**wer (n.)
- **se**ttle (v.)
- thrive /θraɪv/ (v.)

Your words: ....

Culture

- **ce**lebrate (v.)
- cele**bra**tion (n.)
- Christi**a**nity (n.)
- **I**rishness (n.)
- **le**gend (n.)
- pa**rade** (n.)
- Saint **Pa**trick's Day
- **sham**rock (n.)
- wear green

Your words: ....

Tourism

- ad**mire** /əd'maɪə/(v.)
- be a**mazed** = be taken a**back** (adj.)
- **cli**ché = precon**cep**tion (n.)
- con**vey** a **fee**ling
- fan**tas**tic = a**ma**zing (adj.)
- fill your heart with
- go **hi**king / hike (v.)
- go on / take a trip
- go **sight**seeing
- have the time of your life
- **heart**beat (n.)
- **he**ritage /'herɪtɪdʒ/ site (n.)
- over**tou**rism = mass **tou**rism /'tʊərɪzəm/ (n.)
- **tra**vel by plane / by car / on boat / on foot
- **won**derful (adj.)

Your words: ....

MP3
www.lienmini.fr/htr7-u207

LANGUAGE LAB

1 Match the beginning of the sentence with its end.

A. Please, … •
B. Let's… •
C. Drive… •
D. Let's not… •

• 1. … forget to visit the Connemara region. It's really worth it!
• 2. … along the Wild Atlantic Way! It's an amazing experience!
• 3. … come to Galway with me. You will not regret it!
• 4. … take the next flight to Cork. The ticket is really cheap!

2 Complete the sentences with the correct words.

wear • corporate tax rate • mass tourism • celebrate • heritage • booming • settle • attractive

A. On Saint Patrick's Day, Irish people all over the world .... green and .... !
B. Foreign companies .... in Ireland because the .... is the lowest in Europe.
C. Ireland may become Europe's Silicon Valley because of its .... and .... economy.
D. .... risks destroying ecosystems and .... sites.

3 Make imperative sentences. Use the verb and the pronoun in the brackets.

A. *(wear – we)* green clothes on Saint Patrick's Day, we will have fun!
....
B. *(not forget – you)* to bring me back a present from Dublin.
....
C. *(open – you)* your eyes! The view is wonderful!
....
D. *(not invest – we)* in this company. It is a risky business!
....

4 Cross the odd word out. Justify your choice briefly.

A. cathedral – cliff – landscape – waterfall – hill
B. parade – celebrate – wear green – shamrock – hike
C. boost – go sightseeing – tax rate – invest – settle
D. fantastic – wonderful – amazing – horrendous

5 Unit's checkout

Imagine this young woman wants to invite her friends to celebrate St. Patrick's Day in Ireland. Use the imperative.

....

OPEN YOUR EARS!

La prononciation de la lettre *h*

Entraînez-vous à prononcer la lettre *h* en suivant les indications données. Vérifiez à l'écoute.

1. En anglais, la lettre ***h*** est le plus souvent prononcée en expirant de l'air. **MP3 N°2**
heritage • heart • hug • hike • heartbeat
2. Les mots suivants sont des exceptions. Le ***h*** est muet, c'est-à-dire qu'il ne se prononce pas. **MP3 N°3**
hour • heir (héritier) *• honest • honour*
3. Dans certaines phrases, le ***h*** est peu prononcé (forme faible), on fait la liaison avec la syllabe du mot précédent. **MP3 N°4**
Give (h)im the touristic guide. • Tell (h)er what to visit. • Tell (h)im to go to Dublin.

AXE 1

UNIT 3

GLOBAL BRANDING

Have American brands conquered the world?

YOUR PROJECTS

LV

Write an article entitled "The recipe of success" to explain why some American products succeed abroad.

ETLV STMG

As marketing experts, compare how brands adapt their strategies to foreign markets and the consequences it has.

Au menu de cette unité :

DÉCOUVERTES CULTURELLES

- L'influence de la culture américaine à l'étranger
- L'adaptation de marques américaines aux cultures locales
- Des marques américaines implantées sur le marché mondial et leur impact local
- Les échecs d'implantation de marques américaines en Australie et en Inde ETLV STMG

OUTILS LINGUISTIQUES

- Le présent simple
- Le lexique de la mondialisation et du marketing
- La prononciation des diphtongues

GET READY!

WORD CHALLENGE

Use as many of these words as possible throughout the unit.
Tick ✓ the box when you have used the word.

- ☐ abroad = foreign /'fɒrɪn/ (adj.)
- ☐ accommodation /əkɒmə'deɪʃən/ (n.)
- ☐ appealing /ə'piːlɪŋ/ = attractive (adj.)
- ☐ belong to sb / sth (v.)
- ☐ bonds = links (n.)
- ☐ boundary /'baʊndəri/ = frontier (n.)
- ☐ consumer = buyer (n.)
- ☐ consumerism (n.)
- ☐ cross cultural /'kʌltʃərəl/ (adj.)
- ☐ customer /'kʌstəmə/ = client /'klaɪənt/ (n.)
- ☐ eco-friendly /iːkəʊ'frendli/ (adj.)
- ☐ efficient /ɪ'fɪʃənt/ = capable (adj.)
- ☐ empathy /'empəθi/ = care (n.)
- ☐ expand = enlarge (v.)
- ☐ global ≠ local (adj.)
- ☐ habits = routine (n.)
- ☐ host ≠ guest (n.)
- ☐ increase ≠ decrease (v.)
- ☐ localise /'ləʊkəlaɪz/ (v.)
- ☐ loyal /'lɔɪəl/ = faithful (adj.)
- ☐ outlet = factory shop (n.)
- ☐ go overseas = go abroad (v.)
- ☐ settle = establish (v.)
- ☐ store = shop (n.)
- ☐ taste = flavour (n.)
- ☐ thrive /θraɪv/ (v.): *prospérer*

BEFORE CLASS!

A. <u>Before watching</u>: name five American brands you expect to hear about.

www.lienmini.fr/htr7-u301

B. <u>Watch the video</u>. Then answer these questions:

a. What brands were actually mentioned?
Circle the right answers.

Amazon	Colgate	Google
Microsoft	Apple	Disney
Instagram	Tesla	Coca-Cola
Facebook	McDonald's	YouTube

b. Out of the 100 brands, how many are American?

C. Why have American companies been so successful? Recap.

1 Global American Brands

What made brands go from local to global?

1 Coca-Cola, a universal brand

A. **Read the text and underline what makes Coca-Cola a typically American brand.**

B. **Highlight what Coca-Cola did to settle in foreign countries.**

C. **True or False? Justify your answer by circling a quote from the text.**

a. Coca-Cola makes money principally overseas.

T ☐ F ☐

b. Thanks to Coca-Cola, America is more accepted globally.

T ☐ F ☐

c. Coca-Cola is established all over the world.

T ☐ F ☐

D. **In a 1-minute presentation, explain why Coca-Cola is successful worldwide.**

Since the birth of Coca-Cola in 1886, Coca-Cola has grown from small beginnings in Atlanta to becoming the World's most valuable brand. [...] With its push for global reach, Coca-Cola now operates in over 200 countries [...]

Currently, over 70% of Coca-Cola's business income is generated from non-US sources, however, Coca-Cola has always remained true to its roots as an American product, closely linked with the comfort and leisure that has been related to the lifestyle of an American.

The executives at Coca-Cola share the core conviction that the drink would be universally welcomed and celebrated abroad. This conviction which ushered in[1] a large-scale corporate restructuring and global expansion during the first part of the 20th century. The story of Coca-Cola's global expansion and the company's celebration as the model of American corporate success in globalization during the 20th century has its roots in WWII. In 1940, General Dwight Eisenhower requested a shipment[2] of 3 million filled bottles of Coca-Cola and equipment and materials for filling 20,000 bottles per day [...]. Not only did big profit ensue[3] from war-time sales, the company's greatest benefit came from introducing Coca-Cola to new countries with new buyers. Coca-Cola employees remained on location even post war. [...]

By the 1960s, Coca-Cola had a presence in over 110 countries and this earned not only Coca-cola but America a fond presence around the world. [...]

The Coca-Cola Company was successful in securing the highest international presence in the soft-drink[4] industry during the 20th century. Given the current climate of globalization, new technologies have made international business a possibility through remote[5] operations. Coca-Cola is a leader in promoting diversity in the workplace and now operates in all but two countries in the world and has continued to hold a sweet spot in the hearts of people all across the globe.

1 led to • **2** *envoi de marchandises* • **3** result • **4** nonalcoholic beverage • **5** *lointain*

Mixerdirect.com, "Coca-Cola – The drink that unites the world", June 2019

HELP!

Nouns
- consumerism /kən'sjuːmərɪzəm/
- lifestyle
- prosperity
- revenue

Adjective
- mass-market

Verbs & Expressions
- American Dream
- flourish = thrive /θraɪv/
- on a global scale
- sphere of influence

2 McDonald's recipe for success

Founded by Richard and Maurice McDonald in the early 1940s, McDonald's pioneered the "Speedee Service System" – a simple method of preparing hamburgers that used production line efficiency in a restaurant.

The service and the restaurant, which served up simple hamburgers and family meals in a small California town, proved to be a hit. Tired of waiting for hours for their food in other nearby restaurants, visitors flocked to the brothers' restaurant for tasty, affordable food that arrived at their tables in mere minutes. Despite its success, however, it took McDonald's a surprisingly long time to become one of the world's top restaurant brands. The company only filed for a trademark[1] in 1961, describing itself as a "drive through restaurant" and introducing its mascot – Ronald McDonald – in the same year. [...]

Over the next fifty years, McDonald's expanded from a small operation of around ten restaurants into the international juggernaut[2] that it is today. [...]

Today, McDonald's maintains over 34,000 restaurants around the world [...]. Whether you're a health guru or a loyal McDonald's fan, the company's expansion from a single California restaurant into one of the world's largest restaurant chains is undeniably one of America's greatest successes. From corporate culture to ultra-efficient food preparation, McDonald's is a great example of an innovative success.

1 *déposer une marque* • **2** *poids lourd*

SuccessStory, "McDonald's success story"

A. **Read the text. Highlight the three qualities of food sold at McDonald's.**

B. **Cross out the false statements and justify orally.**

a. McDonald's success was fast.

b. The company filed for a trademark in 1961.

c. Ronald McDonald was introduced in the early 1940s.

C. **Describe orally McDonald's concept and origin.**

D. **Use your answers to explain orally why "McDonald's is a great example of an innovative success" (l. 27-28).**

3 McDonald's around the world

www.lienmini.fr/htr7-u302

1'06 to 2'17 — 4'41 to 5'47

A. **Watch the video. Complete the table below with keywords.**

B. **Draw conclusions about McDonald's reasons for success.**

Countries / Cultural specificities	McDonald's offer
Canada:	
India:	
Hawaii, USA:	
South Africa:	
New Zealand:	

HELP!

Nouns
- drive through
- gravy /'greɪvi/ (British sauce)
- production line
- substitution

Adjectives
- affordable /ə'fɔːdəbl/ = cheap
- innovative /'ɪnəvətɪv/
- tasty = delicious /dɪ'lɪʃəs/
- vegetarian /vedʒɪ'teəriən/

Verbs & Expressions
- It is a can't miss! = It is a staple!
- It is mouth-watering! = Yummy!
- pioneer /paɪə'nɪə/

2 The Local Impact of Global Brands

Why do some brands have a negative impact locally?

1 Airbnb's values abroad

www.lienmini.fr/htr7-u303

0'44 to 2'23

A. Give Airbnb's major reason for success (tick the right answer):
"Our business was built ☐ for a purpose ☐ for a good cause."

**B. Describe the founders' story and first experience.
Circle the correct sentences.**

a. They couldn't pay their rent one day.
b. They had nowhere to sleep one day.
c. They offered airbeds in their living room to help visitors in their city.
d. They slept in the same hotel room because all the rooms were booked.
e. They also offered breakfast.
f. They also offered dinner.

C. Cross out what is <u>not</u> among the objectives of the platform.
help owners to make money – help the travellers to save money – sleep in a house instead of hotel room – have a more local and authentic experience – make sure you will be close to museums or attractions – forge bonds with the hosts – increase cross-cultural empathy – decrease cross-cultural boundaries

D. Give the brand's leading value and explain it: "Create a world where people can ...."

2 Not welcome!

Few UK cities have encountered a rise in Airbnb accommodation greater than that in Edinburgh. Scotland's capital also houses many of the country's most popular tourist destinations while its international festival and fringe has become one of the world's foremost cultural and artistic landmarks. According to Airbnb, of its three million or so global listings 6,272, including 4,225 active rentals, are in Edinburgh. These have begun to transform the character of a small city of just over 500,000 people. The Airbnb phenomenon in Edinburgh has led to concerns about the erosion of sustainable communities in the city [...]

The journalist Mike Small is one of the founding members of Citizen, a campaign group seeking to protect Edinburgh from the negative impact of excessive tourism, gentrification, property development and the privatisation of public space. Much of this change has taken place in the shadow of the city's festivals. [...] "Many people have spoken of feeling marginalised and culturally alienated by the encroachment[1] of the festivals into their lives," says Small. "The incidence of unregulated Airbnb and short-term lets has come in the wake of this and wreaked havoc[2] in the Old Town. Old people are feeling isolated as the practice of buying properties for the sole purpose of using them as Airbnb accommodation has risen. "What seems to be driving this is a lust for growth, this being the only metric of value to Edinburgh city council.

1 empiètement • 2 faire des ravages

The Guardian, May 2019

A. Read paragraph one (l. 1 to 12) and describe orally the development of Airbnb in Scotland (city, numbers, reason, consequence).

B. Highlight the main criticisms made by Mike Small about Airbnb in Edinburgh.

C. Underline the locals' feelings. Then summarise why Airbnb is not welcome.

HELP!

Nouns
- lust for wealth /welθ/ = thirst /θɜːst/ for money
- purpose /'pɜːpəs/ = goal = objective
- tourism /'tʊərɪzəm/

Adjectives
- (un)regulated
- marginalised /'mɑːdʒɪnlaɪzd/ = isolated /'aɪsəleɪtɪd/
- sustainable /sə'steɪnəbl/ ≠ short-term

Verbs
- accomodate = host
- rent = let

3 A giant born in a garage

You wouldn't believe that this immense corporation has started out as an online book store based in a garage. [...] The company was founded by Jeff Bezos in 1994, when he [...] moved to Seattle, Washington, where he began to work on a business plan for what would become Amazon.com. [...] In its early days, the company was operated out of the garage of Bezos's house on Northeast 28th Street in Bellevue, Washington. [...]

The company was constantly evolving and opened up to clothing sales as well as magazine subscriptions, electronics, toys, and even kitchenware[1], as it partnered with several major clothing companies to offer 400 apparel[2] brands in its online store. [...]
Basically, in its quarter-century existence, Amazon has revolutionized shopping worldwide. [...] Amazon has become the place where people buy stuff online, regardless[3] of what. Everything is available on Amazon and shipping is done via dedicated and efficient services which run the business to a profit and size maybe even Bezos hadn't dreamt of reaching in 1994.

[...]. Amazon has announced that we will be seeing drone delivery soon – the drones will be able to deliver 5lb packages within a 15-mile radius in 30 minutes. They hope that the drones will reduce the company's environmental impact by encouraging people to stay home.

1 *ustensiles de cuisine* • **2** clothes • **3** without paying attention

Ad-Lister, "Amazon – The success story of the century"

A. Look at the picture. Describe it orally and deduce the cartoonist's message. Use these words for help:
Jeff Bezos – armchair – piggy-bank – drones – deliver – denounce – control.

B. Read the text and underline what refers to the beginnings of Amazon.

C. Highlight the elements that refer to Amazon's success.

HELP!

Nouns
- international retailer
- selective sorting: *tri sélectif*

Adjective
- eco-friendly /iːkəʊˈfrendli/

Verbs
- discard = throw away
- expand
- start from scratch = start anew

4 From garage to garbage

A. Watch the video, then fill in the missing figures.

a. Packages sent in 2019: ....

b. Plastic packaging used in 2019: .... pounds.

c. The Earth could be covered with this plastic more than .... times.

d. Plastic polluting the world's fresh waters and marine ecosystems: .... pounds.

e. Plastic used by Amazon that was recycled: ...... %.

f. Amazon's customers who are worried about that pollution: .... %.

g. People who have signed a petition urging Amazon to offer a plastic-free choice: ....

B. Complete: Amazon has already eliminated non-recyclable plastic packaging in ....

C. Use what you have learnt to explain orally how worried Amazon is about the environment.

D. Recap orally Amazon customers' expectations as regards pollution.

www.lienmini.fr/htr7-u304

YOUR PROJECT BAC

As a reporter, write an article entitled "The recipe for success" to explain why some American products succeed abroad. (150-200 words)

3 Big Brands' Local Corrective Actions

ETLV STMG

Is it always a success to establish a company abroad?

OBJECTIVES STMG

- Analyse strategic choices (internationalisation)
- Identify corrective actions taken by an organisation

1 Starbucks in Australia

Starbucks, the renowned American coffee company, didn't appeal[1] to the Aussies[2]. In 2008, Starbucks had to close down around 70% of its stores down under – leaving only 23 open. [...] Starbucks opened too many outlets too soon. [...] it turned out to be a disaster because Starbucks didn't give the Australians a chance to get well-acquainted[3] with the brand and develop that "need" and "loyalty." Scarcity[4] increases value – but Starbucks wasn't scarce at all and had too many outlets. Starbucks saw coffee as a product, but that's not how Aussies see it. For Australians, coffee is an experience. [...] The Australian coffee culture is more about socializing and probably less about coffee. Most cafes are run by independent owners, therefore personal bond and familiarity is a crucial part of the coffee culture down under. [...] Starbucks' first mistake was to assume that all Australian coffee lovers were going to like them. And the second mistake was to assume that Australians would like the same sugary drinks that their American customers were used to. Again, it backfired – the menu was too sweet for Aussies, not to mention expensive.

1 *séduire* • **2** Australians • **3** *faire connaissance* • **4** *rareté*

Medium, October 2019

A. **Read the text. Say what happened to Starbucks in 2008 and underline two strategic reasons for this.**

B. **Highlight all the mistakes Starbucks made and summarise Starbucks's experience orally.**

HELP!

Verbs
- backfire /bækˈfaɪə/
- close down = shut down
- expect = assume
- get acquainted /əˈkweɪntɪd/ = get to know
- mistake = error
- socialise /ˈsəʊʃəlaɪz/

DEFINITIONS ETLV
- **Internationalisation** is a strategy that consists in taking over new markets in other countries.
- An organisation must take **corrective actions** when its results are not consistent with the objectives given.

2 Dunkin' Donuts in India

A. **Watch the video. Describe Dunkin' Donuts internationalisation.**

B. **Tick the right answers.**

a. Dunkin' Donuts focused its strategy:

☐ on breakfast ☐ on lunch

b. Indian people:

☐ have breakfast at home ☐ don't have breakfast

c. In the morning Indian people do not want to eat:

☐ fast ☐ sweet food

C. **Tick the correct answer and give examples orally.**

Dunkin' Donuts corrective action was to:

☐ delocalise the production of food

☐ localise its menu

www.lienmini.fr/htr7-u305

0'00 to 0'58 | 1'20 to 2'02

YOUR PROJECT

You are marketing experts. Your managers asked you to analyse Dunkin' Donuts' and Starbucks' strategies on foreign markets and the consequences. Suggest corrective actions.

RULE THE GRAMMAR!

LE PRÉSENT SIMPLE

• Formation

Forme affirmative : sujet + BV + complément(s)

*Big brands **adapt** their strategies to foreign markets.*
*She **likes** McDonald's food!*

Forme négative : sujet + *do / does* + *not* + BV + complément(s)

*Some brands **do not succeed** abroad.*
*She **does not like** the food that McDonald's restaurants serve in New Zealand.*

Forme interrogative : *Do / Does* + sujet + BV + complément(s)

***Does** Starbucks **succeed** in Australia?*

• Emploi

Le présent simple s'emploie pour exprimer une habitude, une vérité générale, une action qui se répète, un goût, mais également pour caractériser une action toujours vraie (*the Earth **goes** around the Sun*).

LANGUAGE LAB

MP3
www.lienmini.fr/htr7-u306

1 Tick the correct form in the following sentences.

A. Every day, Australian people ☐ are drinking ☐ drink coffee.

B. The problem is that Starbucks ☐ sees ☐ saw coffee as a product.

C. Australian people ☐ didn't like ☐ don't like too much sugar in their coffee.

D. Unlike Australian customers, American customers ☐ are loving ☐ love sugary drinks.

2 Put the verbs in the brackets in the present simple.

A. In the UK, people usually (*drink*) tea in the afternoon.

....

B. Indian people (*cook*) spicy food. They (*not want*) sweet food for breakfast.

....

C. That is why Dunkin' Donuts now (*serve*) sweet food as snack and (*not focus*) on breakfast anymore.

....

OPEN YOUR EARS!

La prononciation des diphtongues

MP3 N°5

Écoutez les mots suivants, puis notez le numéro correspondant à la prononciation des voyelles en gras.

1 *gl**o**bal* • 2 *l**o**cal* • 3 *fron**tier** (UK)* • 4 *pion**eer*** • 5 *b**ou**ndary* • 6 ***ou**tlet* • 7 *thr**i**ve* • 8 *l**i**festyle* • 9 *f**ai**thful* • 10 *fl**a**vour* • 11 *veget**ar**ian* • 12 *sc**ar**city* • 13 *t**our**ism*

/eɪ/ (taste):	/aɪ/ (fight):	/ʊə/ (poor): ....
/aʊ/ (mouth):	/eə/ (care):	
/ɪə/ (sphere):	/əʊ/ (grow):	

AXE 2

UNIT 4

LET'S BREAK THE GLASS CEILING!

How to empower women in the 21st century?

YOUR PROJECTS

LV Nominate a woman from the English-speaking world for the "person of the year" *Time* cover.

ETLV STMG Nominate the female role model you find the most inspiring.

ETLV ST2S Write an article about a female scientist and her role in science.

Au menu de cette unité :

DÉCOUVERTES CULTURELLES

- Les discriminations faites aux femmes dans le monde professionnel (Australie, États-Unis, Canada)
- La lutte pour l'égalité hommes-femmes (Nouvelle-Zélande, États-Unis, Canada)
- Des femmes inspirantes (justice, éducation, politique)
- Des femmes dirigeantes ETLV STMG
- Des femmes pionnières dans les sciences médicales ETLV ST2S

OUTILS LINGUISTIQUES

- Le *present perfect*
- Le lexique de la discrimination, du monde du travail, de la lutte pour l'égalité, de la réussite
- La prononciation de la lettre *o*

GET READY!

WORD CHALLENGE

Use as many of these words as possible throughout the unit.
Tick ✓ the box when you have used the word.

- ☐ abuse /ə'bjuːs/ (n.)
- ☐ achieve = succeed (v.)
- ☐ achievement = success (n.)
- ☐ address (v.)
- ☐ be biased /'baɪəst/: *avoir des préjugés*
- ☐ break the glass ceiling: *briser le plafond de verre*
- ☐ CEO (Chief Executive Officer)
- ☐ challenge /'tʃælɪndʒ/ (n. / v.)
- ☐ the corporate /'kɔːpərɪt/ world (n.)
- ☐ do business with
- ☐ earn /ɜːn/ (v.)
- ☐ equity /'ekwəti/ (n.)
- ☐ fight (v.)
- ☐ fix = solve (v.)
- ☐ gender pay gap (n.)
- ☐ gender-based discrimination (n.)
- ☐ hire = recruit = employ (v.)
- ☐ (in)equality (n.)
- ☐ leader(ship) position (n.)
- ☐ mindset = mentality (n.)
- ☐ misogynistic /mɪsɒdʒɪ'nɪstɪk/ = sexist (adj.)
- ☐ pave the way for = prepare (v.)
- ☐ recognise = acknowledge /æk'nɒlɪdʒ/ (v.)
- ☐ sector = domain (n.)
- ☐ skill = competence (n.)
- ☐ stereotype = cliché (n.)
- ☐ torchbearer (n.) = *porte-flambeau*
- ☐ trailblazer = pioneer (n.)
- ☐ workplace (n.)

BEFORE CLASS!

A. Watch the video. Say what the riddle is in your own words.

www.lienmini.fr/htr7-u401

B. List the seven people's guesses. People think of:

C. How do the interviewees react once they are given the solution? Explain their reactions.

D. What about you? Did you find the solution? What did you first think of? Be ready to share your experience in class.

1 (In)Equalities in the Workplace

How can we explain the gender pay gap?

1 The gender pay gap in numbers

The Gender Pay Gap In Developed Nations Visualized

% difference in full-time earnings between men/women in selected OECD nations*

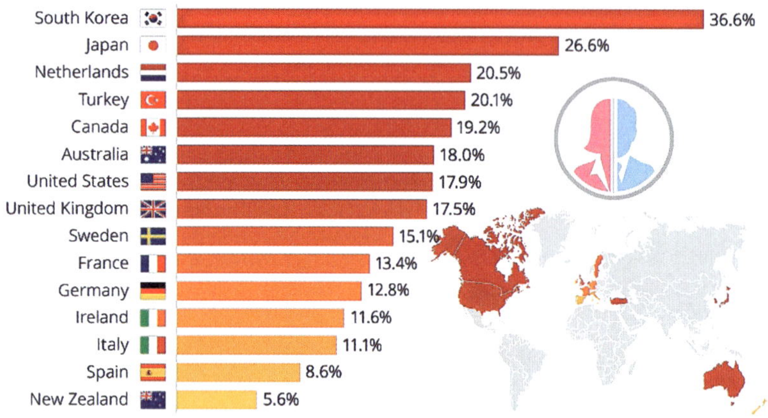

A. Which country among the USA, the UK, Canada, Australia and New Zealand has the highest gender pay gap?

Which country has the lowest one? Answer orally.

B. Imagine what could explain a small gender pay gap.

- ☐ Few women in the workplace
- ☐ The laws in favour of women
- ☐ Most women work part-time
- ☐ People's progressive mindsets

2 The gender pay gap in Australia

A. Watch the video once and say what the lift symbolises.

B. Say what the figure "14%" refers to:

....

....

www.lienmini.fr/htr7-u402

C. Cross out the factor that does not explain the gender pay gap.

a. There are stereotypes about gender roles and in the recruitment and promotion processes.

b. Low-paid sectors are dominated by women.

c. There is a higher proportion of women who are graduated than men.

d. There is not enough flexibility in the workplace.

e. Childcare is an obstacle to female promotion.

D. Comment: why would fixing the gender pay gap benefit us all?

HELP!

Nouns
- **CEO** (Chief Executive Officer): *PDG*
- **childcare**
- the **corporate** /'kɔːpərɪt/ **ladder**: les *échelons d'une entreprise*
- **gender pay gap**
- **lift**: *ascenseur*
- **parental** /pə'rentəl/ **leave**: *congé parental*
- **stereotype** = cliché
- **workplace**

Adjectives
- **flexible**
- **narrow-minded**: *étroit d'esprit* ≠ open-minded
- **prejudiced** (against)

Verbs & Expressions
- **benefit** sb
- **fix / bridge the gap**
- **grant** = give
- **hire** = employ = recruit /rɪ'kruːt/
- **raise salaries**

3 The origins of gender bias in Canada

www.lienmini.fr/htr7-u403

A. Watch the video. Explain the following figures: "$0.87 for $1".

B. Cross out the wrong statements. Justify orally.

a. – Inequalities start when we are teenagers.
– Inequalities start when you are born.

b. – Children are bombarded with false and damaging messages.
– Boys and girls are treated equally.

c. – At 11 years old girls start to think only boys can be brilliant.
– At 6 years old girls start to think only boys can be brilliant.

d. – Only 20% of women are gender biased.
– 80% of women are also gender biased.

C. Pairwork. You are the interviewer, your classmate is Delee Fromm. Act out the interview (in your own words).

Eg: "Delee Fromm, can we say inequalities start at birth or later?" "Well, inequalities start when you are born."

4 The gender gap in American start-ups

A. Watch the video. Find the missing information.

a. Describe the situation in the Pacific Northwest: Out of …… startups, there are only …… women-led companies.

b. Explain the myths about female founders: People think

c. Complete the sentence with a percentage: "Women only receive …… of capital funding."

B. Give two reasons explaining why women struggle more than men in the start-up world, according to the interviewees.

www.lienmini.fr/htr7-u404

0'00 to 2'00

C. Recap orally what you have learnt.

HELP!

Nouns	*Adjectives*	*Verbs & Expressions*
• gender bias /'baɪəs/: *préjugé sexiste*	• biased	• blame sb for sth / V-ing
• patriarchy /'peɪtrɪɑ:kɪ/	• brainwashed (into thinking)	• earn a living = make a living
• self-confidence	• distracted	• shame sb for sth / V-ing
	• harmful = damaging	

2 The Fight for Gender Equality

How do some English-speaking countries fight stereotypes?

1 Equality by law in New Zealand

Unions, employers, and government have come together to develop a fair and sustainable process to guide pay equity claims in Aotearoa[1]. This process is now being incorporated into the Equal Pay Act. [...]

Addressing pay equity means challenging our deeply ingrained assumptions[2] about the value of different types of work. Female-dominated occupations such as nursing, teaching and caring are indispensable around the world. We must recognise and value their skills and contribution. [...]

Globally, women of colour, women with disabilities, and older women face the same challenges of multiple levels of discrimination. If we are serious about addressing inequality, we need to be very honest about who is experiencing the biggest barriers, and make it a priority to remove them.

New Zealand has led the world before. We were the first country in the world where women fought for and won the right to vote. Now we are addressing the systemic undervaluation of work that has mostly been done by women.

1 the Māori name for New Zealand • 2 *suppositions profondément ancrées*

The Guardian, March 2020

A. Read the text and the *Cultural fact*.
Say how New Zealand fights for women's rights.

B. Circle three female-dominated occupations and say how they are considered (one adjective).

C. Underline who faces discrimination the most.

D. Groupwork. Can you think of other ways to achieve pay equity?

> ***Cultural fact***
> The Equal Pay Amendment Bill was introduced in the New Zealand Parliament on 19th September 2018. Under the Act, employers, workers and unions (*syndicats*) negotiate together. It also allows workers to make a pay equity claim.

2 #stoptherobbery campaign

www.lienmini.fr/htr7-u405

A. Watch the video. Take notes and explain the project orally.

B. Describe how people react and why.

C. Say how long it will take to close the gap. What do people do in the end?

D. Give your opinion. What would you have done if you had been one of these people?

HELP!

Nouns	Adjectives	Verbs
• barrier /ˈbæriə/	• (deeply) ingrained	• grant
• equity	• indispensable = essential	• recognise = acknowledge
• robbery	• sustainable	• rob = steal
• undervaluation	• thought-provoking	
• value	• valuable	

3 AOC stands up to sexism

A. Watch the video once and read the *Cultural fact*. Say orally what Alexandria Ocasio-Cortez denounces.

B. Part 1 (0'00 to 1'41): Watch the video again, take notes and cross out the wrong answers.

– Ted Yoho had never insulted any female colleague.
– Power accepts violent language against women.
– Justice regularly punishes misogynistic behaviour.
– An American president and the governor of Florida have already been disrespectful to her.
– Dehumanising language is a strategy to hurt women.

C. Part 2 (1'42 to the end): Watch the video again, take notes and answer.

a. Explain why Alexandria Ocasio-Cortez does not accept Ted Yoho's apology. Underline the right answer.

– Ted Yoho did not really think what he said, because he was angry.
– Ted Yoho does not want to apologise, because he has no remorse.

b. Explain why she says: "give permission to do that to his wife and his daughters".

www.lienmini.fr/htr7-u406

Cultural fact
On July 21st 2020 Republican lawmaker Ted Yoho called Democrat Representative Alexandria Ocasio-Cortez (AOC) a "f... ing b..." and she replied.

4 Justin Trudeau's message

A. Watch the video. Say orally what Canada has been working on for women's rights.

B. Give the other priorities to improve women's rights in Canada. Tick what you hear.

- ☐ gender-based violence
- ☐ access to university
- ☐ pay equity
- ☐ fair treatment with their brothers at home
- ☐ choice of what they do with their own body
- ☐ arranged marriages
- ☐ discrimination against women from minorities

www.lienmini.fr/htr7-u407

HELP!

Nouns
- abuse /ə'bjuːs/
- ethics
- harm
- misogynist /mɪ'sɒdʒɪnɪst/= sexist
- spokesperson: *porte-parole*

Adjectives
- abusive
- harmful = damaging
- offended
- relevant: *pertinent(e)*
- worthy of sb / sth: *digne de qqn / qqch*

Verbs
- appeal to: *attirer*
- deserve: *mériter*
- draw attention
- get / be involved: *être impliqué(e)*
- point out

YOUR TURN! 5 Write an article BAC

On International Women's Day, write an article entitled "Progress still needed for women's rights."

3 Female Game Changers

How can women empower today's girls?

1 Ruth Bader Ginsburg: a pioneer

A. Observe the film poster.

a. Circle the title and the catchphrase and imagine the story.

b. What message is conveyed? Focus on the woman's hands on the building (The US Supreme Court).

B. Watch the trailer online and take notes.

a. Heroine (name, studies): ....

....

....

b. Men's opinions: ....

....

....

c. Her husband's attitude: ....

....

....

d. Her actions: ....

....

....

C. Recap orally what you have understood.

D. Comment on the last sentences about the US Constitution.

2 Leadership Academy for Girls

www.lienmini.fr/htr7-u408

0'00 to 2'04

HELP!

Nouns
- **boa**rding school: *internat*
- **ca**reer path: *voie professionnelle*

Adjectives
- **gra**teful (to sb for V-ing): *reconnaissant (envers qqn)*
- (under)**pri**vileged

Verbs & Expressions
- give an oppor**tu**nity
- **gra**duate: *être diplômé(e)*
- lift sb out of **po**verty
- over**co**me: *surmonter*
- own one's space
- pave the way (for): *ouvrir la voie (à)*
- show the way

A. Watch the video and summarise the programme of the Leadership Academy for Girls (who, why, when, where).

B. Take notes about Oprah Winfrey's motivations. She wanted to:

....

....

C. Listen to Kimberly Brooks, take notes and summarise why Oprah changed her life.

Oprah changed her life, because ....

....

3 Kamala Harris

We are so grateful to Joe and Jill [Biden] for welcoming our family into theirs on this incredible journey. And to the woman most responsible for my presence here today – my mother, Shyamala Gopalan Harris, who is always in our hearts. [...]

And so, I'm thinking about her and about the generations of women – Black Women, Asian, White, Latina, Native American women who throughout our nation's history have paved the way for this moment tonight. [...] All the women who have worked to secure and protect the right to vote for over a century: 100 years ago with the 19th Amendment, 55 years ago with the Voting Rights Act, and now, in 2020, with a new generation of women in our country who cast their ballots[1] and continue the fight for their fundamental right to vote and be heard.

Tonight, I reflect on their struggle, their determination and the strength of their vision – to see what can be unburdened[2] by what has been – and I stand on their shoulders. [...] But while I may be the first woman in this office, I will not be the last. Because every little girl watching tonight sees that this is a country of possibilities.

1 *votent* • **2** *soulagé*

Vice President Kamala Harris's victory speech,
7 November 2020

A. **Say who Kamala Harris is and why she is addressing the nation.**

....

....

B. **Highlight who she is thinking about and circle their actions. Explain: "and I stand on their shoulders" (l. 18-19).**

....

....

....

....

C. **Do you find Kamala Harris empowering for other girls? Why (not)?**

....

....

....

YOUR PROJECT

Nominate a woman from the English-speaking world for the "person of the year" *Time* cover.

4 Female Leaders

ETLV STMG *What is the evolution of women in leadership today?*

OBJECTIVE STMG

➤ Recognise a leadership style

Female CEOs to boost companies

www.lienmini.fr/htr7-u409

A. Watch the video. Describe orally Helen Hamilton-James's job (name of company, mission, place).

B. Give the valuable skills she sees in women. Tick what you hear.

☐ collaborative ☐ patient ☐ understanding

☐ bring diverse teams together

☐ manage different teams throughout the world

☐ bring effective methods

☐ have a different perspective

C. Take notes and summarise the results of the data collected by Australian companies about women in business.

....

....

....

....

....

D. Tick the sentences that reflect the ideas of this report. Correct orally the one that does not.

☐ Having more women at the top brings new perspectives in a company.

☐ Women reflect the needs and desires of half a society.

☐ A company with more women is more likely to meet the needs of a larger consumer group.

☐ The companies that reduce the number of female managers gain 3% of market value.

HELP!

Nouns

- **CEO** (Chief Executive Officer): *PDG*
- **curriculum** /kəˈrɪkjʊləm/ = programme
- **leadership** (style)
- **self-confidence**
- **target**

Adjectives

- **effective**
- **efficient**
- **profitable**
- **self-confident**

Verbs & Expressions

- **believe** in oneself
- **improve**
- **pave** the way for
- **set** sb on the path to success
- **trust** sb

DEFINITION ETLV

Leadership style is the art of managing a team. It differs from one manager to another, according to his/her personality, skills, culture, etc.

E. As there is a paternalistic leadership, do you think there is a maternalistic one?

....

....

....

....

....

....

....

....

YOUR PROJECT

UN Women is going to award the prize for the best leadership project to promote the rise of women in companies. Nominate the female role model you find the most inspiring. Explain your choice in a video. You will include the woman's education and diplomas, her career, her skills, and her successes. Go on the *CEO magazine* website to find information about female CEOs.

5 Sexism and Socialisation

ETLV ST2S

Are we still living in a sexist world?

OBJECTIVES ST2S

- Explain why sexism is a discriminatory social norm
- Explain how gender influences socialisation

Fighting diseases... and sexism

In 2005 [Katalin Karikó] discovered a way to configure messenger RNA – a molecule that kickstarts **the production of proteins – so that it slipped past the body's natural defenses, unannounced**[1]. That paved the way for what has recently turned out to be one of modern science's greatest achievements: the world's first mRNA vaccines. [...]

In 1997, Karikó met Drew Weissman, an immunologist who'd just joined the university. They [...] began working together to address the mRNA immune-response problem. [...] Karikó and Weissman filed a patent[2] for their work shortly after their research was published. When the patent was originally submitted, Karikó's name was listed second. But she fought to get first billing. "I said, 'No, it was my idea,'" she said. "I insisted – change it back." Her insistence was, perhaps, a reaction to sexism she'd faced earlier in her career. Once, Karikó said, she was asked for the name of her supervisor while running her own lab. She was referred to as "Mrs." in an article in which her male colleagues were given the title "professor." Another article confused her as a postdoc in Weissman's lab. "I don't work in anybody's lab," Karikó said. "I created my own field." [...]

After UPenn[3] declined to promote her to a faculty role in 2013, she joined BioNTech as senior vice president. [...] UPenn faculty said they'd "concluded that I was not of faculty quality." "When I told them I was leaving, they laughed at me and said, 'BioNTech doesn't even have a website,'" she said. [...] "When people are saying, 'There is no messenger RNA vaccine that's ever been,' it is very critical and very important to know that not because it failed," Karikó said. "It just didn't have time to be advanced by many people." [...] Karikó said she got the call about the Pfizer-BioNTech results the night before they were publicly announced.

1 *inattendu* • 2 *brevet* • 3 University of Pennsylvania

Business Insider, December 2020

A. Say why Katalin Karikó is in the spotlight.

B. Tick the obstacles she has met in her career. Comment.

- ☐ She was awarded a Nobel Prize.
- ☐ Her name was listed second on the patent although she had made the discovery.
- ☐ The university congratulated her and promoted her.
- ☐ She was mentioned as a postdoc in the scientific press and piece of writing.

C. Highlight other obstacles she has met to have her work recognised.

D. Why could Katalin Karikó be nominated for a Nobel Prize?

HELP!

DEFINITION ETLV

Socialisation refers to the set of processes by which individuals acquire and internalise the norms, values and roles that govern social life, thus building their psychological and social identity.

YOUR PROJECT

The AAAS (American Association for the Advancement of Science) plans to pay tribute to English-speaking female pioneers who advanced science. Choose one female scientist, do some research and write an article about her role in science. Here are a few of them: Nettie Stevens - Ada Lovelace - Rosalind Franklin - Elizabeth and Emily Blackwell - Miriam Menkin - K. Sumathi - Sarah Gilbert - Kizzmekia Corbett - Nita Patel - Lisa A. Jackson.

RULE THE GRAMMAR!

LE *PRESENT PERFECT*

• Formation

Auxiliaire ***have*** au présent + **participe passé** du verbe

Rappel : Participe passé = base verbale (verbe sans *to*) + *-ed* **ou** 3e colonne des verbes irréguliers

• Emploi

Le ***present perfect*** est un **temps du présent**.

Attention : Il n'est pas l'équivalent du passé composé français, même si sa structure y ressemble.

1. Il exprime le résultat, ou le bilan dans le présent d'actions ou d'événements passés.
   *Women **have fought** for their rights for decades. => Women have rights now.*

Remarque : Avec l'adverbe ***just***, on peut renvoyer à une action d'un **passé récent**.
   *New Zealand **has just started** to work on new laws in favour of more equity at work.*

2. Il exprime la continuité d'actions ou d'événements débutés dans le passé, qui se poursuivent dans le présent.
   *Katalin Karikó **has worked** on the messenger RNA since 2005. => She still works on it.*

VOCABULARY

Women

Discrimination

- abuse /ə'bjuːs/ (n.)
- biased /'baɪəst/ = prejudiced (against) (adj.)
- gender-based discrimination = gender bias (n.)
- harmful = damaging (adj.)
- inequity ≠ equity /'ekwɪti/ (n.)
- mindset = mentality (n.)
- misogynist /mɪ'sɒdʒɪnɪst/ (n.)
- misogynistic /mɪsɒdʒɪ'nɪstɪk/ = sexist (adj.)
- narrow-minded ≠ open-minded (adj.)
- stereotype /'steriətaɪp/ = cliché (n.)

Your words: ....

The workplace

- career /kə'rɪə/ path (n.)
- CEO (Chief Executive Officer) (n.)
- the corporate world (n.)
- the corporate ladder (n.)
- do business with
- earn /ɜːn/ (v.)
- gender pay gap
- hire = recruit = employ (v.)
- (in)equality (n.)
- leader(ship) position (n.)
- maternity / parental leave (n.)
- skill = competence (n.)

Your words: ....

Fight for equality

- address (v.)
- challenge (v.)
- fix / bridge the gap (v.)
- law / legislation (n.)
- overcome ≠ fail (v.)
- struggle = fight (n. / v.)
- support (v.)

Your words: ....

Success

- achieve = succeed (v.)
- believe in oneself
- break the glass ceiling /'siːlɪŋ/
- inspiring (adj.)
- lift sb out of poverty (v.)
- life-changing (adj.)
- pave the way for = show the way (v.)
- recognise = acknowledge /æk'nɒlɪdʒ/ (v.)
- trailblazer /'treɪlbleɪzə/ = pioneer /paɪə'nɪə/ = torchbearer (n.)

Your words: ....

LANGUAGE LAB

MP3
www.lienmini.fr/htr7-u410

1 Complete the sentences with the following nouns:
mindsets • *biased* • *break the glass ceiling* • *gender-based discrimination* • *misogynist*

A. The difference in treatment between men and women is called ....

B. People are .... when they judge others on their appearance, gender or race.

C. A .... is someone who dislikes women.

D. To allow women to .... , people have to change their ....

2 Give the synonyms (=) or antonyms (≠) of these words.

A. pioneer = ...

B. reduce the difference in salary between men and women = ...

C. recognise = ...

D. fail ≠ ....

Now, make a sentence for each one.

A. ....

B. ....

C. ....

D. ....

3 Put the verb in brackets in the present perfect.

A. Stereotypes against women (*be*) ingrained in society for centuries. ....

B. Childcare (*become*) a major obstacle to women's promotion for years. ....

C. Unfortunately, the gender pay gap (*not decrease*) yet. ....

4 Choose the appropriate verb tense. Tick the right answer.

A. The Oprah Winfrey Leadership Academy for Girls ☐ provides ☐ has provided education for girls since 2007.

B. Oprah Winfrey ☐ always wants ☐ has always wanted to help girls like herself.

C. Few women ☐ have won ☐ win Nobel Prizes since they have been awarded.

D. Women's rights ☐ have evolved ☐ evolved over the last century.

5 Unit's checkout

Comment on this photo taking into account the result of the American presidential election in November 2020 and also the fight for gender equality. Use the present perfect.

....

OPEN YOUR EARS!

La prononciation de la lettre *o* MP3 N°6

Écoutez les mots et surlignez pour chacun la prononciation de la lettre *o* qui lui correspond.

a. *woman* /ʊ/ *would* /ʌ/ *company*
b. *women* /ʊ/ *would* /ɪ/ *win*
c. *corporate* /ɒ/ *body* /ɔː/ *support*
d. *overcome* /ʌ/ *company* /əʊ/ *show*
e. *obstacle* /ɒ/ *body* /ɔː/ *support*
f. *improve* /uː/ *to* /ʌ/ *company*
g. *work* /ɜː/ *world* /ɔː/ *support*

AXE 2

UNIT 5

NEW WAYS OF WORKING

How are today's trends transforming jobs and workspaces?

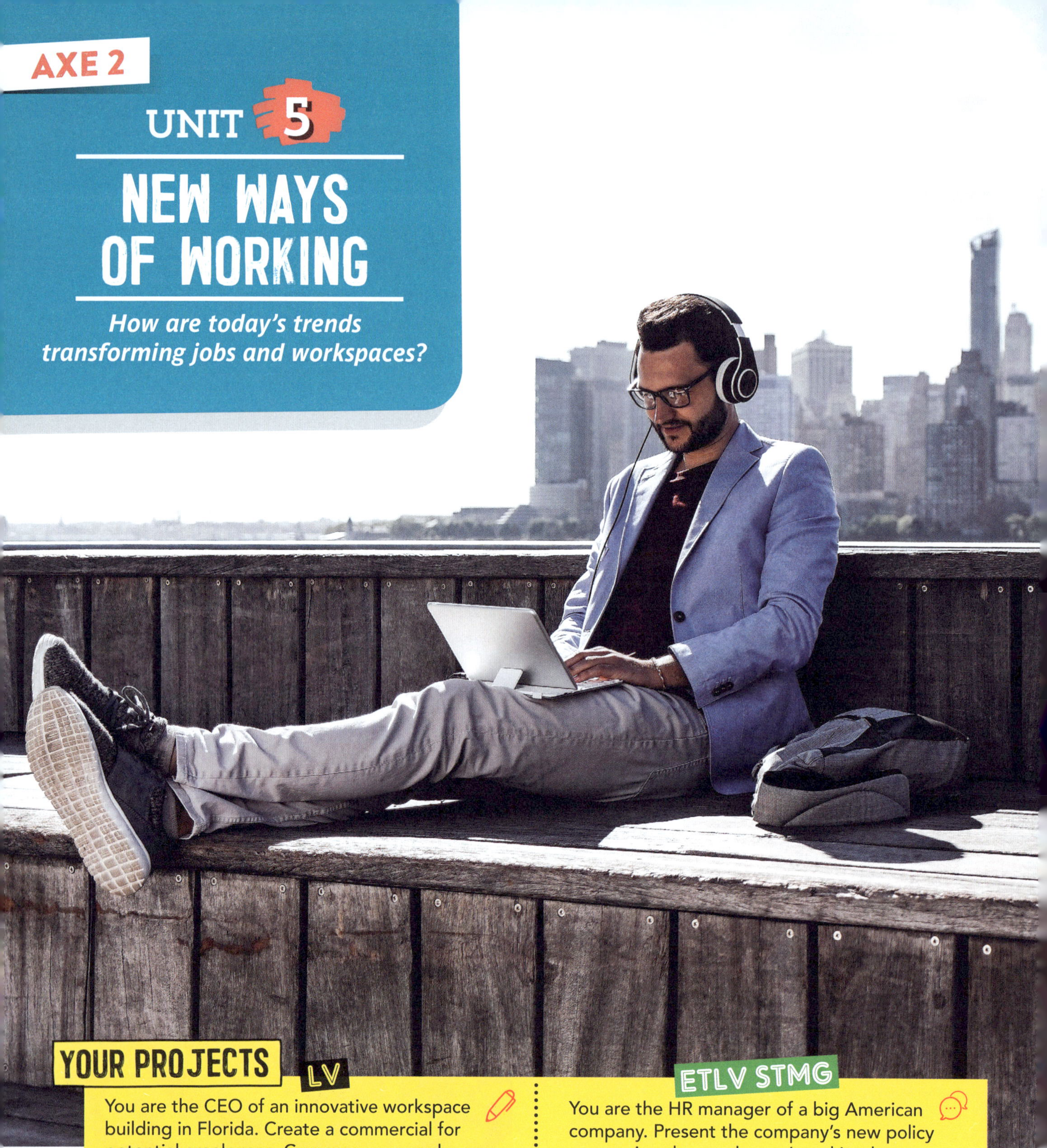

YOUR PROJECTS

LV

You are the CEO of an innovative workspace building in Florida. Create a commercial for potential employees. Compare your workspace to traditional offices.

ETLV STMG

You are the HR manager of a big American company. Present the company's new policy concerning the employees' working hours to the board of directors who react to the project.

Au menu de cette unité :

DÉCOUVERTES CULTURELLES

- Les nouveaux espaces de travail aux États-Unis (Dallas, Hawaï)
- L'équilibre travail-vie personnelle aux États-Unis
- Le bonheur au travail
- Le temps de travail aux États-Unis et au Royaume-Uni ETLV STMG

OUTILS LINGUISTIQUES

- Les quantifieurs
- Le présent simple
- Le lexique des espaces de travail, des conditions de travail, de l'équilibre travail-vie personnelle et du temps de travail
- La prononciation de la lettre *e*

GET READY!

WORD CHALLENGE

Use as many of these words as possible throughout the unit.
Tick ✓ the box when you have used the word.

- ☐ career /kəˈrɪə/ (n.)
- ☐ colleague /ˈkɒliːg/ = coworker (n.)
- ☐ commute /kəˈmjuːt/ (v.)
- ☐ coworking space (n.)
- ☐ digital /ˈdɪdʒɪtəl/ (*numérique*) nomad (n.)
- ☐ entitled (to) (adj.)
- ☐ flexible hours (n.)
- ☐ get a promotion /prəˈməʊʃən/
- ☐ get a raise (n.)
- ☐ health (n.)
- ☐ increase ≠ decrease (v. / n.)
- ☐ look after (v.)
- ☐ maternity/paternity/parental leave (n.)
- ☐ nine-to-five job (n.)
- ☐ policy (n.)
- ☐ reliable /rɪˈlaɪəbəl/ (adj.)
- ☐ remote = distant (adj.)
- ☐ right to disconnect
- ☐ schedule UK: /ˈʃedjuːl/ US: /ˈskedʒul/ (n.)
- ☐ telecommuting (n.)
- ☐ teleworking /ˈtelɪwɜːkɪŋ/ (n.)
- ☐ work-life balance (n.)
- ☐ working hours (n.)

BEFORE CLASS!

A. Watch the video and find out the information about:

a. Company name: ....

b. Reason for its recent success: ....

....

c. Number of participants in December 2019 and in April 2020:

....

....

www.lienmini.fr/htr7-u501

B. The future of office work: Explain:

a. The meaning of "hybrid model":

....

....

....

b. The limits of this system:

1. ....

....

2. ....

....

c. The possible solutions in the future:

1. ....

....

2. ....

....

3. ....

....

1 Is the Office Obsolete?

Why do some people choose not to work in a traditional office?

1 Sharing an office space

A. Watch the video without the sound on and focus on what you see. Describe the workspace orally.

B. Watch and listen, then find information about:

a. The company's founders: ....

b. Its location: ....

C. Tick the correct statements.

a. There you can:

- ☐ have your table at the coffee shop
- ☐ attend events and workshops
- ☐ see some friends
- ☐ meet leading female CEOs

b. When working there, people feel:

☐ comfortable ☐ discouraged ☐ safe
☐ worried ☐ encouraged

D. Complete your notes and use them to present the Riveter orally.

www.lienmini.fr/htr7-u502

HELP!

Nouns	*Adjectives*	*Verbs & Expressions*
• productivity	• efficient /ɪ'fɪʃənt/	• meet deadlines
• schedule /'ʃedjuːl/	• reliable /rɪ'laɪəbəl/	• overwork /əʊvə'wɜːk/
• work station	• remote = distant	• take a break
• work-life balance		• unplug /ʌn'plʌg/

2 Teleworking

A. **Pairwork.** Try to find arguments for or against teleworking. Report to the class.

B. Check your findings: focus on the two graphs dealing with remote working around the world in 2020. Focus on advantages and drawbacks and sum up in your own words.

C. Read the text. Highlight words or expressions related to the benefits of teleworking.

What's the biggest benefit you see to working remotely?

What's your biggest struggle with working remotely?

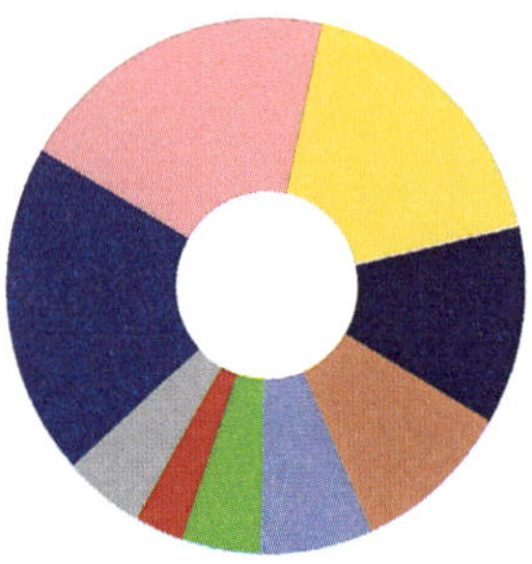

New research suggests the coronavirus will have a lasting impact on the way we work, with almost half of the workforce expected to work remotely after the virus is contained. But [Gartner's[1] vice president of research and advisory Aaron McEwan] told *The New Daily* the benefits of remote working outweighed[2] the downsides as workers were typically happier and more productive.

This is mainly because they save lots of time by not commuting and can attack their work with a clear state of mind as soon as they wake up, when their mind is at its sharpest, Mr McEwan said.

[...] Remote workers were more productive than office workers when their managers refrained from micro-managing[3] and – aside from setting reasonable deadlines – allowed workers to determine their own schedules and way of working.

1 Global research and advisory firm • **2** were more important than • **3** controlling every detail

The New Daily, April 2020

3 Digital nomadism

A. Pairwork. Before watching the video: use the photo to imagine what digital nomadism might be. Start your sentences with: *I suppose… I imagine… I guess… It might / may be…*

B. Check if you were right by watching the video.

www.lienmini.fr/htr7-u503

0'00 to 2'38

C. Tick the correct answer(s):

a. David's schedule:

- ☐ He shares his time between the island and the mainland.
- ☐ He works all the time on the island.

b. According to David, in order to be a successful remote worker, you need to be:

☐ focused ☐ dedicated ☐ relaxed

c. The island is 2 to 3 hours behind Pacific Time, so it means that he can start to work:

☐ whenever he wants to ☐ early ☐ late

D. How do David's colleagues on the continent feel when they see his work environment?

....

E. Would you be ready to work remotely like David? Explain why (not).

4 A growing trend

There has been a sharp increase in the number of people who no longer work from a set office – be they writers, marketeers, HR professionals, software programmers – and who can do their job by opening a laptop in any location. These online workers can be seen in coffee shops and short-term workspaces around the world, and rely on digital tools to be able to travel as they please.

Putting an exact figure on the number is difficult, though a 2018 study by research firm MBO Partners found that 4.8 million US citizens identified as "digital nomads".

In response, countries have offered special visas to attract the workers. [...] Barbados launched its "Welcome Stamp" [which] costs $2,000 [£1,500], and applicants must earn $50,000 [£37,500] a year, but they are exempt from paying Barbados income tax. The new initiative comes as the island is grappling with the drastic effect that the coronavirus has had on its tourism industry. [...]

While it may appear to be as simple a process as gathering up a few possessions and hopping on a flight, the reality of shifting your work to a new country can be a lot more complex, and the costs can mount up. [...]

Luckily there is an extensive community of digital nomads to tap for experience on how much different cities cost to live in. The website Nomadlist.com ranks cities via an extensive list of demands that digital workers typically have – from the overall monthly cost to the standard of free wifi, how friendly it is to women and what the air quality is like.

The Guardian, August 2020

A. Highlight the words or expressions related to travelling and explain orally why these words are important in this article.

B. What is needed to become a digital worker? Circle the answers in the text.

C. Underline the limits of this new trend.

D. Report about what you understood from the article.

YOUR TURN! 5 Write a report BAC

Groupwork. The New Zealand Ministry of Business, Innovation and Employment has asked you to promote new work trends: coworking, teleworking and digital nomadism.
List their advantages and drawbacks. Write a report about your conclusions.

2 American Workers' Situation

How do American workers balance their career and their family?

1 Time for your family

A resurfaced letter from Joe Biden when he was Vice President addressed to staffers has revealed how he encouraged employees not to miss family commitments for work.

The letter, which surfaced on Twitter on Monday, was sent from Mr Biden to his staff before Thanksgiving in 2014 under the then Obama administration.

In the note addressed to his "Wonderful Staff" the then Vice President urged his employees not to miss any family commitments for work, saying it is "very important to him" that people do not.

"I would like to take a moment to make something clear to everyone," the memo begins. "I do not expect nor do I want any of you to miss or sacrifice important family obligations for work."

"Family obligations include but are not limited to family birthdays, anniversaries, weddings, any religious ceremonies such as first communions and bar mitzvahs, graduations, and times of need such as illness or a loss in the family," the letter continues.

He adds: "This is very important to me. In fact, I will go so far as to say that if I find out that you are working with me while missing important family responsibilities, it will disappoint me greatly. "This has been an unwritten rule since my days in the senate."

The Independent, November 2020

A. Read the article and say what "family commitments" (l. 3-4) may mean: circle several answers.

time to support your family – working with your family – time devoted to family events – choosing a career over family

B. Highlight the words related to "family commitments" and underline the sentences showing how important they are to Joe Biden.

2 Time to relax

www.lienmini.fr/htr7-u504

HELP!

Nouns
- company policy
- health /helθ/
- time off
- vacation /veɪˈkeɪʃən/ (US)/ holiday(s) (UK)

Adjectives
- afraid of (+ V-ing)
- entitled (to)
- exhausted
- required

Verbs & Expressions
- get a promotion / get a raise
- go on vacation / on holiday
- lose out on: *perdre*
- take a day off

A. Watch the video and write key information about:

a. What happens during summer in Europe:

b. When it started and why:

c. Duration of paid vacation, Europeans are entitled to:

d. Situation in the US:

e. Place where workers are the most productive in the world:

f. List all the advantages of taking a vacation:

g. Reasons why some people refuse to go on vacation:

B. Use your notes to sum up orally what you have learnt.

3 Time to raise your children

The share of moms who are working either full or part time in the United States has increased over the past half-century from 51% to 72%, and almost half of two-parent families now include two full-time working parents. At the same time, fathers – virtually all of whom are working – are taking on more childcare responsibilities, as fatherhood has grown to encompass far more than just bringing home the bacon.

Despite these transformations, the U.S. is the only country among 41 nations that does not mandate any paid leave for new parents, according to data compiled by the Organization for Economic Cooperation and Development (OECD) and current as of April 2018. The smallest amount of paid leave required in any of the other 40 nations is about two months. [...]

It's important to note that while the U.S. is the only country that does not have a national paid leave mandate, California, New Jersey, New York, Rhode Island and the District of Columbia all have state-mandated paid leave plans in place. The state of Washington passed a state-mandated paid leave program in 2017; it will take effect at the start of 2020.

Pew Research Center, December 2019

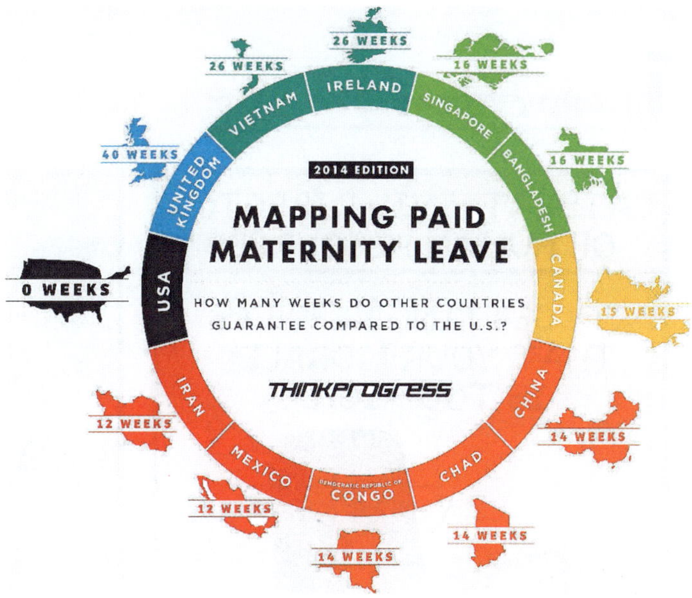

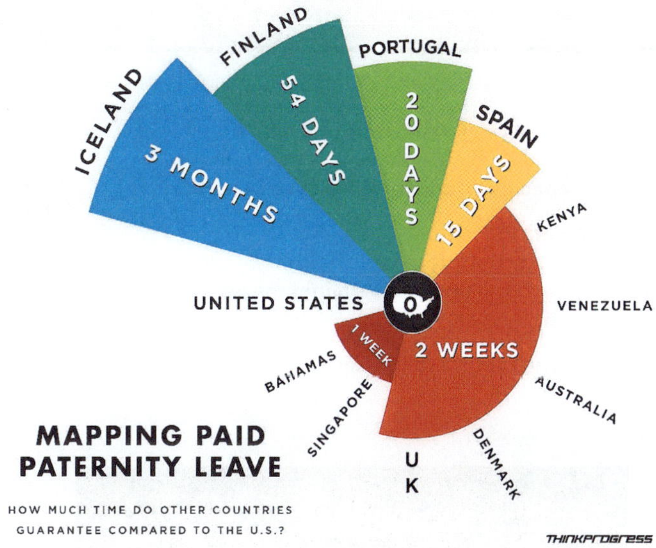

A. Read the article and highlight the transformations in the work-life balance of American parents.

B. What can you say about the American workers' situation?

C. Focus on the infographics above to compare the parents' situations in Canada, the US, the UK, Singapore and Ireland. Use: *fewer weeks than…; less time than…; more weeks than…; the least time…*

HELP!

Nouns	**Adjectives**
• breadwinner • childcare • day care /keə/ (US) = crèche (UK) • housewife • maternity / paternity / parental leave • stay-at-home mum	• allocated • available /ə'veɪləbəl/ **Verbs & Expressions** • allocate /'æləkeɪt/ • bring home the bacon • earn a living / a salary • increase ≠ decrease • look after: *garder*

D. Sum up your findings orally.

3 Happy at Work

Can you achieve happiness at work?

1 Happy workers

Dilbert, by Scott Adams, 2010

A. Read the cartoon. What is the cat's job? Explain what he says in your own words. Can you guess his conclusion and the employee's reaction?

B. **Groupwork.**
Group 1: Study the infographic below.
Group 2: Read the text and highlight the key information.

C. Each group reports to the class.

HELP!

Nouns	Adjectives	Verbs
• atmosphere	• cynical	• criticise
• Human Resources (HR)	• low ≠ high	• denounce
• well-being	• scornful	• despise
• wage		• ignore = overlook

So what does a 'Director of Happiness' or a 'Chief Happiness Officer' (CHO) actually do?

First of all, it is not their job to keep people happy 24/7. Frankly, it is impossible for people to be happy 100% of the time. Their role, that is not necessarily a completely new role is like a HR[1] Manager with additional special features. According to Mallory Bartz, it is the job of a CHO to create work environments where freedom can exist and flourish. This means allowing employees to be themselves and fulfil their personal aspirations.

Kiera Lawlor, Director of Happiness at Social Chain, supports the above points and adds that it is her duty to create a fun and enjoyable workplace for staff. She also enforces celebrating all staff achievements, both personal and professional, no matter how big or small. Other important aspects of her job include organising group activities, arranging classes on valuable life skills and creating welcoming spaces that encourage creativity.

1 Human Resources

Hire Hive Blog

2 I need a friend...

Having friends at work is not only key to your personal happiness, but it's vital for having a successful career. In fact, it makes you seven times more likely to be engaged in your job.

A new survey by job site *Comparably* found that of over 33,000 workers across the tech industry, more than half of them report having best friends at work. While 60 percent of women said they have a close friend at work, 56 percent of men admitted having work BFFs[1] as well.

"One of the most important things to have in the workplace is a close relationship," *Comparably* CEO Jason Nazar tells CNBC *Make It*. "So very often the largest source of stress for people is a boss, co-worker or the day-to-day pressures of work."

[...] Interestingly, *Comparably* also found that the likelihood of having a best friend at work declines with age. Gen Zers and millennials[2] – those between the age of 18 and 30 – reported the highest percentage of workplace friendships (62 percent), while people in their early-to-mid 50s reported the lowest rates (50 percent). The reason behind this decline, *Comparably* explains, is presumably because as people age, they hold higher job titles with dramatically increased responsibilities at work and in life. As a result, they have less time for socializing and creating close social relationships at work. [...]

1 best friends for ever • 2 Generation Z: born after 2000, millennials: born between 1980 and 2000

Cnbc.com, March 2018

A. Pairwork. Before reading: is it possible to make friends at work? Think of the advantages and drawbacks, then share with the class.

B. Read the text and check your hypotheses.

a. Advantages: ....

....

....

b. Drawbacks: ....

....

....

C. Say which age groups are concerned and find out if the percentages are similar whatever the workers' ages. Explain why.

....

....

....

....

YOUR PROJECT BAC

You are the CEO of an innovative workspace building in Florida, near the Atlantic Ocean. Imagine a commercial targeting potential employees: mention the location, history, main characteristics, number of employees, work atmosphere, potential work schedules. Compare your workspace to traditional office spaces. You may also add illustrations.

4 Reducing Working Time

ETLV STMG

Is working less a viable option for businesses?

OBJECTIVES STMG

- Study the link between working conditions and staff behaviour
- Identify motivation factors at work

1 A case study: Kellogg's

At the end of 1930, just after the start of the Great Depression, the Kellogg's cereal plant in Battle Creek, Michigan, replaced its three eight-hour shifts[1] per day with four six-hour shifts [...] to achieve several goals at the same time: to reduce unemployment in the community, to increase worker efficiency, and to provide employees "greater opportunity for recreation and enjoyment – outside of business hours," which would "mean better living and working conditions generally." [...]

After World War II, however, new management began to push for an eight-hour day, and workers became increasingly divided as management made new shifts be available to all "those who want it." They offered benefits to senior workers willing to advocate longer hours and offered to increase hourly wages if the union would give up shorter hours. [...]

Finally, in the mid-1980s, Kellogg's threatened to move jobs out of state if the remaining six-hour departments would not switch to eight hours. Workers who still loved their six-hour days held a funeral eulogizing[1] the shorter shift. [...]

Though Kellogg's six-hour day is a thing of the past that few can now remember, many of today's advocates consider it an innovation that was clearly ahead of its time.

1 trois périodes de travail de 8 heures • *2 éloge funèbre*

Feminists for life of America

A. Read the text. What do the following dates correspond to?

a. 1930: ....

b. After WWII: ....

c. The mid-1980s: ....

B. Tick the right statements and justify.

a. Goals of the company when reducing the working hours:

- ☐ decrease unemployment
- ☐ increase production
- ☐ save the company money
- ☐ improve its workers' living conditions
- ☐ control its workers' lives

b. Reasons why the workers finally accepted to work longer hours in the end:

- ☐ The company offered benefits to the new employees.
- ☐ Some employees wished to earn more by working more.
- ☐ Kellogg's threatened its workers to move from Michigan if they didn't change their minds.

C. Sum up the story of shorter hours at Kellogg's.

HELP!

Nouns
- **burnout**
- **efficiency** /ɪ'fɪʃənsi/
- **Human Resources** (HR)
- **nine-to-fiver/nine-to-five job**
- **plant** = **factory**
- **scheme** /skiːm/
- **staff**
- (trade) **union**: *syndicat*
- (trade) **unionist**
- (un)**employment**

Adjectives
- **flexible**
- **jobless** = **unemployed**
- **productive**

Verbs & Expressions
- **be out of work**
- **boost**
- **clock in** ≠ **clock out**
- **work in shifts**
- **work long hours** / **work shorter hours**
- **work extra hours** = **work overtime** / **overwork**

DEFINITION ETLV

Motivation at work depends on internal and external factors that impact the workers' behaviour. Working conditions, wages, communication, job missions can increase involvement, motivation and satisfaction.

2 Working hours in the United Kingdom

A. Pairwork. Do you believe that working longer hours makes you more productive?

B. Watch the video about working hours in the UK and fill in the table.

Type of document	....
Aim	....
Advantages of working less	....
Working hours in the past	....
Effects of overwork	....

www.lienmini.fr/htr7-u505

3 Netflix: inspiration over supervision

www.lienmini.fr/htr7-u506

A. Watch the video, then tick the correct answers and justify orally with words from the video.

a. ☐ Thanks to this system Netflix employees can take as much vacation and time off as they want.

b. ☐ The number of hours is more important than new ideas and creativity.

c. ☐ The company does not check the number of hours or weeks its employees do.

d. ☐ Unlimited vacation means people can live more flexibly as long as they get their work done.

B. What is good management according to Reed Hastings? Is this system possible in any other industry?

....

....

....

YOUR PROJECT BAC

You are the HR manager of a big American company. Present the company's new policy concerning employees' working hours to the board of directors. List all the advantages for the employees and the company. The rest of the class is the board of directors: react to the project (ask questions / agree or disagree).

RULE THE GRAMMAR!

1. LES QUANTIFIEURS

Rappel : Un **nom indénombrable** désigne un ensemble, une notion abstraite, une idée qui est toujours au singulier. Un **nom dénombrable** désigne des éléments que l'on peut compter et mettre au pluriel.

	Indénombrable (sing.)	**Dénombrable (pl.)**
(si) peu de	*(So) little time is devoted to the employees' well-being.*	*(So) few Americans are willing to take a vacation.*
un peu de / quelques	*A little consideration would be nice.*	*A few employees have decided to work from home all the time.*
beaucoup de	*A lot of / (So) much money has been invested in new technology to help workers telework.*	*A lot of / Many CEOs have reduced their office space.*

2. LE PRÉSENT SIMPLE

• Formation
Voir page 41.

• Emploi
Il permet d'exprimer une vérité générale, une habitude, une action qui se répète, un goût, mais également de caractériser une action toujours vraie (*The Earth goes around the Sun*).

VOCABULARY

Work

Working spaces

- commute (n. / v.)
- coworking /ˈkəʊwɜːkɪŋ/ (n.)
- digital nomadism /ˈdɪdʒɪtəl ˈnəʊmædizəm/ (n.)
- office buildings (n.)
- relocate = move (v.)
- teleworking = working from home = remote / distant working (n.)
- workplace (n.)
- work station (n.)

Your words:

Working conditions

- efficient (adj.)
- exhausted (adj.)
- get a promotion / a raise
- loneliness (n.)
- motivated (adj.)
- productive (adj.) / productivity (n.)
- overwork (n.)
- socialise /ˈsəʊʃəlaɪz/ (v.)
- supervision (n.)

Your words:

Working time

- 4-day workweek
- 6-hour day
- clock in ≠ clock out (v.)
- flexible hours / schedule /ˈskedʒul/ /ˈʃedjuːl/ (n.)
- flexibility (n.)
- meet deadlines
- nine-to-five job (n.)
- paid time off (n)
- part-time ≠ full-time (adj.)
- work in shifts
- work longer hours ≠ work shorter hours
- working days (n.)

Your words:

Work-life balance

- burnout (n.)
- Chief Happiness Officer = Director of Happiness (n.)
- childcare (n.)
- devote (time) (v.)
- parental leave (n.)
- right to disconnect
- take a break
- unplug (v.)
- vacation /veɪˈkeɪʃən/ holiday(s) (n.)

Your words:

MP3
www.lienmini.fr/htr7-u507

LANGUAGE LAB

1 Use the present simple to describe an employee's typical working day.

A. She usually (*commute*) to work three days a week.

B. He (*not travel*) to the office two days a week because he (*work*) from home.

C. What you (*think*) about this organisation? We (*agree*) with you: teleworking is the right choice.

D. They (*believe*) this schedule is perfect!

2 Match the underlined words with the correct quantifiers.

few • a few • much • many • little • a little

A. Only two employees have accepted to take some time off.

B. Thousands of parents enjoy working from home.

C. I made two friends out of the fifty employees in the company.

D. We don't need a lot of money to make employees more comfortable at work.

E. Only 5 minutes left before the meeting? Hurry! We have almost no time left!

F. Employees need a bit of comfort to be more productive at work.

3 Fill in the blanks with the following words.

loneliness • devote • nine-to-five jobs • get a raise • productive

A. Studies have shown that workers who take vacations .... more easily.

B. Some people are unhappy working from home because of ....

C. Most jobs in this city are ....

D. Happy employees are often more .... in their professional activities.

4 Find the synonyms (=) or antonyms (≠) of these words.

A. working from home = ... B. full-time ≠ ....

C. clock in ≠ .... D. move = ...

5 Unit's checkout

Describe the man's working conditions in this cartoon. Use *(a) few, (a) little, much, many, a lot of*, and the present simple.

OPEN YOUR EARS!

La prononciation de la lettre *e* MP3 N°7

Écoutez les mots suivants, puis notez le numéro correspondant à la prononciation de la voyelle *e*.

1 teleworking (2x) • 2 supervision • 3 chosen • 4 remote • 5 serious • 6 relocate • 7 creativity • 8 atmosphere • 9 equipped • 10 schedule

/ɪ/ (pretty): ....

/iː/ (region): ....

/e/ (get): ....

/ɪə/ (here): ....

/ə/ (enemy): ....

AXE 2

UNIT 6

THE WATER GAP

What makes toilet and water access an issue for human health?

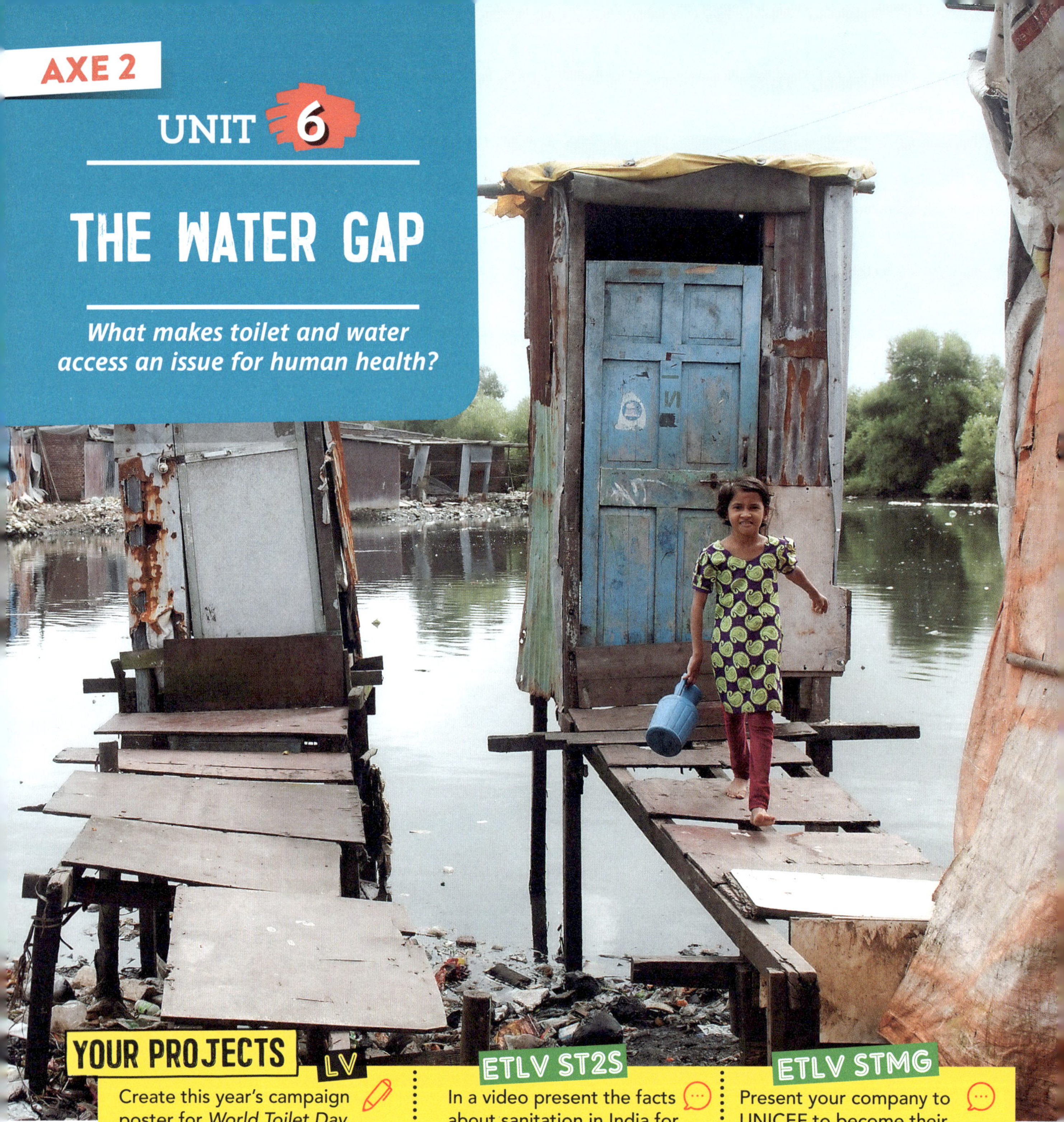

YOUR PROJECTS

LV

Create this year's campaign poster for *World Toilet Day*.

ETLV ST2S

In a video present the facts about sanitation in India for an awareness campaign.

ETLV STMG

Present your company to UNICEF to become their *#Toilets4All* partner.

Au menu de cette unité :

DÉCOUVERTES CULTURELLES

- La campagne de Bill Gates pour des W.-C accessibles à tous
- Le cas de l'Inde
- La situation des États-Unis
- La campagne *World Toilet Day*
- Le projet *#Toilets4All* ETLV ST2S
- L'engagement des entreprises dans l'humanitaire ETLV STMG

OUTILS LINGUISTIQUES

- L'obligation et la possibilité
- Le comparatif et le superlatif
- Le lexique des sanitaires et de l'accès à l'eau, des conséquences sur la santé, des actions à mener et des solutions
- La prononciation du *th*

GET READY!

WORD CHALLENGE

Use as many of these words as possible throughout the unit.
Tick ✓ the box when you have used the word.

- ☐ a drop in the bucket: *une goutte d'eau dans l'océan*
- ☐ affect (v.)
- ☐ affordable ≠ unaffordable (adj.)
- ☐ contaminated /kən'tæmɪneɪtɪd/ (adj.)
- ☐ disease = illness (n.)
- ☐ give a crap (slang)
- ☐ have access to (v.)
- ☐ healthy ≠ unhealthy /ʌn'helθi/ (adj.)
- ☐ household (n.)
- ☐ human waste /weɪst/ (n.)
- ☐ hygiene /'haɪdʒiːn/ (n.)
- ☐ hygienic /haɪ'dʒiːnɪk/ ≠ unhygienic (adj.)
- ☐ in the open = outdoors (adv.)
- ☐ indoor plumbing /'plʌmɪŋ/ (n.)
- ☐ issue = problem (n.)
- ☐ lack (v.)
- ☐ make a change / a difference (v.)
- ☐ privacy UK: /'prɪvəsi/ US: /'praɪvəsi/ (n.)
- ☐ processed waste (n.)
- ☐ provide /prə'vaɪd/ (v.)
- ☐ sanitary ≠ unsanitary (adj.)
- ☐ sewage /'suːɪdʒ/ / sewer /'sʊːə/ (n.)
- ☐ toilet /'tɔɪlət/ = latrine /lə'triːn/ (n.)

BEFORE CLASS!

A. Watch the video and tick the words you hear for each item.

a.	☐ a sewer system	☐ a newer system
b.	☐ placed	☐ waste
c.	☐ 2.5 million	☐ 2.5 billion
d.	☐ affordable	☐ unaffordable
e.	☐ a big latrine	☐ a pit latrine
f.	☐ processed	☐ unprocessed
g.	☐ human health	☐ human wealth
h.	☐ malnourished	☐ malpractice
i.	☐ sensation	☐ sanitation
j.	☐ oxygen	☐ pathogen

www.lienmini.fr/htr7-u601

B. Watch again and take notes.

C. Classify your notes using the grid below.

Toilet issues	Possible solutions

D. Get ready to recap orally what you have learnt about this issue.

1 Talking about Toilets in India

How does India deal with its sanitation and water problems?

1 Investigating the issue

Santoshi Tiwari educates villagers from North Bhopal on the subject of open defecation and offers to build them toilets. Photo by Andrea Bruce.

After years covering wars in Iraq and Afghanistan, Andrea Bruce was asked by *National Geographic* in 2016 to undertake one of the most difficult assignments[1] of her career. The subject? Open defecation.

"It almost seemed so ridiculous that I had to do it," Ms. Bruce said. "But once you start researching you realize that it's among the most important issues today, affecting nearly a billion people. If you don't have proper sanitation, you don't have clean drinking water, and then you don't have a healthy population." [...]

1 jobs, missions

The New York Times, September 2018

A. Read the text and say what is surprising about Andrea Bruce's mission.

B. How did she react to it?

C. Observe the picture and read the caption. Comment on what Santoshi Tiwari does.

D. Groupwork. Brainstorm with your classmates on the solutions that can be found to solve the problem.

2 For women, it's personal

Listen to Jodie Foster and pick out the reasons why the water crisis affects women first. Quote keywords and recap orally.

www.lienmini.fr/htr7-u602

3 The Bollywood approach

Akshay Kumar, film director of the highly successful Bollywood film Toilet – Ek Pram Khatha, *talks about his source of inspiration for the plot.*

We need to change our minds about toilets. A woman from a small village in rural India, Anita Narre, shocked the nation when she left her husband two days after her wedding. But it wasn't the speed of her decision that caused the astonishment; it was the reason. Outraged that her new home lacked a toilet, Narre refused to return until her husband built her one. Her story, which inspired my latest film, cuts to the very heart of one of the biggest crises facing my country today.

It wasn't until I met Narre and other women like her that I understood the true scale of the issue. During my research for the film, I found out that half of India's population – 564 million people – defecate in the open because they lack access to a toilet. But I didn't know what this means for millions of women across the country. I had no idea about the fear these women experience every single time nature calls, or that so many women face assault and rape[1] while going to the toilet outdoors. The threat of violence and the leers[2] of men mean that most women wait until nightfall before trudging out[3] into the open. Many hold their bladders[4] for up to 13 hours at a time, exposing them to urinary tract infections and other health problems.

This isn't the only awful consequence of India's lack of toilets. Defecating in the open spreads disease and pollutes drinking water, damaging the health of millions of my countrymen and women.

1 viol • 2 regards lubriques • 3 marcher péniblement • 4 vessies

The Guardian, November 2017

A. **Read the text and explain what true story inspired Akshay Kumar for his Bollywood film.**

B. **Highlight problems caused by the lack of toilets. Which part of the population is the most affected?**

C. **In your opinion, why was Akshay Kumar unaware of this situation? Make hypotheses.**

HELP!

Nouns
- **assault** /ə'sɔːlt/
- **health problem**
- **human waste**
- **hygiene** /'haɪdʒiːn/
- **open defecation**
- **privacy** UK: /'prɪvəsi/ US: /'praɪvəsi/
- **rape**
- **sanitation** /sænɪ'teɪʃən/
- **solar panel**

Adjective
- **contaminated** /kən'tæmɪneɪtɪd/

Verbs & Expressions
- **process the waste**
- **provide**

YOUR TURN!

4 Prepare a podcast

As a reporter for *Times of India*, prepare a two-minute podcast for the news website, titled "Indian toilets: issues and solutions."

2 American Dream Down the Drain

Is there a water access problem in the United States?

1 Make America flush again

A. Watch the report and take notes. Then explain the situation.

B. How do American citizens cope with the problem?

a. ☐ They use their neighbours' water systems.

b. ☐ They fill buckets at a water point and boil their drinking water.

c. ☐ They collect and drink rainwater.

d. ☐ They do not really cope and have daily problems.

www.lienmini.fr/htr7-u603

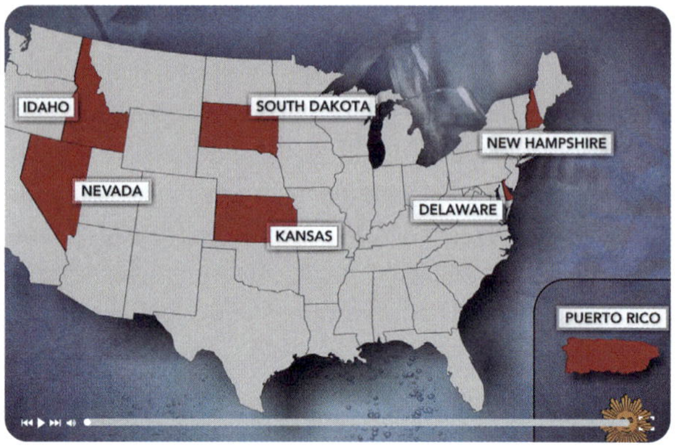

C. Is the situation improving? Explain.

☐ Yes ☐ No

2 The water scandal

Today, more than two million Americans live without running water and basic indoor plumbing, and many more without sanitation. On the Navajo Nation in the Southwest, families drive for hours to haul[1] barrels of water to meet their basic needs. [...] In West Virginia, they drink from polluted streams. In Alabama, parents warn their children not to play outside because their yards are flooded[2] with sewage[3]. [...] Families living in Texas border towns worry because there is no running water to fight fires. [...] The United States is home to some of the most reliable water and wastewater systems on earth, and many Americans believe access is universal. But in fact, millions of the most vulnerable people in the country – low-income[4] people in rural areas, people of color, tribal communities, immigrants – have fallen through the cracks[5].

- Native American households are 19 times more likely than white households to lack indoor plumbing.
- 17% of people living in rural areas report having experienced issues with safe drinking water.
- African American and Latino households are nearly twice as likely.
- 12% of people living in rural areas report issues with their sewage system.
- Communities facing water access challenges exist in every state. Alaska, Maine and New Mexico are among the states hardest hit.

1 *transporter* • **2** inundated • **3** *eaux usées* • **4** *à faible revenu* • **5** have been forgotten

Dig Deep, US Water Alliance,
"Closing the Water Access Gap in the United States",
March 2020

A. Read the text. Highlight all the elements that relate to the title, "The water scandal".

B. Tick the categories of the population which are the most affected.

☐ High-income people in cities ☐ Low-income people in rural areas ☐ People who belong to ethnic minorities ☐ Immigrants

C. Does this situation surprise you? Why (not)?

3 A drop in the bucket

A. Take notes and talk about the cartoon for one minute.

....

....

....

....

....

....

....

B. What could the characters be thinking or saying? Write the speech balloons.

HELP!

Nouns
- hose /həʊz/: *tuyau d'arrosage*
- water drops: *gouttes d'eau*
- water guns
- puddle: *flaque*

Adjectives
- derelict: *délabré*
- fenced: *clôturé*

Expression
- shower under

4 World Toilet Day

A. Read the *Cultural fact*. Complete the caption with the following words: *banner – catchphrase – illustration – quote*. Explain the role of each element.

....

....

....

B. Using the caption and the *Cultural fact*, present this poster orally.

C. In this context, what is the meaning of "I give a crap"?

☐ I care about this problem ☐ I don't care about this problem

Cultural fact
Since 2013, the United Nations has observed November 19th as *World Toilet Day* to draw the world's attention to the importance of accessible toilets and their role in improving hygiene and health around the world.

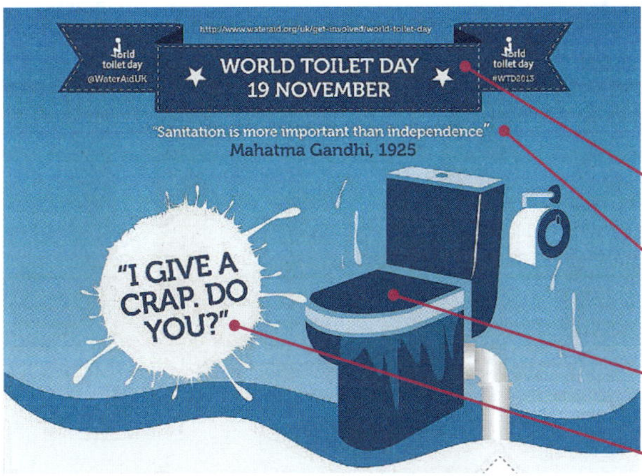

....

....

....

....

YOUR PROJECT

Create a campaign poster for *World Toilet Day*. Find a quote, a catchphrase and an illustration for your poster. You can either design it yourself or on your computer.

3 Sanitation in India

ETLV ST2S

Is hygiene a social marker for health?

OBJECTIVES ST2S

- Define a social marker for health
- Present the influence of social markers on health

1 Making progress

India has made rapid progress in ending open defecation across the country. [...] By 2019, according to the latest estimates, the number of people without access to toilets has reduced significantly by an estimated 450 million people. [...] Whether in the cities or the countryside, open defecation has historically been most prevalent among the poorest citizens. [...] The situation contributed to nearly 100,000 diarrheal deaths of children under five years in India. [...] Recent reports also showed that 22% [of schools] did not have appropriate toilets for girls, 58% of preschools had no toilet at all and 56% of preschools had no water on the premises. Less than 50% of the population has access to safely managed drinking water (located on premises, available when needed and free of contamination).

Unicef, "Water, sanitation and hygiene"

Read the text and take notes.

a. Relevant facts and figures: ....

b. What makes access to sanitation vital: ....

c. Link between toilets and social status: ....

2 The heart of the matter

Watch the video and note the different elements and methods used to build an awareness campaign.

....

www.lienmini.fr/htr7-u604

YOUR PROJECT BAC

As a UNICEF delegate, you have been tasked with creating the next awareness campaign for #*Toilets4All* in India. Using what you have learnt, make a video that provides facts about sanitation in India and encourages access to a private toilet for all.

HELP!

DEFINITIONS ETLV

Social marker for health: Specific factors that influence or are connected to the state of health.

4 A Company that Cares about Ethics

ETLV STMG

How can a company combine profit and ethics?

OBJECTIVES STMG

- Identify a CSR action and explain its objectives
- Show ethical issues addressed by an organisation

A business helping NGOs

A. Watch this crowdfunding video campaign and take notes. What do you learn about the company's product? Present "Who Gives a Crap", its activity and its purpose.

....

....

....

....

....

www.lienmini.fr/htr7-u605

B. Read the text about the UNICEF sanitation projects. Highlight the elements that would help "Who Gives a Crap" to suggest a partnership.

C. In your opinion, why should UNICEF accept to cooperate with "Who Gives a Crap"?

UNICEF promotes community-based handwashing through a variety of media and through campaigns like Global Handwashing Day, which reaches hundreds of millions of people every year. Our people-based approach has helped entire communities eliminate the dangerous practice of open defecation. [...]

We work directly with schools and healthcare facilities to improve access to basic water, sanitation and handwashing facilities, and to establish protocols for preventing and controlling infections. We support menstrual health and hygiene in schools, including the construction of private and secure sanitation and washing facilities, menstrual pad disposal facilities, and education and support services, to help more girls better manage their menstruation cycle.

Unicef, "Water, sanitation and hygiene"

HELP!

Nouns
- disease = illness
- ethics /'eθɪks/
- facilities
- healthcare
- hygiene /'haɪdʒiːn/
- open defecation
- purpose = goal
- sanitation /sænɪ'teɪʃən/

Adjectives
- eco-friendly
- menstrual

Verb
- have access to

DEFINITIONS ETLV
- **Crowdfunding** aims at collecting money from individuals to finance a project thanks to a web platform.
- **Corporate Social Responsibility (CSR)** is a management concept that includes social and environmental concerns in businesses.

YOUR PROJECT BAC

As the new spokesperson for the company "Who Gives a Crap", present it to UNICEF to become their newest partner in their *#Toilets4All* project.

RULE THE GRAMMAR!

1. L'OBLIGATION, LA POSSIBILITÉ

Pour exprimer l'obligation ou la possibilité, on peut utiliser des auxiliaires de modalité (ou modaux).
Les modaux illustrent l'opinion ou le jugement de l'énonciateur.

- **Obligation : *must / must not (mustn't)***
  *India **must** find a solution to develop water and sanitation access.*
  *They **mustn't** give up their fight to get drinking water access.*

On peut également utiliser *have to*, qui est un verbe et doit être conjugué.
*People from Keystone **have to** boil their water before using it.*

- **Possibilité : *can / can not (can't)***
  *Villages **can** ask NGOs like Dig Deep for help.*

2. LE COMPARATIF ET LE SUPERLATIF

- **Formation** Voir page 20.
- **Le comparatif** permet de comparer un élément à un autre. L'élément de comparaison peut être omis si le contexte le permet.
  *India is a poor**er** country **than** the United States but they share similar problems.*
  *Access to private toilets is **more** secure **than** open defecation.*
- **Le superlatif** permet de comparer un élément par rapport à un ensemble.
  *Only **the** wealthi**est** American families have never wondered about water access in their country.*

VOCABULARY

The water gap

Sanitation & water access

- aff**o**rdable ≠ unaff**o**rdable (adj.)
- dr**i**nking w**a**ter (n.)
- have **a**ccess to (v.)
- h**u**man waste /weɪst/ (n.)
- **i**ndoor pl**u**mbing /ˈplʌmɪŋ/ (n.)
- in the **o**pen = outd**oo**rs (adv.)
- low **i**ncome h**o**usehold (n.)
- **o**pen defec**a**tion (n.)
- pr**o**cessed waste (n.)
- s**a**nitary ≠ uns**a**nitary (adj.)
- s**e**wage /ˈsuːɪdʒ/ / s**e**wer /ˈsʊːə/ (n.)
- t**oi**let /ˈtɔɪlət/ = latr**i**ne /ləˈtriːn/ (n.)

Your words: ....

Consequences

- aff**e**ct (v.)
- ass**au**lt /əˈsɔːlt/ (n.)
- cont**a**minated /kənˈtæmɪneɪtɪd/ (adj.)
- dis**ea**se = **i**llness (n.)
- h**ea**lthy ≠ unh**ea**lthy /ʌnˈhelθi/ (adj.)
- h**y**giene /ˈhaɪdʒiːn/ (n.)
- hygi**e**nic /haɪˈdʒiːnɪk/ ≠ unhygi**e**nic (adj.)
- **i**ssue = pr**o**blem (n.)
- pr**i**vacy
  (US) /ˈpraɪvəsi/ (UK) /ˈprɪvəsi/ (n.)
- r**a**pe

Your words: ....

Actions

- campa**i**gn (v.)
- **e**ducate (v.)
- get **a**ccess to (v.)
- have a p**u**rpose / a goal
- make a ch**a**nge
- make a d**i**fference
- prov**i**de /prəˈvaɪd/ (v.)
- raise aw**a**reness
- take **a**ction
- undert**a**ke (v.): *entreprendre*

Your words: ....

Solutions

- aw**a**reness campa**i**gn (n.)
- comm**u**nity-based (adj.)
- c**o**pe = overc**o**me d**i**fficulties (v.)
- cr**o**wdfunding /ˈkraʊdfʌndɪŋ/ (n.)
- humanit**a**rian pr**o**jects
- p**a**rtnership (n.)
- prev**e**ntion (n.)
- raise m**o**ney

Your words: ....

LANGUAGE LAB

1 Compare the following elements in a full sentence, using the adjectives provided.

A. dry toilets – affordable – water toilets.

B. low-income households – poor water access – rich households.

C. healthy – have access to water and sanitation.

D. I feel – informed – now – before.

2 Obligation or possibility? Complete the following sentences.

A. NGOs .... organise campaigns to raise people's awareness.

B. A solution .... be found now to process contaminated water.

C. When there is no water access, inhabitants .... fill their buckets at a water point.

D. NGOs .... find partnerships with community-based companies to build toilets.

3 Cross the odd word out. Explain your choice orally.

A. hygienic – healthy – contaminated – sanitary

B. undertake – wait – take action – act

C. self-financing – raising money – crowdfunding – financing collectively

D. disease – health – illness – sickness

OPEN YOUR EARS!

La prononciation du *th* MP3 N°8

Écoutez les mots suivants et notez le numéro correspondant à la prononciation de *th*.

1 healthy • 2 their • 3 mother • 4 think • 5 they • 6 thousand

/θ/ (three): ....

/ð/ (the): ....

Attention de ne pas confondre : MP3 N°9

/s/ **et** /θ/ **:** *I think that there is no sink in this house.*
He is terribly sick ≠ He is terribly thick.

/z/ **et** /ð/ **:** *This child is close to his mother.*
This child is clothed by his mother.

4 Complete the following sentences by putting the adjective in the superlative form.

A. Learning that there are water access problems in the US was (*surprising*) element to me.

B. Households with (*low*) income have (*serious*) problems.

C. Unicef is optimistic that the situation will improve in (*affected*) areas.

5 Unit's checkout

React to this picture taken in South Africa and write a short speech to raise villagers' awareness using the following words. Use *must* and *can*.

unhygienic • secure • affordable • affect children and women first • human waste • disease • make a change • build dry toilets • private • take action

AXE 3

UNIT 7

BLACK ART MATTERS

How has the art world been portraying America's racial tensions?

YOUR PROJECTS

LV

Choose a work of art and imagine the post of a Black Lives Matter activist, explaining why it is important to support the movement and push for change.

ETLV STMG

In teams, choose an American brand and imagine its official statement supporting the Black Lives Matter movement.

Au menu de cette unité :

DÉCOUVERTES CULTURELLES

- Les tensions raciales aux États-Unis
- Le Ku Klux Klan
- Le cinéma afro-américain
- Des artistes engagés (Billie Holiday, Kadir Nelson…)
- L'afrofuturisme et le film *Black Panther*
- Les entreprises et le mouvement Black Lives Matter (marketing, subventions) ETLV STMG

OUTILS LINGUISTIQUES

- La voix passive
- Le lexique de la contestation, de la discrimination, de l'art et de la justice
- Les homographes et les mots transparents

GET READY!

WORD CHALLENGE

Use as many of these words as possible throughout the unit.
Tick ✓ the box when you have used the word.

- ☐ (be) prejudiced against (adj.)
- ☐ bias /'baɪəs/ (n.)
- ☐ brutality (n.)
- ☐ celebrate (v.)
- ☐ degrading (adj.)
- ☐ demonstrate (v.)
- ☐ denounce (v.)
- ☐ discriminate against (v.)
- ☐ discrimination (n.)
- ☐ empower /ɪm'paʊə/ (v.)
- ☐ look down on ≠ look up to (v.)
- ☐ painting (n.)
- ☐ piece of art = work of art (n.)
- ☐ portray
- ☐ prejudice (n.)
- ☐ pride / dignity /'dɪgnɪti/ (n.)
- ☐ protest /'prəʊtest/ song (n.)
- ☐ racism /'reɪsɪzm/ (n.)
- ☐ rise up for = stand up for = defend (v.)
- ☐ target (n. / v.)
- ☐ trauma /'trɔːmə/ (n.)

BEFORE CLASS!

A. **Watch the video and write what you have understood.**

www.lienmini.fr/htr7-u701

0'11 to 1'20 — 1'45 to 2'27

a. Principles / Ideology: ....

....

....

b. Symbols: ....

....

....

....

c. Actions: ....

....

....

B. **True or False? Tick the right anwer and justify with an element from the video.**

a. The white costume has always been the only symbol of the KKK.

T ☐ F ☐

....

....

....

b. The KKK has established connections with other hate groups in America.

T ☐ F ☐

....

....

....

C. **Now watch the trailer for Spike Lee's *BlacKkKlansman* (2018) online. What strikes you? Use what you have learnt about the KKK to sum up the story.**

1 Expressing the Trauma of Racism

How does art depict America's racial issues?

1 Singing the pain away

Lloyd G. Wade, *Strange Fruit*, 2019

A. React to Lloyd G. Wade's painting, inspired by the song *Strange Fruit*.

a. Identify the characters and their environment. Say what strikes you about the painting, using the following words:

hang from *(être pendu(e) à qqch)*, curled up *(recroquevillé(e))*, braids / plaits /'plæts/ *(tresses)*

b. Guess what the singer's song could be about. Justify your answer with elements from the painting.

B. Listen to the protest song online and read the lyrics.

Strange Fruit

Southern trees bear strange fruit,
Blood on the leaves and blood at the root[1],
Black bodies swinging in the southern breeze,
Strange fruit hanging from the poplar trees.

Pastoral[2] scene of the gallant South,
The bulging[3] eyes and the twisted mouth,
Scent[4] of magnolias, sweet and fresh,
Then the sudden smell of burning flesh.

Here is the fruit for the crows[5] to pluck[6],
For the rain to gather, for the wind to suck,
For the sun to rot[7], for the trees to drop,
Here is a strange and bitter crop[8].

1 *racine* • **2** *rural* • **3** *exorbités* • **4** smell • **5** *corbeaux* • **6** *picorer*
7 *pourrir* • **8** *récolte*

Recorded by **Billie Holliday** in 1939
Music and lyrics by Lewis Allan (Abel Meeropol)

C. a. Underline the references to the place where the story of the song is set.

b. Highlight the words / images describing the "strange fruit" and identify what the fruit is.

c. What feelings does the song express? Use two words of your choice. Justify with quotations.

fury / sadness / kindness / pain / disgust / compassion / bravery / surprise

D. Pairwork. Do you think that the painting is a good illustration for the song? Why (not)?

2 A Tale of Two Hoodies

Cultural fact

- This painting was created during the Trayvon Martin case (2012). Trayvon Martin was a 17-year-old African-American student who was shot by a man who claimed self-defence, but was ultimately charged with murder. He was acquitted at the end of the trial.

Michael D'Antuono's painting was controversial. He put his painting on eBay, planning to give half of the profits to the Trayvon Martin Foundation, but eBay censored his work.

- **Confederate flag:** Symbol of white supremacy / slavery for Southerners since the Civil War (1861-1865).

Michael D'Antuono, *A Tale of Two Hoodies*, 2012

A. React to the painting. Identify the symbols and the contrasts between the characters' clothes and attitudes.

B. Find a link with recent US history.

C. Identify the artist's intention and give your opinion about it.

HELP!

Nouns
- candy bar
- hooded sweatshirt /ˈswetʃɜːt/ = hoodie
- Ku Klux Klan /kuː klʌks ˈklæn/ / KKK hood
- police uniform / officer

Adjective
- threatening

Verbs & Expressions
- aim at sb with a gun
- offer / hand sth to sb
- point a gun at sb / at point-blank range (*à bout portant*)

YOUR TURN! 3 Group debate

Is some form of exaggeration necessary to make people react?
Give your opinion about the impact of Michael D'Antuono's representation of racism.

HELP!

Adjectives
- beneficial ≠ detrimental to a cause
- biased /ˈbaɪəst/
- distorted
- exaggerated
- provocative
- shocking
- simplistic

Verbs & Expressions
- caricature
- raise awareness
- shock sb into awareness / understanding sth
- shock sb out of indifference
- scare sb into action / reacting

❷ Black Lives Matter Protest Art

How have American artists used the Civil Rights Movement to push for change?

1 The need for a movement

www.lienmini.fr/htr7-u702

A. Watch the video and gather information about Black Lives Matter:

a. Pick out the reasons for the movement.

b. Identify the circumstances of George Floyd's death.

B. Create a timeline of the major events in recent African-American history, from segregation to George Floyd's death.

2 The call for change in the press

Kadir Nelson (www.kadirnelson.com), *American Uprising*, 2020

Eugène Delacroix, *La Liberté guidant le peuple*, 1830

A. React to the original oil painting by American artist Kadir Nelson on the cover of *Rolling Stone magazine* after the killing of George Floyd (2020). What strikes you about the structure of the illustration and the characters' postures?

B. In groups, share your interpretation of the artist's message.

C. Find an alternative title for this work of art. Justify your choice.

HELP!

Nouns
- allegory
- demonstration
- icon
- march
- protest sign
- revolution
- symbol
- tribute to

Verbs & Expressions
- demand: *exiger*
- lead
- protest
- raise (one's) fist

3 When a whole system needs to change

Scott Stantis, 2020

Dave Whamond, 2020

A. Look at the cartoons and react to the representation of the US justice system.

Focus on the characteristics of the two monuments. What strikes you?

HELP!

Nouns
- cartoon
- court of justice
- justice system
- pediment: *fronton*
- the scales of justice: *la balance de la justice*

Adjectives
- blind
- ironic

Verbs & Expressions
- be charged with (a crime)
- be condemned ≠ be acquitted
- be treated equally before the law
- be prosecuted
- stick: *rester collé(e) / accroché(e)*
- turn a blind eye to sb / sth

B. Draw a parallel between the characters' thoughts and the Black Lives Matter movement.

C. What common point can you see between the cartoons?

D. Groupwork. Which cartoon better represents the subject, according to you? Justify your choice.

www.lienmini.fr/htr7-u703

4 Taking art to the street

A. Watch the video and take notes to collect as much information as you can.
Title of the piece: "Black Lives Matter Mural Unveiled in Brooklyn".

B. Write a 100-word article describing the artistic event.

3 Victims No More

How do artists celebrate Black culture?

1 Afrofuturism

B*lack Panther* is the first mainstream superhero film to feature a predominantly Black all-star cast, a Black director (Ryan Coogler [...]), Black screenwriters, and an immensely Black supporting cast and crew. From the imagery, the colours, the natural hairstyles, the fashion, to the action-packed fight scenes [...] and dynamic storyline, *Black Panther* came through in all its afrofuturistic glory.

While *Black Panther* didn't invent Afrofuturism, the film adds to the already rich artistic history of those who kept the movement alive. [...] Afrofuturism is a cultural and artistic movement that seeks to insert Blackness and African identity into science-fiction. It is a type of mystical reimagining of our past, present and future as Africans or African Americans, by combining traditional culture with futuristic elements. It is a political movement, and it is a feminist movement as it often emphasizes the idea of liberation from oppressive institutions.

K. Yusuf, LGA, 2018

A. **Read the article and highlight the characteristics which make the film *Black Panther* special.**

B. **Underline the elements describing Afrofuturism then explain why the film is Afrofuturistic.**

....

....

....

C. Groupwork. **Look at the poster and watch the scene. Study the elements from Afrofuturism in the representation of Black culture in *Black Panther*. How does the film represent the future of Black culture?**

....

....

....

....

....

....

....

....

....

....

....

....

www.lienmini.fr/htr7-u704

HELP!

Nouns & Adjectives
- futuristic
- headdress
- skyscraper
- spaceship
- technologically-advanced
- tribal /'traɪbəl/ costumes / jewellery /'dʒu:əlri/
- weaponry /'wepənri/: *armes, arsenal*

2 Kehinde Wiley

In 2017, Nigerian-American portrait painter Kehinde Wiley made history when he became the first Black artist to paint an official presidential portrait. [...] Since this major project, Wiley has continued to reimagine traditional portraiture. Most recently, he challenged the expectations of equestrian painting with *Rumors of War*, a monumental sculpture [...]. With this piece, Wiley rethinks the concept of a "hero" – and of American identity. "Today," he said during the sculpture's unveiling in Times Square, "we say yes to something that looks like us. We say yes to inclusivity. We say yes to broader notions of what it means to be an American."

Kelly Richman-Abdou, ***mymodernmet.com***

Rumors of War, by Kehinde Wiley, 2019, New York

HELP!

Nouns
- celebration
- dignity /ˈdɪgnɪti/
- inclusitivity
- pride

Verbs & Expressions
- crown /kraʊn/ oneself
- honour = pay tribute to = celebrate

A. Read the text. Highlight information about Kehinde Wiley and share your answers.

B. Underline the words / expressions describing the sculpture and its message.

C. Draw a parallel between the text and the picture. What strikes you in the artist's intention?

3 A musical celebration of Blackness

The Carters [*a.k.a.* Beyoncé and Jay-Z] [...] took over the famous Louvre museum in Paris and made it their property [in their music video]. By choosing a location that is directly linked to royalty and international art, the power couple crowned themselves as the worldwide king and queen of popular music. Their proclamation of Blackness in an often inaccessible space like the Louvre is a statement in itself. [...] The Carters are making – as well as honoring – history by crafting art and showing it to be, at its core, for Black people.

Brooklyn White, Adapted from ***hellogiggles.com***

A. Read the text describing Beyoncé and Jay-Z's music video.

a. Highlight the elements describing the place where the video clip was shot.

b. Underline the elements referring to the couple.

B. Go online and watch the video clip. Focus on the representation of the couple and Black culture and identify the goal of this project.

YOUR PROJECT BAC

Choose an American work of art (cinema, painting, music, street art...) and imagine the post of a Black Lives Matter activist, explaining why the piece is important to support the movement and talk people into change (120 words). Do some research if necessary.

4 US Corporations Support Black Lives Matter

ETLV STMG

How do companies try to reconnect with the African-American reality?

OBJECTIVES STMG

- Identify a CSR action and explain its objectives
- Identify perceived value indicators

1 The need for US companies to respond

Not too long ago, few companies paid much attention to Black Lives Matter. Today, in the wake of the George Floyd protests, it seems as if most major companies including Apple, Amazon and Facebook have endorsed the movement – or at a minimum pledged millions of dollars to fight racism and vowed to do more to end discrimination in their workplaces.

So how did companies so swiftly decide to align with Black Lives Matter?

As with anything, there usually are lots of reasons. But, as a scholar who studies the psychology of consumer behavior and how companies respond to it, I believe that one stands out: young people.

A post-Floyd poll found that nearly 90% of members of Generation Z[1] – those born from 1997 to 2005 – believe African Americans are treated differently and support Black Lives Matter. [...] More than two-thirds of Generation Z and millennials think brands should be even more involved in Black Lives Matter.

[T]he views of generations Y and Z are particularly significant because attracting younger consumers is so vital to brands' future growth. [...] And the vast majority of millennials say it's important that the companies they buy from share their values, which is also true for Gen Z.

It's also noteworthy that brands are expressing their support for the movement largely via social media, which is the primary place millennials learn about brands.

The Conversation, 2020

1 Generation X = those born between 1965 and 1980,
Generation Y = those born between 1981 and 1996,
Generation Z = those born between 1997 and 2005.

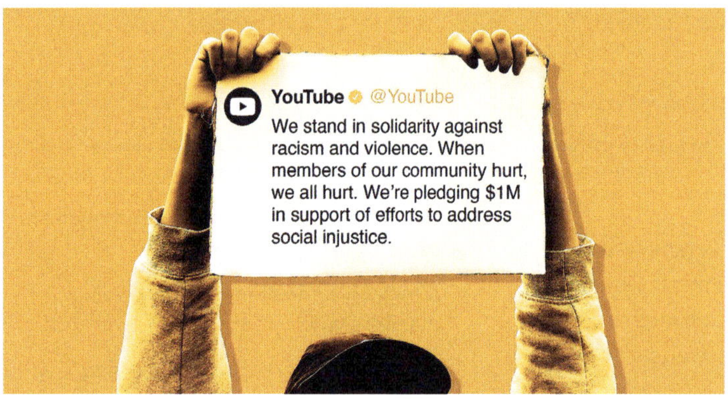

HELP!

Verbs & Expressions

- address an issue
- commit oneself (to a cause): *s'engager pour*
- donate
- endorse = support
- make a statement: *faire une déclaration*
- pledge = promise /'prɒmɪs/
- raise funds /fʌndz/

A. React to the picture. What strikes you about the brand's statement? Discuss the impact of such a message on the consumers.

....

....

....

B. Read the article and focus on the response of US companies to Black Lives Matter. Identify their reactions and pick out the reasons why they support the movement.

....

....

....

2 The brands that are doing it right

Many brands are now making Black Lives Matter statements, but a rare few are actually contributing to change. [...] Some brands, however, are making real clear statements and helpful commitments – here are some things other brands can learn from them:

BE CLEAR

[...] Ben & Jerry's stand out for their no-quarter-given boldness[1] [...] Their social media post states: "What happened to George Floyd was not the result of a bad apple; it was the predictable consequence of a racist and prejudiced system and culture that has treated Black bodies as the enemy from the beginning."The brand, who have long been champions of various social causes, from equal marriage [for the LGBTQ community] to climate activism, [in response to the Floyd murder] also called for 4 concrete actions including demanding the Department of Justice reinvigorate its Civil Rights Division [...].

SUPPORT YOUR OWN PEOPLE

[...] Niantic, the company behind Pokemon Go, announced that the company will be donating $5 million to racial justice causes. Half of that will go towards funding new projects from Black creators, and the other half will go towards US nonprofits. In addition, it will donate $100,000 [...], match employee contributions up to $50,000, and provide all employees with 5 'Flex' days a year to volunteer for the cause of their choice.

UPLIFT BLACK BUSINESS

Another way to support Black people is through promoting Black-owned businesses, often side-lined[2] in white, big brand-dominated industries. [...] To that end, Glossier[3] set aside $500,000 in the form of grants that will be distributed to Black-owned beauty businesses, and delayed the launch of their latest product 'in an effort to focus attention, and that of their audience, on the ongoing fight against racial injustice.'

1 courage • **2** *mis de côté* • **3** cosmetics company

The Marketing Society, 2020

A. Read the text and highlight the words describing the ways some US brands react to Black Lives Matter.

B. Identify the different types of power companies can have to support a cause, and explain them with quotations.

....

....

....

....

....

Cultural fact

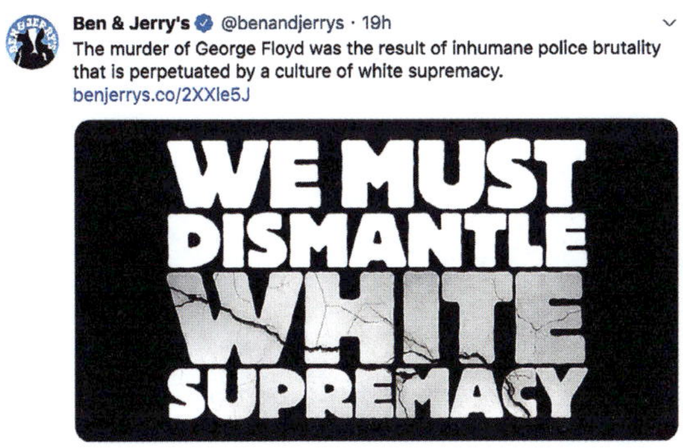

Ben & Jerry's, founded in 1978 in Burlington, Vermont, has a history of commitment in social, environmental and political causes. The brand has been working deeply on racial justice issues over the past 5 years, signing up to support the Black Lives Matter movement in 2016.

C. Express your personal opinion about these companies' strategies in connection with their CSR.

HELP!

Nouns
- grant = financial award
- non-profit: *organisation à but non lucratif*
- statement = declaration

Expression
- talk sb into sth /doing sth: *convaincre qqn de qqch / de faire qqch*

DEFINITIONS ETLV
- Corporate Social Responsibility (CSR) is a management concept that includes social and environmental concerns in business.
- The brand image and the reputation of an organisation are part of its **perceived value**.

YOUR PROJECT

In teams, choose an American brand and imagine its official statement supporting the BLM movement (100 words). Find a link between the brand's identity and their support of the BLM movement. The goal will be to talk the American government, customers or users into making a real change. Include your statement in a poster, a TV commercial or a speech.

RULE THE GRAMMAR!

LA VOIX PASSIVE

• Formation

Auxiliaire ***be*** conjugué au temps souhaité + **participe passé** (verbes réguliers + ***-ed*** / 3e colonne verbes irréguliers (+ *by* + agent)

• Emploi

Voix active	Voix passive
La personne à l'origine de l'action (agent) est davantage mise en valeur que l'action ou ceux qui la subissent. *The KKK persecuted African Americans for decades after the Civil War.*	**On insiste sur l'action et le sujet qui la subit**, plutôt que sur la personne qui est à l'origine de l'action (l'agent). *African Americans **were persecuted** for decades (**by** the KKK) after the Civil War.*

VOCABULARY

Black Art Matters

Art

- caricature /'kærɪkətʃʊə/ (v.)
- committed (art) (adj.)
- controversial /kɒntrə'vɜːʃəl/ (adj.)
- convey a message (v.)
- mural / graffiti /grə'fiːti/ (n.)
- portray = represent = depict (v.)
- protest song
- sculpture /'skʌlptʃə/ (n.)
- street art (n.)
- subversive /səb'vɜːsɪv/ (adj.)
- work of art (n.)

Your words: ....

Racial tensions

- discriminate against (v.)
- persecution (n.)
- (be) prejudiced (against) (adj.)
- prejudice (n.)
- segregation (n.)
- target (n.) (v.)

Your words: ....

Justice

- (be) (wrongfully) accused of sth / V-ing (adj.)
- (be) acquitted /ə'kwɪtɪd/ (adj.)
- (be) brought to justice (adj.)
- (be) charged with (adj.)
- civil rights (n.)
- court of justice (n.)
- justice system (n.)
- put sb under arrest (v.)
- stand trial /'traɪəl/
- trial / prosecution (n.)
- (un)fairly (adv.)

Your words: ....

Protest

- activist (n.)
- demand equal rights
- demonstration = protest (n.)
- denounce /dɪ'naʊns/ (v.)
- raise awareness of (v.)
- riot /'raɪət/ (n.): *émeute*
- spark sth (off) (v.): *déclencher*
- stand up for = rise up for (v.)

Your words: ....

LANGUAGE LAB

1 Cross the odd word out. Explain your choice orally.

A. street art – sport – sculpture – mural – protest song

B. separation – division – segregation – exclusion – connection

C. preconception – prejudice – bias – tolerance – stereotype

D. indifferent – committed – engaged – involved – dedicated

2 Complete the sentences with the following elements.

prejudiced • demonstration • under arrest • trial • controversial

A. Tomorrow at the court, the prisoner will stand .... for his crimes.

B. The artist's work of art was .... because it was a caricature of police brutality.

C. Yesterday's Black Lives Matter .... was crushed (*écrasée*) by the National Guard.

D. The officer put the woman .... for no known reasons.

E. The US justice system seems to have a .... conception of African Americans.

3 Translate the sentences using the passive voice.

A. *Les Afro-Américains sont souvent ciblés par les autorités.*

....

B. *Trop d'Afro-Américains sont discriminés injustement.*

....

C. *Le mouvement Black Lives Matter fut créé par des militants des droits civiques.*

....

D. *La chanson de Beyoncé est inspirée du mouvement BLM.*

....

4 Rewrite the sentences using the passive voice.

A. Spike Lee directed *BlacKkKlansman* in 2018.

....

B. The death of George Floyd sparked the revival of the BLM movement. ....

C. The Black Lives Matter movement has changed America.

....

D. A street artist painted a mural to pay tribute to George Floyd. ....

E. The police shooting sparked the riot.

....

5 Unit's checkout

Use what you have learnt to imagine the woman's words.

....

Nicole Wandera / the omicollective

OPEN YOUR EARS!

Les homographes et les mots transparents

MP3 N°10

1. Écoutez les mots suivants dont l'orthographe ressemble à leurs équivalents français.
2. Soulignez les syllabes accentuées et surlignez les consonnes muettes (que l'on ne prononce pas).
3. Lisez à voix haute chaque mot après avoir écouté le modèle.

brutality • caricature • celebrate • celebration • costume • court • demonstration • dignity • discrimination • honour • icon • ironic • justice • movement • police • promise • racism • revolution • symbol • uniform

AXE 4

UNIT 8

CITIZEN GAME

How do video games create bonds between individuals?

YOUR PROJECTS

LV
Make a commercial for a virtual world inside a video game.

ETLV STI2D
Create an infographic about A/R and V/R for *Popular Science*.

ETLV STMG
Write an article revealing the business strategies of an American video games company.

Au menu de cette unité :

DÉCOUVERTES CULTURELLES

- La socialisation par le jeu vidéo
- L'engagement caritatif et politique grâce au jeu vidéo
- Le jeu vidéo, source d'inspiration des auteurs de science-fiction
- Réalité virtuelle/augmentée, du jeu vidéo aux applications dans la médecine et l'armée ETLV STI2D
- L'industrie du jeu vidéo et le placement de produits ETLV STMG

OUTILS LINGUISTIQUES

- Les structures causatives (« faire faire qqch à qqn »)
- L'expression du futur
- Le lexique des technologies du jeu vidéo, de la pratique du jeu vidéo, de la socialisation et de l'industrie du jeu vidéo
- La prononciation de *ea*

GET READY!

WORD CHALLENGE

**Use as many of these words as possible throughout the unit.
Tick ✓ the box when you have used the word.**

- ☐ abilities (n.)
- ☐ addicted to (adj.)
- ☐ addiction (n.)
- ☐ augmented reality (A/R) (n.)
- ☐ cheer on (v.)
- ☐ controversial /kɒntrəˈvɜːʃl/ (adj.)
- ☐ digital /ˈdɪdʒɪtl/ (adj.): *numérique*
- ☐ e-sport (n.)
- ☐ gaming (n.)
- ☐ product placement (n.)
- ☐ relationships / connections / bonds (n.)
- ☐ social /ˈsəʊʃl/ networks / platforms (n.)
- ☐ social skills (n.)
- ☐ socialising /ˈsəʊʃəlaɪzɪŋ/ (n.)
- ☐ stay / keep in touch (v.)
- ☐ (un)healthy (adj.)
- ☐ virtual /ˈvɜːtʃuəl/ reality (V/R) (n.)

BEFORE CLASS!

A. Watch the video. Write keywords.

a. Bad news about video games:

....

....

....

....

....

b. Good news about video games:

....

....

....

....

....

....

....

....

www.lienmini.fr/htr7-u801

B. Explain the experts' advice for a good use of video games.

....

....

....

C. Are video games bad for you? Give your opinion.

....

....

....

....

1 Socialising by Playing Video Games

How do video games improve social skills?

1 The power of games

A. Study the infographic for 5 minutes.

B. True or False? Tick the right answer. Justify with an element from the infographic.

a. Video games can boost general knowledge. T ☐ F ☐

....

....

b. Playing games is beneficial to Australian economy. T ☐ F ☐

....

....

c. Video games can help players to manage stress and pain. T ☐ F ☐

....

....

d. All gamers are boys. T ☐ F ☐

....

C. Pick out three surprising or interesting facts about the powers of gaming. Explain your choice orally.

HELP!

Nouns
- 2/3 = two thirds of...
- 20% = 20 percent of...
- skills = abilities

Verbs & Expressions
- allow /əˈlaʊ/
- connect with people
- help sb (to) + BV
- improve = make sth / sb better
- make people do sth
- socialise /ˈsəʊʃəlaɪz/

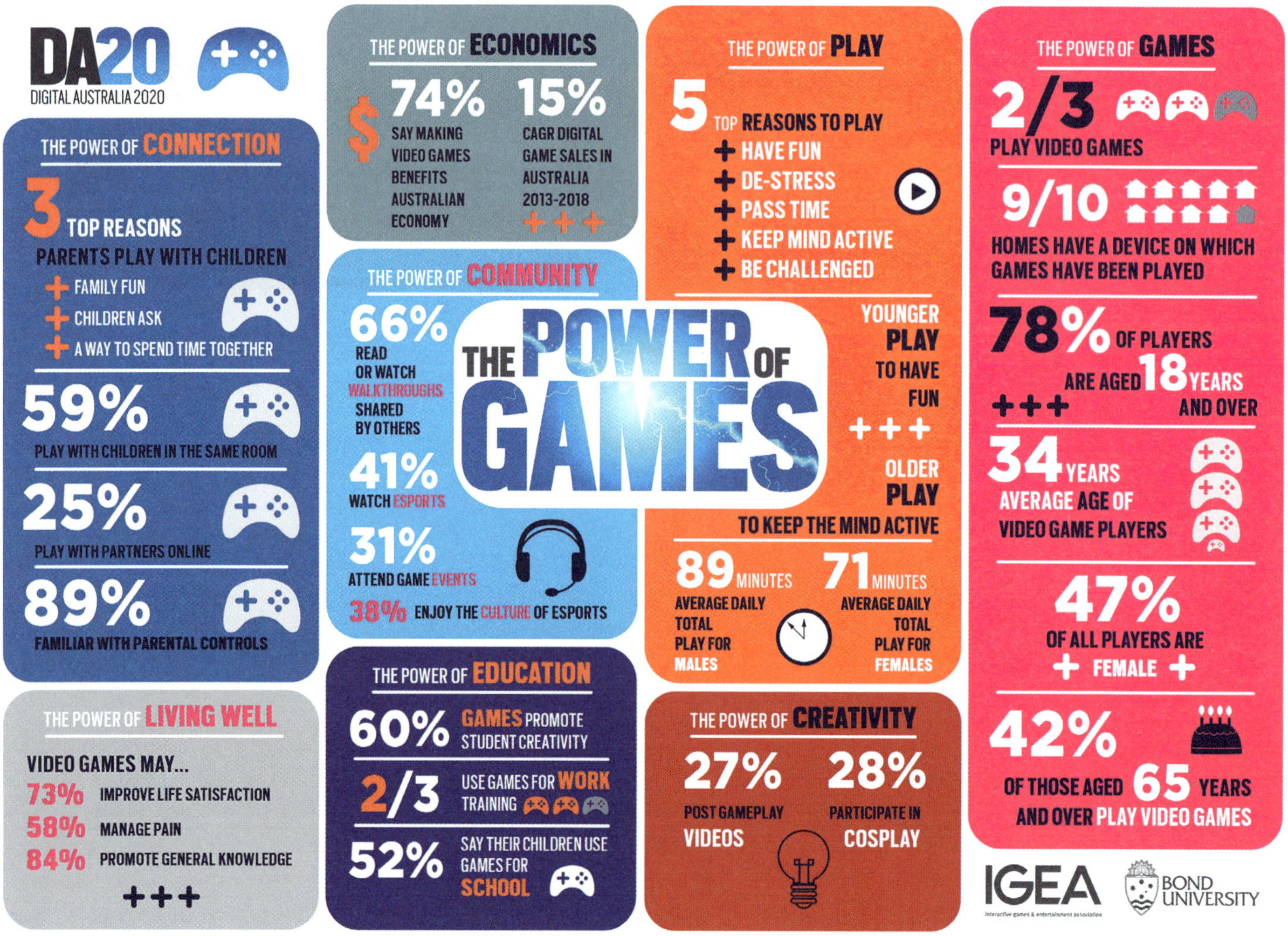

2 Gaming and sharing

A. Watch the video and take notes. Focus on the keywords about gaming and social interactions to organise your notes in a mind map, or a chart.

B. **Groupwork.** Share what you have understood. Say why the document breaks clichés about gaming.

www.lienmini.fr/htr7-u802

0'10 to 1'26

1'46 to 2'29

3 Games as multiple-experience spaces

A narrative[1] has been allowed to swirl[2] in media circles that *Fortnite, Roblox*[3] *et al.*, are the social networks of the future. Sure, engagement and socializing are what makes those games tick[4] but they're more than just a place to add friends and collect likes and followers. In fact, *Fortnite* and *Roblox* are closer to what the theme parks of the future will look like. [...]

The Marvel-themed fourth season of the game concluded last week when *Fortnite* players were pitted against[5] the planet-sized supervillain Galactus. [...] A record 15.3 million concurrent players took part in the event, while more than 3.4 million watched it all unfold on YouTube and Twitch according to *Fortnite's* creators. For context, the final episode of the final season of *Game of Thrones* was watched by 13.6 million viewers live on the HBO channel. *Fortnite's* lofty numbers reveal a key point. It isn't a video game so much as it is a destination with a myriad of entertainment experiences and social interactions available, depending on what someone feels like doing, and who they're hanging out with. Yes, there are gamers who only play, but there are others also watching people play, influencing those matches and talking about doing so while streaming to hundreds of thousands of people.

1 story • 2 *(ici) tourner en boucle* • 3 *Roblox* is an online game platform that brings people together • 4 make (sth) work • 5 confronted with

digiday.com, December 2020

A. Read the text and highlight the keywords describing *Fortnite* and *Roblox*. What is striking?

B. Focus on the social aspect and underline the types of interactions which are made possible in the games. What are the benefits?

YOUR TURN! 4 Advertise an online game platform

BAC

You have been asked to write a promotional text for the official website of *Fortnite* (100 words). Your goal is to show that your game breaks the clichés about gaming.

2 Global Gaming Citizens

How have video games become a place for social involvement?

1 Playing for charities

There has been a quiet revolution in the world of philanthropy[1] over recent years, driven by the fact that sitting down to play a video game [...] can raise thousands or even millions of dollars for charity – as long as you do it live on the internet.

"The impact is big and getting bigger," says Jeremy Wells, fundraising[2] events manager for Médecins sans frontières, a popular partner for charity streams. "Summer Games Done Quick is our biggest fundraiser of the year – it brought in $2.1m last year out of $4.7m for our whole events program."

Charity streaming is similar to old-school telethons or donation drives: streamers broadcast[3] themselves playing games live on the internet while urging[4] viewers to donate to charity. Games Done Quick – a twice-a-year multiday showcase[5] where speedrunners utilise technical knowledge, well-honed[6] skills and physics-defying glitches[7] to race through games as fast as possible – is one of the scene's biggest events. But it's far from the only charity stream out there. Streaming platform Twitch estimates between 2012 and 2017, more than $75m was raised for various charities on its service alone.

1 being charitable • 2 collecting money • 3 *diffuser*
4 encourage • 5 event • 6 *bien aiguisées* • 7 *bug*

The Guardian, February 2019

The *League of Legends* "Streamathon" (May 2020) gathered gamers from many countries to raise funds to help fight the COVID-19 pandemic. The tournament's prize amounted to US$600,000.

A. Read the text and highlight the words, expressions and figures, related to charity in the video gaming world.

B. Circle the words describing charity streams (type of shows, people involved, goal…).
Explain what they are in your own words. Give an example.

C. Pick out an example of a cause defended by charity streams.

D. Watch the video *AGDQ 2019 Finale* online and take notes to complete the chart.

Players	
Reasons for participating	Feelings about the event

AGDQ (Awesome Games Done Quick)	
The organisation	Social benefits

2 Politics and video games

Watch the video and take notes.

a. Identify the two political gaming events of 2020 described in the video.

b. Give information about younger voters in America.

c. What was the goal of the video game event?

d. Identify the key ideas of the other political gaming events mentioned at the end of the video.

www.lienmini.fr/htr7-u804

0'00 to 1'06

2'20 to 2'52

3 The gamer vote

On Tuesday night, US members of Congress Alexandria Ocasio-Cortez and Ilhan Omar held what is perhaps the most unusual voter outreach[1] event in recent memory. They signed on to play a livestreamed video game on Twitch [...]. They were playing the incredibly popular *Among Us* [...] And it was [...] an incredible success. Ocasio-Cortez's Twitch channel garnered[2] a staggering audience of 439,000 viewers, all watching her in real time [...] with approximately 5.2 million viewers watching the stream [...].

But Ocasio-Cortez and Omar aren't just famous people playing an unusually popular video game; they're members of Congress trying to get out the vote. And in this, they achieved something most politicians attempt[3] and fail at daily: they looked like completely normal people. [...]. Credibility goes a long way here: AOC, in particular, has an established online presence [...]. This, like the notion of playing a video game when she and Omar ostensibly have "more important" things to do, has earned her the scorn[4] of others in Congress, but consider the things other candidates do to get out the vote: fish fries, baby kissing and benefit concerts. You go where people are, and in 2020, young people are watching video games played on Twitch.

1 *rayonnement* • 2 collect • 3 try • 4 *mépris*

The Guardian, October 2020

A. **Read the text and highlight the information about the streaming event mentioned in the text (players, game, audience, reception, goal…). Rephrase the event in your words.**

B. **Focus on the politicians' strategies to attract voters and say what makes this event special.**

C. **What do you think of this type of political events?**

3 An Inspiring Form of Entertainment

How is American science-fiction inspired by the social benefits of gaming?

1 Reality 3.0

A. Study the poster of *Ready Player One*, by Steven Spielberg (2018). Say what strikes you.

B. Guess the role of the video game in this story.

HELP!

Nouns
- escape
- headset / head-up display
- hope
- poverty
- slums: *bidonvilles*
- V/R (Virtual Reality)

Adjectives
- desolate /'desələt/
- dirty

Expression
- full of opportunities

2 The only place to be?

The OASIS[1] contained hundreds (and eventually thousands) of high-resolution 3-D worlds for people to explore, and each one was beautifully rendered in meticulous graphical detail [...]. Users could circumnavigate each of these planets and never see the same terrain twice. [...] Halliday and Morrow referred to the OASIS as an "open-source reality," a malleable[2] online universe that anyone could access via the Internet, using their existing home computer or videogame console. You could log in and instantly escape the drudgery[3] of your day-to-day life. You could create an entirely new persona for yourself, with complete control over how you looked and sounded to others. In the OASIS, the fat could become thin, the ugly could become beautiful, and the shy, extroverted. Or vice versa. You could change your name, age, sex, race, height, weight, voice, hair color, and bone structure. Or you could cease being human altogether, and become an elf, ogre, alien, or any other creature from literature, movies, or mythology. In the OASIS, you could become whomever and whatever you wanted to be, without ever revealing your true identity, because your anonymity was guaranteed. [...] The OASIS was what people had been dreaming of for decades. The "virtual reality" they had been promised for so long was finally here, and it was even better than they'd imagined. The OASIS was an online utopia.

1 /əʊ'eɪsɪs/ • 2 flexible • 3 *corvée*

Ready Player One,
by Ernest Cline, 2011

A. Read the text from *Ready Player One* (opposite page) and highlight the technological characteristics of the OASIS.

B. Use your findings to complete the following information.

a. Type of platform the OASIS is:

b. How it works:

C. Focus on the visual appearance of the OASIS. What surprises you about the game environment?

D. Underline the expressions describing the opportunities offered by the OASIS. Explain why it is seen as a utopia.

E. React to the name. Why is the game called the "OASIS"?

F. Watch the trailer for Steven Spielberg's adaptation online. Is it faithful to the text? Give your opinion.

3 The message behind the story

A. Read the text about the novel *Ready Player One*.

B. Focus on the relationship between Aech and Wade. How does the game facilitate friendship?

C. Pick out information about Aech. Highlight the elements about the character's identity and story. Explain the benefits of the OASIS for the character according to the journalist.

D. **Groupwork.** Share your answers and discuss the advantages of this type of relationships. Can you think about some drawbacks?

Surely, the big idea friendships have been shown throughout *Ready Player One*. The big idea friendships are portrayed by Aech and Wade. First meeting online [...] Aech and Wade quickly bonded. Playing video games, watching movies, or completing quests is how they would spend their days together. Since they are best friends online and not in the outside or real world, they've never met and are unsure of what their actual appearances are. [...] Aech's character online can be described as a tall, broad shouldered Caucasian male with dark hair and brown eyes. She reveals her true identity to Wade, Helen Harris, in reality, is a girl, an African American, and lesbian. She wasn't accepted for herself, so she made it possible for her to be somebody on the online world. Even though Aech lied completely about her appearance, it wouldn't change their relationship.

weebly.com

YOUR PROJECT BAC

Make a commercial for the OASIS. You are about to launch an essential update of the OASIS that will offer new opportunities. Promote the game by introducing its concept and the new possibilities related to your update, and attract some new players! Your commercial can be a short scene performed live, a video with a voice-over, or a poster with a text...

4 Video Game-Inspired Technologies

ETLV STI2D

How can Augmented and Virtual Realities have useful applications for society?

OBJECTIVES STI2D

- Share an idea, a project, a hypothesis or a technical solution
- Choose and use the right technological communication tool

www.lienmini.fr/htr7-u805

0'00 to 2'38

1 From V/R to A/R

A. Groupwork. Watch the video and pick out information about A/R (group 1), or V/R (group 2).
Focus on the devices and their key functions.

B. Share your findings and make a mind map with the key information corresponding to each technology.

C. Group 1 reads Text 1. Group 2 reads Text 2. Each group completes the chart.

Text 1	Text 2
Characteristics of A/R using 5G	Ingredients of social V/R
....	....
....	....
....	....
....	....
Benefits for the players	Benefits for the players
....	....
....	....
....	....

Text 1

Mobile 5G: the AR game changer

With 5G capabilities, you will be able to pull up an AR game, look through your screen and [...] get instantaneous data on the world around you.

For example, [Kevin Mack, a VR game developer] said, "Imagine that people are in a social AR experience, and they created custom avatars for themselves, so anybody else who's using the same application [...] sees this person in whatever costume they designed for themselves. You're going to need to have some fast way to make that data available." The technology behind 5G promises to answer that. This breakthrough will not only make mobile gaming better, it will likely create a network effect in which more and more people get into mobile gaming [...] due to an increase in cultural buzz about the high-quality experience of AR gaming.

builtin.com, February 2020

Text 2

The social VR

Here's how it works. Players gather in a physical space, like the inside of a warehouse, and strap on helmets and computers that double as backpacks. They proceed to participate in a virtual activity together, a mission. But unlike the typical VR experience, where everything takes place inside the goggles[1], hyperreality game players will notice that what they see in their headsets[2] actually corresponds to the physical space of the room. So they can run around, duck[3] and, in some cases, even reach for a virtual object and feel it – in the form of a strategically placed physical prop[4]. The interplay between virtual reality and tactile feedback[5] creates a uniquely immersive experience.

1 glasses • **2** helmet • **3** *esquiver* • **4** accessory • **5** reaction

builtin.com, February 2020

2 From "video gaming" to "video training"

A. **Groupwork.** Discover two different real-life applications of A/R and V/R.

Group 1 works on Video 1.
Group 2 works on Video 2.

B. Take notes and share your findings in groups to organise the information.

C. Each group presents one real-life application of A/R or V/R.

D. Explain how video games inspired a real technology beneficial to society.

1

www.lienmini.fr/htr7-u806

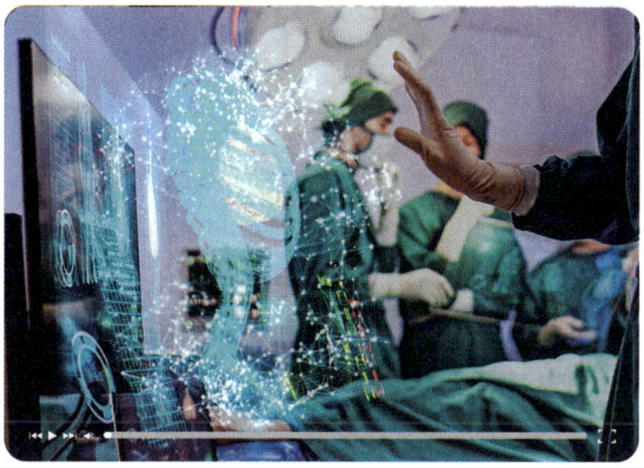

2

www.lienmini.fr/htr7-u807

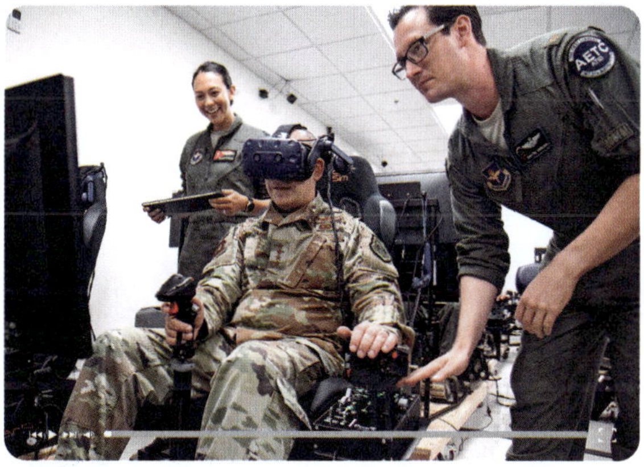

HELP!

How to talk about a technology's application

- Teachers have their students practise with…
- The device will help… (to) + BV
- Using… gets students to + BV / makes them + BV

DEFINITION ETLV

- A **network** consists of multiple devices that communicate with one another. It can be as small as two computers or as large as billions of devices. While a traditional network includes desktop computers, modern networks may include laptops, tablets, smartphones, connected TV sets, gaming consoles, smart appliances, and other electronic devices.

YOUR PROJECT BAC

You have been asked to create an infographic on the differences between A/R and V/R for *Popular Science* magazine.
The infographic will include illustrations, explanations and examples to show why these new technologies may potentially change our lives.

5 The Business of Video Games

ETLV STMG

How has gaming become a valuable industry?

OBJECTIVES STMG

- Make a connection between working conditions and staff behaviour
- Analyse a communication strategy
- Evaluate the impact of a digital technology on a company's communication

1 The gaming industry

A. Study the infographic. Compare the gaming industry with other entertainment industries. What is striking?

....

....

....

....

B. True or False? Tick the right answer. Justify orally.

Video games are more lucrative than the box office and music industries combined.

T ☐ F ☐

Gaming: The Most Lucrative Entertainment Industry By Far

Global revenue of selected entertainment industy sectors in 2019

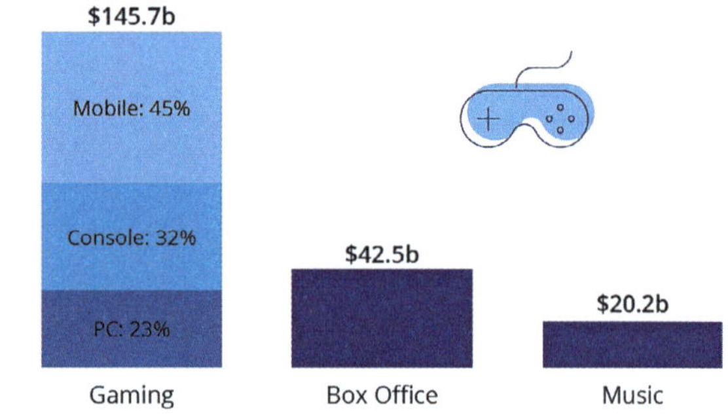

Sources: Newzoo, Comscore, IFPI

2 An exciting industry?

www.lienmini.fr/htr7-u808

1'43 to 2'43 — 3'07 to 3'46

HELP!

Nouns
- advertising
- brand
- layoff: *licenciement*

Expression
- (be) laid off = *être licencié(e)*

DEFINITION ETLV

A communication strategy is the scheme of planning how to share information for an organisation. If it targets consumers, it is called external communication.

A. Watch the video and take notes about the gaming industry.

B. Share your findings and complete the following information about the workers of the industry.

Pros: ....

....

....

....

Cons: ....

....

....

....

....

....

C. Why is the position of women paradoxical in the gaming industry?

....

....

....

....

....

3 Embedded marketing strategies

Video games are often ad-free[1], but increasingly they're not brand-free. Branded characters. One-off[2] events. Programmatic ads. Marketers are finding more ways to get their brands into games – big picture, gaming has gone mainstream[3]. [...]

It's a far cry from[4] a decade ago when Microsoft tried to convince advertisers to buy ads in Xbox games. Back then, the infrastructure wasn't in place to make in-game advertisers a cost-effective[5] endeavour[6]. [...] Video game publishers weren't as open to working with advertisers as they are now and it was expensive to hard code ads into games. As the infrastructure around in-game ads has matured, they're getting more experimental – and more frequent.

"Over the course of 2020, we've had 21 partners participate in our new in-game SR Arena Banners programs including Mastercard, Spotify, and Mercedes-Benz," said Naz Aletaha, head of global e-sports partnerships at Riot Games. "Our partnerships enable brands to be woven throughout the fabric[7] of our game and sport in ways that are meaningful and drive value to them and our community." [...] Take Duracell for example. Earlier this month, the advertiser became the first-shirt sponsor of footballer Gareth Bale's Eleven Sports team inside the *Fifa 21* game. [...]

There was a time when the idea of L'Oréal targeting gamers was pretty much unimaginable – not least because so few of them were believed to be women. While that may have been true for a time, it isn't anymore. Indeed, women now represent more than four in ten (41%) gamers in the U.S., per Statista. [...] "We want our brands to be where people are and increasingly women are spending more of their time on the gaming platforms," said L'Oréal's chief digital officer Lubomira Rochet. "We're thinking about doing product placements in games where the player or the viewer is able to buy what they see through micro-transactions."

1 *sans publicité* • 2 unique • 3 ordinary • 4 different from • 5 *rentable* • 6 *effort* • 7 *tissées (à l'intérieur du jeu)*

digiday.com, December 2020

A. Read the text and highlight the words and expressions about brands' strategies in video games.

B. Say what you have understood about the brands' strategies.

C. Focus on the evolution of marketing in video games and explain the changes with examples.

D. How have product placements changed with society?

YOUR PROJECT BAC

You are a journalist for an American video games magazine and you have investigated an American gaming company for two months. Write an article revealing the company's business strategies, and the pros and cons of working there.

RULE THE GRAMMAR!

1. STRUCTURES CAUSATIVES (« FAIRE FAIRE QQCH À QQN »)

• ***Make*** **(à conjuguer) + COD + BV**
Insiste sur un lien de cause à effet, ou une contrainte.
*She **made** me play her game.*

• ***Have*** **(à conjuguer) + COD + BV**
Intervention d'une tierce personne pour faire une action.
*He **had** the owner of the shop repair his computer.*

• ***Get / Order*** **(à conjuguer) COD + to + BV**
Quelqu'un va demander à quelqu'un d'autre de faire quelque chose.
*They **got / ordered** their children to turn off their computers after 9pm every evening.*

2. L'EXPRESSION DU FUTUR

• ***Will*** **+ BV** est utilisé pour exprimer une action qui se réalisera dans l'avenir.
*V/R **will** revolutionise the world of video games.*

• **Le présent *be* + *going to* + BV** peut être utilisé lorsque l'action qui se déroulera est en lien direct avec le présent.
*Wait for me, **I'm going to** help you complete your mission!*

VOCABULARY

Gaming

Gaming technologies

- app(lication) (n.)
- Augmented Reality (A/**R**) (n.)
- console/kən'səʊl/ (n.)
- head-up display (n.)
- online gaming (n.)
- streaming platform (n.)
- three-dimensional (3-D) /θriːdaɪ'menʃənəl/ (adj.)
- Virtual /'vɜːtʃuəl/ Reality (V/**R**) (n.)

Your words: ....

The gaming experience

- be addicted to (adj.)
- beneficial (to sb) (adj.)
- cut oneself off = isolate /'aɪsəleɪt/ oneself from (v.)
- detrimental (to) (adj.)
- educational (adj.)
- entertaining (adj.)
- harmful (adj.)
- immersive /ɪ'mɜːsɪv/ (adj.)
- lifelike = realistic /rɪə'lɪstɪk/ (adj.)
- rewarding /rɪ'wɔːdɪŋ/ (adj.)
- stimulating (adj.)
- unhealthy /ʌn'helθi/ (adj.)

Your words: ....

Social life

- charity (n.)
- connection (n.)
- create bonds (v.)
- dedicate oneself to sth / to V-ing (v.)
- e-sport event / competition (n.)
- interact (v.)
- involvement (n.)
- make friends with sb (v.)
- non-profit (adj. / n.)
- raise funds /fʌndz/
- self-isolation (n.)
- social /'səʊʃəl/ platform (n.)
- socialise /'səʊʃəlaɪz/ (v.)
- support a cause
- team spirit (n.)

Your words: ....

The gaming industry

- (be) laid off
- coder (n.)
- crunch time (n.)
- developer /dɪ'veləpə/ (n.)
- entertainment /entə'teɪnmənt/ (n.)
- lucrative /'luːkrətɪv/ (adj.)
- product placement

Your words: ....

MP3
www.lienmini.fr/htr7-u809

LANGUAGE LAB

1 Complete the sentences using the right terms.
V/R technology • head-up display • benefits • skills • addiction

A. Video game .... is a real issue among teenagers.

B. Video games will use .... to build realistic worlds for the players.

C. The user has to wear a .... in order to have a more immersive experience.

D. The .... of gaming are often ignored. They improve people's ....

2 Cross the odd word out. Justify your choice briefly.

A. competition – match – hobby – tournament – battle

B. real – natural – artificial – lifelike – realistic

C. unhealthy – harmful – advantageous – isolating – dangerous

D. bond – isolation – relationship – connection – attachment

3 Make sentences using the right causative structures with the help of the prompts.

A. The team worked very hard to design the latest video game.

The director of this video game company made the team ....

B. His parents now believe that playing video games in English will improve his speaking and listening skills.

He got his parents ....

C. Tomorrow, the technician will fix my internet access.

Tomorrow, I will have ....

4 Translate these sentences into English. Use *be going to* + BV, or *will* + BV to express the future. Get some help with the mind map p. 100.

A. *Les jeux vidéo seront bientôt le meilleur moyen de rencontrer des amis.*

....

B. *Fais attention, tu vas être accro aux écrans !*

....

C. *Dans le futur, les gens porteront des casques de réalité virtuelle pour s'amuser.*

....

D. *La prochaine compétition d'e-sport va lever des fonds contre le cancer.*

....

5 Unit's checkout

You are going to take part in this event.
Post this picture with a 50-word comment explaining why you will participate.

....

OPEN YOUR EARS!

La prononciation de *ea* MP3 N°11

Écoutez les mots suivants, puis notez le numéro correspondant à la prononciation de *ea*.
1 head • 2 realistic • 3 team • 4 streaming • 5 real • 6 wear • 7 unhealthy

/e/ (felt): ....

/iː/ (deal): ....

/ɪə/ (near): ....

/eə/ (share): ....

AXE 4

UNIT 9

THE WILD WILD WEB

Is there much privacy left in today's world?

YOUR PROJECTS

LV

Create a poster to give a list of tips for a safe use of social media.

ETLV STMG

Make a video dealing with the use of personal data by potential employers. Give examples and tips.

Au menu de cette unité :

DÉCOUVERTES CULTURELLES

- L'empreinte numérique
- L'utilisation des données personnelles
- Facebook et Cambridge Analytica
- Les *deepfakes* et le cas de la reine Elizabeth
- L'utilisation des réseaux sociaux par deux entreprises américaines ETLV STMG

OUTILS LINGUISTIQUES

- Le conseil et la suggestion
- La voix passive
- Le lexique de l'empreinte numérique, de l'utilisation des données, des fausses données et du monde du travail
- La prononciation de la lettre *i*

GET READY!

WORD CHALLENGE

**Use as many of these words as possible throughout the unit.
Tick ✓ the box when you have used the word.**

- ☐ advice /əd'vaɪs/ (n.)
- ☐ applicant (n.)
- ☐ bully /'bʊli/ (n. / v.)
- ☐ content /kən'tent/ (n.): *contenu*
- ☐ cyberbullying /'saɪbəbʊliɪŋ/ (n.)
- ☐ data /'deɪtə/ (n.)
- ☐ deepfake (n.)
- ☐ digital /'dɪdʒɪtəl/ footprint (n.): *empreinte numérique*
- ☐ employ (v.)
- ☐ employer (n.)
- ☐ employee (n.)
- ☐ hire /'haɪə/ = recruit /rɪ'kruːt/ (v.)
- ☐ millennials /mɪ'lenɪəlz/ (n.)
- ☐ monetise /'mʌnətaɪz/ (v.)
- ☐ policy (n.)
- ☐ post (v. / n.)
- ☐ privacy UK: /'prɪvəsi/ US: /'praɪvəsi/ (n.)
- ☐ private (adj.)
- ☐ provide (v.)
- ☐ raise awareness
- ☐ recruitment (n.)
- ☐ share (v. / n.)
- ☐ social media /'səʊʃəl 'miːdiə/ (n.)
- ☐ user /'juːzə/ (n.)

BEFORE CLASS!

A. Watch the video. Make a list of how teens are impacted by their phone usage in everyday life. Write keywords.

www.lienmini.fr/htr7-u901

a. Phone usage:

When:

Where:

b. Consequences (feelings, emotions, everyday life):

c. How has phone usage changed the way teens communicate?

B. How do you react to this report? Is this how you feel about your phone usage? Why (not)?

1 What Is on the Net, Stays on the Net

Is there a way to protect our privacy online?

1 Digital footprint

The Internet is a very powerful tool used by billions of people every second of the day. We can now communicate very easily with people that are half way across the world just by the click of a button.

While access to information, forums, chat rooms, gaming groups, social networks, shopping and emails is so easy by using a variety of different devices, the need for us to be aware of what is happening when we use the Internet is becoming increasingly important.

When we walk across mud, snow or sand we leave footprints that are visible. The same applies when we use the Internet – we leave a digital footprint trail. Every click, every post, every submit leaves a trace. As soon as you post something online it is available for other users to do with it what they want. Even with the best privacy settings, you are no longer in control of the information once you have posted it. Other users can save it, share it, comment on it or use it in a negative way against you. Once it is on the World Wide Web it is potentially there forever. Even if you delete a post, remove a picture or a comment they will still be present on a server somewhere.

Bullies Out, "Digital footprint"

A. **Read the text.**

a. Highlight all the positive aspects of internet usage.

b. Underline all the facts proving that we need to be aware of its threats.

c. Cross out the statements that are not mentioned in the text. Justify your answers orally.

– Everything you do on the Internet is visible forever.

– You are always in control of what you post.

– If you delete a post, then it will totally disappear.

– Some people may use your personal information in a negative way.

B. **Now observe the poster. Explain the message in your own words.**

....

....

....

....

....

....

....

....

HELP!

Nouns	*Adjectives & Adverb*	*Verbs & Expressions*	
• network	• available /ə'veɪləbəl/	• agree to = accept to	• post
• privacy UK: /'prɪvəsi/ US: /'praɪvəsi/	• aware	• delete /dɪ'liːt/ = erase	• protect
• threat /θret/	• private	• give access	• raise awareness
	• increasingly	• make sb aware of	• share
			• threaten sb

2 Enjoy social media responsibly

A. **What kind of personal data can social networks collect about you?**

....

B. Groupwork.

Group 1:

a. Check by <u>watching Video 1</u> about Facebook.

b. Recap orally to group 2 what you have learnt.

Group 2:

a. <u>Watch Video 2</u>. Find out the solutions to enjoy social media responsibly.

c. Complete the three questions you should ask yourself before posting:

Am I ok with…

1. … ....
2. … ....
3. … ....

c. Recap orally to group 1 what you have learnt.

1

www.lienmini.fr/htr7-u902

0'00 to 2'28

2

www.lienmini.fr/htr7-u903

3 Tips to protect yourself

Social media can be a great way to connect with friends and family and gives people an outlet for self-expression and entertainment. Social media can also get you in a lot of trouble. Here are a few tips and advice to remember when using social media.

Think about what you post. Sharing provocative photos or intimate details online, even in private emails, can cause you problems later on. [...]

Passwords are private. Don't share your password even with friends [...]

Don't measure your own life based on what others post. [...] Don't assume that others have better lives than you do, based on what they post.

Don't post or send anything you would be embarrassed for certain others to see. [...]

Do be considerate of others when posting and interacting. [...] don't post pictures of others without their permission. [...]

Watauga High School, "Social media tips"

A. **Read the text and give the lines corresponding to each sentence.**

a. Social media enable you to socialise, have fun and be creative. ....

b. Don't compare your life to what people post about their lives on the Internet. ....

c. Post pictures of other people only if they allow you to do so. ....

B. **Do you approve of these rules? Are you ready to follow them? Why (not)? Share your opinion with the class.**

C. Pairwork. **Give advice to your classmate by using the tips from the document.**
Start your sentence with the following expressions:
I advise you to… You should….
Why don't you… If I were you, I would / wouldn't…

YOUR TURN! 4 Conduct a class survey

Are you aware of the sort of personal information you are leaving on social media?

2 Precious Data (Real or Fake)

Can tech companies buy or sell our data?

1 Cambridge Analytica

A. Watch the video and find the key information (who, when, what, why).

B. Match the words to prepare an oral summary of the story.

Alexander Kogan •	• 2016 campaign
Cambridge Analytica •	• sent to 300,000 Americans
Donald Trump's •	• a British academic
personality quizzes •	• in favour of D. Trump
access to •	• a British research firm
your profile sent to •	• Cambridge Analytica
your friends' personal data •	• were taken
send political messages •	• your data and your likes

C. With the help of your notes, sum up orally. Organise your summary with the following words:
first / first of all / firstly; second / secondly; then; as a consequence / so / consequently /thus; to conclude /lastly / finally.

www.lienmini.fr/htr7-u904

HELP!

Nouns
- commodity = merchandise /mɜːtʃəndaɪz/
- interference /ɪntəˈfɪərəns/
- profit

Adjectives
- profitable
- valuable /ˈvæljʊəbəl/
- worth /wɜːθ/

Verbs
- advertise /ˈædvətaɪz/
- collect = harvest
- intrude on
- make money
- monetise /ˈmʌnətaɪz/
- spy on sb

2 Data for sale

A. Read the text and underline information showing that people are the product.

B. Highlight the reasons why tech giants should pay for our data.

C. Pairwork. Discuss why our data has become precious. Then share your ideas.

I hope you enjoy this article – maybe even enough to like it on Facebook, leave a comment and share it with your friends. Then, let's imagine your friends do the same. Suddenly, the article has over 100 engagements from your network. What if I told you that Facebook, on average, just made $10.00 from advertisers based on those engagements?

What if you could get in on some of that cheddar? [...]

Facebook and other platforms are free for us to use because they generate billions of dollars in revenue from advertisers. But remember this: If you don't pay for it, you are the product. Our data is their currency [...]. What would it look like if these companies had to pay us for data? [...]

When they can put together an intimate portrait of you – your age, gender, interests and so on – they can give other companies the chance to show you ads that are highly relevant to you. [...]

At this point, the idea of big tech paying you for your data is still hypothetical – but some people are working hard to make it a reality. Andrew Yang recently launched the Data Dividend Project to try to establish data-as-property rights. He wants to "pave the way for a future in which all Americans can claim their data as a property right and receive payment" if a platform profits from it. [...] Realistically, the only way anything like this could ever come to fruition[1] is if consumers demand it at mass scale. I just hope that we start to recognize the massive value our data generates on social platforms. We're giving Facebook and other companies a lot – and when you start to put a dollar amount on each engagement, it drives home the point: Free platforms aren't free.

1 come to life

Forbes, October 2020

3 Dealing with fake personal data

Personal information is currently collected primarily through screens, when people use computers and smartphones. [...] And as scientists push the boundaries[1] of what's possible with artificial intelligence, we will also need to learn to make sense of personal data that isn't even real, at least in that it didn't come from humans. For example, algorithms are already generating "fake" data for other algorithms to train on. So-called deepfake technology allows propagandists and hoaxers[2] to leverage[3] social media photos to make videos depicting events that never happened.

1 limits • 2 *plaisantins* • 3 *exploiter*

Wired, February 2019

A. **Read the text. Highlight where your personal information is collected.**

B. **Underline the sentence meaning: We have to be careful where so-called personal data come from because it can be fake.**

C. **What can Artificial Intelligence do with your data?**

HELP!

Adjectives
- genuine /'dʒenjuɪn/ = authentic
- reliable /rɪ'laɪəbəl/ ≠ unreliable

Verbs
- mislead = fool = deceive: *tromper*
- pretend: *faire semblant*

4 The Queen's message

The real British monarch traditionally delivers a Christmas Day speech aired[1] around the world. But her speech on Friday at 3 p.m. was followed by a digitally-created fake of the Queen, aired on Channel 4 and voiced by an actor, warning[2] viewers to question "whether what we see and hear is always what it seems."

Channel 4 [...] said the video was supposed to offer "a stark[3] warning about the advanced technology that is enabling[4] the proliferation of misinformation and fake news in a digital age."

Channel 4 annually accompanies the Queen's traditional speech with an "alternative Christmas message." [...] This year Channel 4 hired[5] VFX studio Framestore to create a fake Queen Elizabeth, who spoke candidly about personal matters.

The video was manipulated using artificial intelligence technology. [...]

"Deepfake technology is the frightening new frontier in the battle between misinformation and truth," Channel 4 Director of Programmes Ian Katz said in a statement.

"This year's Alternative Christmas Address – seemingly delivered by one of the most familiar and trusted figures in the nation – is a powerful reminder[6] that we can no longer trust our own eyes."

1 broadcast • 2 alert • 3 clear • 4 permitting • 5 recruited • 6 *rappel*

CNN, December 2020

A. **Read the text.**

a. Underline the sentence explaining what happened to the Queen's message on Channel 4.

b. Circle the sentence showing the goal of the channel.

B. **Look at the picture: what makes you think it is a fake picture?**

C. **Do you agree with the following quote from the text when dealing with artificial intelligence?**

"Deepfake technology is the frightening new frontier in the battle between misinformation and truth [...]" (l. 18-19)

YOUR PROJECT

You are a member of your school council. Create a poster to give a list of tips for a safe use of social media to your schoolmates.

3 Business and Social Media

ETLV
STMG

How do potential employers use social media for their businesses?

OBJECTIVES STMG
- Understand the diversity of digital technology uses and its impacts
- Identify good practices in digital identity management

1 A tool for business

Text 1

If current studies are to be believed, millennials check their smartphones more than 150 times a day, or once every five or six minutes. Much of that time is spent on social media.

Companies know they can't control their employees' smartphone obsession or what they post to their personal accounts, but there is one thing they can control: whether to hire a person, based on their social media history.

"We, as an agency, look at everyone's social media postings when we're considering hiring people," says [Beth Monaghan, co-founder and CEO of Inkhouse, the Waltham-based PR[1] and content marketing firm]. "I'm sure we're not alone in that."

They're not. Recent survey results from Career Builder.com and Harris Poll showed that 70 percent of employers nationwide consider social media activity when screening job applicants, and more than half reject a potential hire because of some content they uncovered.

So what should these prospective employees keep in mind before they tap "post?"

[...] "How you want to be seen on social media should be informed by your goals," [Monaghan] says. "In my own case, I care about creating a more modern workplace; I care about equality for minorities and women and I care about public relations. So those are things I feature on social media."

Monaghan also says authenticity is important.

"You can't be somebody on social media and somebody else in the real-world," she says.

1 public relation

The Boston Globe, August 2017

A. Groupwork.

Group 1:

a. Focus on Text 1 and highlight useful tips for future employees.

b. Think of some advice that would be useful to potential applicants.

c. Share your findings with group 2.

Group 2:

a. Focus on Text 2 and underline useful tips for business owners.

b. How important is the Internet to companies?

c. Share your findings with group 1.

B. Discuss the advantages and drawbacks of using social networks for business.

HELP!

Nouns
- account
- applicant: *candidat(e)*
- content
- employee
- employer
- employment
- social media /ˈsəʊʃəl ˈmiːdiə/
- value

Adjectives
- corporate /ˈkɔːpərɪt/
- offensive
- respectful ≠ disrespectful
- rude /ruːd/

Verbs & Expressions
- apply /əˈplaɪ/ for a job
- hire /ˈhaɪə/ = recruit /rɪˈkruːt/
- lack of respect
- land a job = get a job
- look for a job
- screen = select: *filtrer*

DEFINITION ETLV

Digital identity includes any **personal data** existing online that can be traced back to the real you (for example, photos uploaded to **social media** posts and comments, search engine history, etc.).

Text 2

Joanne Chang, the award-winning chef, author, and owner of Flour Bakery and Cafe in Boston and Cambridge uses social media to share behind-the-scenes looks at her business and also feels it's a good way to represent her values and interests.

"I take pictures all day long of things that delight me," she says. "And then when I have a moment – usually about once a day – I pick one of the pictures and post what I love about it. It becomes representative of the brand."

She doesn't have specific disqualifiers like Monaghan, but instead relies more on her gut – and the "Mom Test." Her mom worked at Flour briefly in its early days and Chang valued her opinions on what worked and what didn't. She approaches social media similarly. Would mom approve? If not, don't post.

A challenging but necessary component of a company's social media outreach[1] is designating employees to also post for the business.

"We have a few people in the company who post for us," says Chang. "I think they have the same philosophy idea – it's a great way to send a message about something you are excited about."

Some companies have more strict policies on who can post content and what they can say. [...]

Still, making sure the right messages go out, either on the corporate social media sites or individual accounts, takes some level of monitoring.

Chang recalled one incident involving an employee who complained about her boss in a pretty detailed manner on social media. "I pulled that person aside and let her know that I had read her posts, and did she want to talk to me about how we could work through this."

1 *accompagnement*

The Boston Globe, August 2017

2 How to remove negative reviews

A. Watch the video. Find out:

a. why five-star reviews are important to your business;

b. who posts fake reviews and why.

B. At home: guess how to delete negative reviews. Check your answers by watching the end of the video.

www.lienmini.fr/htr7-u905

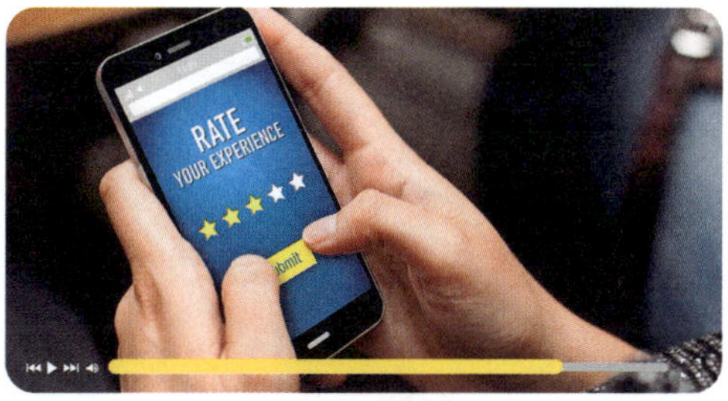

0'00 to 1'05

YOUR PROJECT BAC

You are a YouTuber specialised in work-related issues. Make a video dealing with the use of personal data by potential employers. Give examples and tips.

RULE THE GRAMMAR!

1. LE CONSEIL ET LA SUGGESTION

On peut formuler des conseils et des suggestions à l'aide d'auxiliaires de modalité (modaux) ou d'expressions.

	Modaux	Expressions
Le conseil	• *should* + BV : *You **should think** twice before posting anything on Twitter.* • *ought to* + BV : *They **ought to fight** hacking to protect personal data.* => obligation morale, conseil insistant	• *had better ('d better)* + BV : ***You'd better have** a good antivirus system not to get hacked.* => fort conseil • *If I were you, I would* + BV : ***If I were you, I would denounce** cyberbullying.*
La suggestion	*could / might try* + V-ing : *She **might try checking** her employees' online activities.*	• *Why don't you… / Why not* + BV : ***Why not learn** how to fight cyber criminals?* • *What / How about* + V-ing : ***How about taking** computer lessons?*

2. LA VOIX PASSIVE

La voix passive permet de mettre en avant la personne ou la chose qui subit l'action.

• Formation

Be conjugué au même temps que le verbe à la forme active + participe passé (+ *by* + agent) (voir aussi p. 86).

*Too many personal details **are posted** on the Internet.*

*The Queen's speech **was manipulated** by Artificial Intelligence.*

VOCABULARY

The wild wild web

Digital footprint

- advice /əd'vaɪs/ (n.)
- application = app (n.)
- aware ≠ unaware (adj.)
- bully /'bʊli/ (n. / v.)
- cyberbullying /'saɪbəbʊliɪŋ/ (n.)
- data /'deɪtə/ (n.)
- delete = erase (v.)
- give access (v.)
- post (v.)
- privacy /'prɪvəsi/ (UK) /'praɪvəsi/ (US) (n.)
- share (v.)
- social media /'səʊʃəl 'mi:diə/ / network
- threat (n.) / threaten /'θretən/ (v.)
- user (n.)

Your words: ....

Precious data

- advertise /'ædvətaɪz/ (v.)
- agree = accept (v.)
- available (adj.)
- collect = harvest (v.)
- commodity = merchandise /'mɜ:tʃəndaɪz/ (n.)
- consumer /kən'sju:mə/ (n.)
- currency (n.)
- monetise /'mʌnətaɪz/ (v.)
- product (n.)
- value = worth (n.)

Your words: ....

Business

- applicant = candidate (n.)
- apply /ə'plaɪ/ for a job
- employ (v.)
- employee (n.)
- employer (n.)
- hire /'haɪə/ = recruit /rɪ'kru:t/ (v.)
- screen = select (v.): *filtrer*
- social media history

Your words: ....

Fake data

- Artificial Intelligence (AI) /ˌeɪ'aɪ/ (n.)
- deepfake (n.)
- digitally-created (adj.)
- fake ≠ real (adj.)
- hoax /həʊks/ (n.)
- manipulate /mə'nɪpjəleɪt/ (n.)
- misinformation ≠ truth (n.)
- reliable /rɪ'laɪəbəl/ ≠ unreliable (adj.)
- warning (n.)

Your words: ....

MP3
www.lienmini.fr/htr7-u906

LANGUAGE LAB

1 Rephrase the sentences using the prompts.

Tell your parents each time you are cyberbullied.

A. You should…

B. You might try…

C. If I were you, I would…

D. You ought to…

2 Cross the odd word out.

A. privacy – share – private data – personal information
B. fake – truth – hoax – manipulation
C. recruit – hire – consumer – applicant
D. threat – value – product – advertiser

3 Translate with the help of the mind map p. 110.

A. *Tu devrais vérifier si c'est un canular.*

B. *Si j'étais toi, je ne partagerais pas mes photos.*

C. *L'intelligence artificielle permet de* (enables to) *recruter des candidats.*

D. *Les données sont collectées par les réseaux sociaux.*

4 Turn each sentence into the passive. Use the underlined elements to start.

Google collects our data. → Our data is collected by Google.

A. Channel 4 transformed the Queen's speech.
→

B. They use a deepfake app to manipulate the viewers.
→

C. Managers screen potential employees with the help of their social network history. →

D. Social media sell our personal information to make money.
→

5 Unit's checkout

Write a 50-word paragraph that could be illustrated by this cartoon. Use the passive voice, advice and suggestion.

OPEN YOUR EARS!

La prononciation de la lettre *i* MP3 N°12

Écoutez les mots suivants et notez la lettre correspondant à la prononciation de la lettre *i*.

1 *hire* • 2 *privacy (UK)* • 3 *privacy (US)* • 4 *empire* • 5 *provide* • 6 *availability* • 7 *media* • 8 *digital* • 9 *firm* • 10 *private*

/ɪ/ (profit): ……… /aɪ/ (website): ……… /iː/ (feel): ………
/aɪə/ (fire): ……… /ɜː/ (world): ………

AXE 5

UNIT 10

THE MAGIC OF DISNEY'S EMPIRE

How has Disney established and spread its influence?

YOUR PROJECTS

LV
Imagine the front page of a special issue of *Forbes* magazine entitled: "Disney: the most influential company of our time".

ETLV STMG
Record a 2-minute presentation for the book trailer for Disney CEO Bob Iger's memoirs: *The Ride of a Lifetime.*

ETLV STMG
Imagine the first episode of a *Disney* employee's podcast entitled: "My 1st month working for the Mouse".

Au menu de cette unité :

DÉCOUVERTES CULTURELLES

- La multinationale Disney
- L'évolution des personnages féminins dans les productions Disney
- Le détournement de l'univers féerique par des artistes (D. Goldstein, Banksy)
- Bob Iger, patron visionnaire **ETLV STMG**
- Travailler chez Disney **ETLV STMG**

OUTILS LINGUISTIQUES

- Le *present perfect*
- Le lexique des médias, de l'entreprise, du monde du travail, des stéréotypes et de l'égalité hommes-femmes
- La prononciation des mots en *-ion*

GET READY!

WORD CHALLENGE

**Use as many of these words as possible throughout the unit.
Tick ✓ the box when you have used the word.**

- ☐ acquisition /ækwɪ'zɪʃən/ (n.)
- ☐ advertising /'ædvətaɪzɪŋ/ (n.)
- ☐ archetype /'ɑːkɪtaɪp/ (n.)
- ☐ brand/brand image /'ɪmɪdʒ/ (n.)
- ☐ business (n.)
- ☐ Chief Executive Officer (CEO) (n.)
- ☐ consumer (n.)
- ☐ corporation = company = firm /fɜːrn/ (n.)
- ☐ Disney /'dɪzni/
- ☐ emancipation (n.)
- ☐ entertainment industry
- ☐ expand (v.)
- ☐ franchise /'fræntʃaɪz/ (n.)
- ☐ gender cliché (n.)
- ☐ marketing strategy
- ☐ media /'midiə/ empire /'empaɪə/ (n.)
- ☐ merchandise /'mɜːtʃəndaɪz/ (n.)
- ☐ Mickey /'mɪki/
- ☐ profit (n.)
- ☐ sexism /'seksɪzəm/ (n.)
- ☐ stereotype /'steriətaɪp/ (n.)
- ☐ storytelling (n.)
- ☐ takeover (n.)

BEFORE CLASS!

A. Watch Disney's short animated film entitled *From Our Family to Yours* online.

B. Focus on the way Disney promotes its image and its products. Tick the statements you agree with. Justify orally.

a. ☐ Disney characters bring generations together.

b. ☐ Disney appeals to people's nostalgia to touch every member of the family.

c. ☐ Disney is mostly a company for kids.

d. ☐ Disney influences our lives with its stories and products.

e. ☐ Disney uses emotions / storytelling to sell its products.

C. What image does Disney give in this short animated film? Do you find it effective / convincing? Why (not)?

....

....

....

....

D. Storytelling challenge. Use all the following words to sum up the story:

Mickey Mouse plush / cuddly toy – across generations – touching – tradition – connection – nostalgic – gift – paper lanterns – mend/fix – broken ear.

....

....

....

....

....

....

....

....

1 Disney's Omnipresence

How has Disney's power taken over our lives?

1 Disney and the entertainment industry

www.lienmini.fr/htr7-u1001

A. Watch the video released by Disney and look at the infographic.

B. Identify the major types of entertainment Disney controls in both documents, and comment on the company's goal and targeted audience.

C. Draw your conclusions about the way Disney tries to impact people's lives.

1 *Participation majoritaire*

HELP!

Nouns
- acquisition
- franchise /ˈfræntʃaɪz/
- media /ˈmiːdiə/
- platform

Adjectives
- diverse
- eclectic
- omnipresent

Verbs & Expressions
- expand a brand
- modernise
- reach audiences
- spread an influence

2 Disney in Ron English's art

I remember making a painting of Mickey Mouse as a young child. I didn't think of it as a subversive[1] act. I was just rendering a beloved character that dominated my little world. Mickey Mouse was omnipresent. Mickey was America's mouse. Mickey was everybody's mouse. By the time I had kids of my own Mickey Mouse was stamped[2] on everything from plates to diapers[3]. Without any effort of proactive will on my part my house filled with images of the mouse.

At times it seemed that every available surface was brandished with Mickey the Trojan[4] mouse. The Disney Corporation wanted to brand every square inch of our lives and had been quite successful at it. They wanted to make the mouse an American Icon, and they did. They wanted children to adore the mouse; they wanted them to have the same deep-rooted love for Mickey as they did for their parents, and they do. [...] The Disney Corporation wanted their characters to be beloved; to be omnipresent yet remain untouchable. [...] I look out my window and I don't see a mountain, I see an advertisement. I am surrounded by the cartoon mascots of the corporations that rule the planet. The way I have come to terms with[5] them is by making them my own through the process of art.

1 trying to destroy an established system • **2** *estampillé* • **3** *couches pour bébés* • **4** something designed to have a damaging effect even if it appears inoffensive • **5** *se faire à une idée*

Ron English, ***popaganda.com***

American Depress Card, **by Ron English, 2015**

A. **<u>Read the text</u> by American artist Ron English, focusing on his relationship with Mickey Mouse.**

B. **Underline the words associated with Mickey Mouse and draw your conclusions.**

C. **Highlight the strategies of the Disney corporation with children and rephrase them.**

D. **<u>React to the picture</u>: identify the message of Ron English's art.**

HELP!

Nouns
- capitalism
- credit card
- financial power
- mousetrap

Verbs & Expressions
- be a symbol of
- fall into the trap

3 The secret of Disney's brand

For Disney, storytelling is key. Storytelling requires an emotional component that will appeal to consumers of all ages [...] Every advertisement, commercial, and billboard must remind consumers of those emotions and stories. [...] But how does Disney manage to separate itself from its competitors? The answer lies in a unique content marketing strategy. Disney has a one-two approach by first creating the story and then building a whole line of products around that story.

As an article from *Forbes* states, "Disney's 'content marketing' strategy goes in reverse compared to most brands. Meaning, where most brands start with a physical product and then build a story around it in the form of 'content marketing,' companies like Disney do exactly the opposite."

medium.com, March 2020

A. **Read the text and highlight the words associated with Disney's storytelling and marketing strategy.**

B. **Use your findings to explain orally what makes Disney's strategy special.**

2 The Rise of Disney's Heroines

How does Disney keep up with the evolution of society?

1 The evolution of Disney's female characters

Look at the documents. Comment on the evolution of Disney's female characters. Justify with elements from the three documents.

1 A visual chronology of emancipation

Snow White
1937

Cinderella
1950

The Little Mermaid (Ariel)
1989

The Princess and the Frog (Tiana)
2009

Tangled (Rapunzel)
2010

Brave (Merida)
2012

Frozen (Elsa and Anna)
2013/2019

Moana
2016

Raya and the Last Dragon
2021

2 How princesses spend their time (1937-2010)

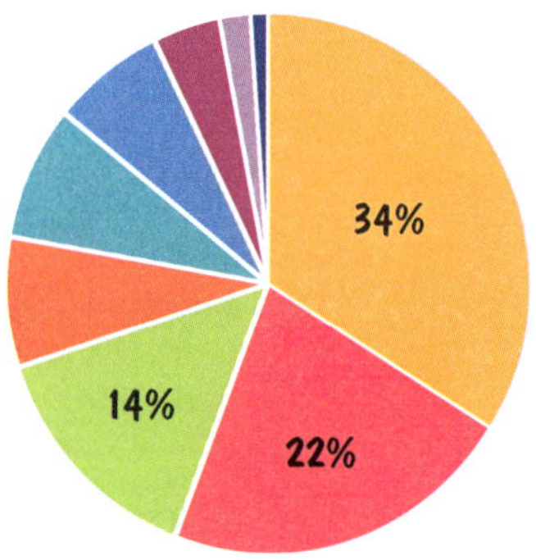

1 *se faire belle*

Source: J. Ewert, Montana State University

3 Heroines' quotes (2012-2021)

"I want my freedom." **Merida** (*Brave*)

"I will lead with pride; I will make us strong." **Moana**

"Yes, I'm alone, but I'm alone and free!" **Elsa** (*Frozen*)

"My whole life, I trained to become a guardian of the dragon gem, but this world has changed, and its people are divided. Now, to restore peace, I must find the last dragon." **Raya**

HELP!

Nouns & Adjectives
- bold = daring = audacious
- gender clichés / stereotypes
- patriarchal society

Verbs & Expressions
- (not) have a say in sth
- fulfil one's dream
- (be) silenced
- (be) subjected to
- (be) submissive

2 Captain Marvel

www.lienmini.fr/htr7-u1002

0'00 to 1'15 — 1'38 to the end

HELP!

Nouns
- army suit
- clenched fists
- inspiration
- national symbol
- power
- strength

Adjectives
- godlike / all-powerful / mighty
- superhuman (abilities)
- female-led (film)
- invincible

Verbs & Expressions
- empowering vision
- low-angle shot (camera shot pointing upward)
- shake things up
- take leadership
- look up to sb

A. Watch the video and complete the table below with keywords.

Captain Marvel	The representation of women	Impact & message of the film

B. Groupwork. Share your findings in pairs and discuss the importance of this film for Disney.

C. React to the poster in a 1-minute presentation. Focus on the representation of the character.

a. Symbols: ....

b. Style / Attitude: ....

c. Colours / Light: ....

d. Angle: ....

YOUR TURN! 3 Write an article BAC

Write a 100-word article for *The Hollywood Reporter* about the changes the company has made over the years in its representation of heroines. Give your opinion.

3 Happily Ever After?

How do some artists use Disney's world to make us think about society?

1 Fallen princesses

Snowy, by Dina Goldstein, 2008

Fallen Princesses (2007-2009) is a 10-piece series featuring humanized fairy tale Princesses dealing with modern-day scourges[1] such as cancer, addiction, obesity, war and environmental degradation. As a feminist and new mother, Dina was disturbed about the stereotypical societal tropes[2] Disney was perpetrating about women and girls; the work is critical of the "happily ever after" motif, exploited by Walt Disney and embraced by Western society.

1 *fléaux* • 2 repeated themes

dinagoldstein.com

A. Read the text. Pick out the characteristics of Dina Goldstein's princesses and react to them.

B. Pick out information about the reason for Dina Goldstein's project and identify her goal.

Reasons:

Goal:

C. Groupwork. React to the picture from the *Fallen Princesses* project. Take notes before the group conversation.

2 "Dismaland"

▶ www.lienmini.fr/htr7-u1003

HELP!

Noun
- bumper cars: *auto-tamponneuses*

Adjectives
- dismal /ˈdɪzmlə/: *lugubre*
- shattered = broken

Verbs & Expressions
- denounce = criticise = point an accusing finger at…
- laugh at = mock = parody = caricature (sb / sth)
- the truth beyond appearances
- turn… into ridicule

Express your opinion
- I agree with you…
- I disagree with you…
- I share the same opinion…
- In my opinion…

A. Watch the video above on Banksy's temporary exhibition. Take notes.

B. Groupwork. Share what you have understood about Dismaland.

a. Exhibition: ……………………………………………

b. Subjects: ……………………………………………

c. Goals: ……………………………………………

C. Discuss Banksy's message. Take notes before the group conversation.

……………………………………………

D. Dubbing task. Record a funny voice-over for the trailer of Banksy's theme park.

Complete the original voice-over for the second part of the video below.

Use what you have understood from the park to match the voice with the images.

▶ www.lienmini.fr/htr7-u1004

0'32 to 1'25

YOUR PROJECT BAC

Imagine the front page of a special issue of *Forbes* magazine entitled: "Disney: the most influential company of our time". The cover will include a picture of the company's power and a 100-word explanatory text on its influence in our lives (role in the media, gender representation…).

4 Inside the "Mouse-opoly"

ETLV
STMG *What strategic decisions has Disney made to build its success?*

OBJECTIVES STMG
- Identify strategic decisions
- Evaluate management efficiency

1 Disney's most daring CEO

www.lienmini.fr/htr7-u1005

0'00 to 1'45 — 3'38 to 4'27

HELP!

Nouns
- Bob Iger /'aɪgə/
- CEO = Chief Executive Officer (head of a company)

Adjectives
- bold = courageous and audacious

DEFINITION ETLV

A **strategic decision** is made by top managers in the long term, is irreversible and requires numerous resources.

Useful expressions
- acquisition = takeover = when one company purchases another one to gain control of that company
- deal = a mutual agreement between two parties that want to do business
- expand a brand / a company's scope
- make profit = increase a company's profit

A. **Watch the documentary about former Disney CEO Bob Iger.**

B. **Take notes and pick out as much information as you can about the entrepreneur.**

a. Bob Iger's career history and professional experience:

....

....

....

....

b. His personality and values:

....

....

....

....

c. His impact on Disney and its acquisitions:

....

....

....

....

....

....

C. Groupwork. **Share your findings and discuss Bob Iger's strategy as Disney's former CEO. Say what strikes you the most about his story and expansion strategy.**

2 Inside the iconic CEO's strategy

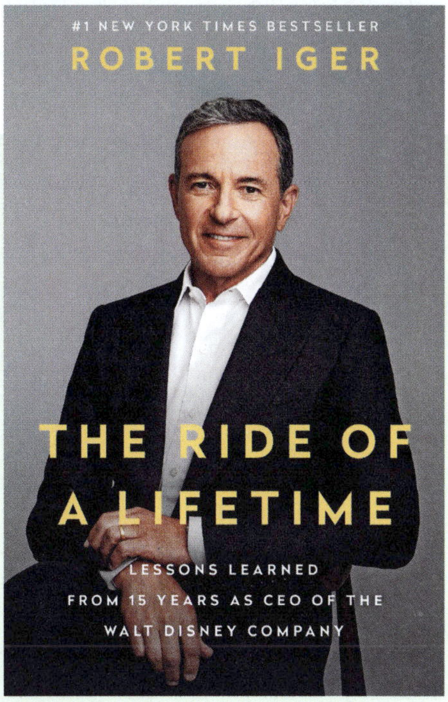

I quickly landed on three clear strategic priorities. They have guided the company since the moment I was named CEO:

1. We needed to devote most of our time and capital to the creation of high-quality branded content. In an age when more and more "content" was being created and distributed, we needed to bet on the fact that quality will matter more and more. [...] With an explosion of choice, consumers needed an ability to make decisions about how to spend their time and money. [...]

2. We needed to embrace technology to the fullest extent [...] to reach more consumers in more modern, more relevant[1] ways. [...] Unless[2] consumers had the ability to consume our content in more user-friendly, more mobile, and more digital ways, our relevance would be challenged. In short, we needed to view technology as more of an opportunity than a threat[3], and we had to do so with commitment[4], enthusiasm, and a sense of urgency.

3. We needed to become a truly global company. We were broad[5] with our reach, doing business in numerous markets around the world, but we needed to better penetrate certain markets, particularly the world's most populous countries, like China and India. If our primary focus was on creating excellent branded content, the next step was to bring that content to a global audience, firmly planting our roots[6] in those markets and creating a strong foundation to grow significantly in scale. [...]

That was the vision. It was about the future, not the past [...].

1 *pertinent* • **2** *à moins que* • **3** *menace* • **4** *engagement* • **5** *large* • **6** *racines*

The Ride of a Lifetime, by Robert Iger, 2019

A. Read the text from Bob Iger's book.

B. Highlight the keywords associated with each "strategic priority". Use your findings to rephrase the strategic priorities as follows:

a. Bob Iger was convinced that Disney had to:

....

....

b. According to Bob Iger, it was necessary for Disney to:

....

....

c. Iger wanted Disney to:

....

....

C. True or False? Justify each answer with elements from the text.

a. On his arrival, Bob Iger thought that Disney was already present in every market.

T ☐ F ☐

....

b. Some priorities were motivated by the strong competition faced by Disney.

T ☐ F ☐

....

....

....

YOUR PROJECT

Imagine and record a 2-minute presentation for the book trailer for Bob Iger's memoirs: *The Ride of a Lifetime*. You will introduce him and talk about his greatest achievements as Disney's CEO. Your aim is to make people want to know more about Bob Iger and buy the book.

5 Working for the Mouse

ETLV STMG

What is it like to work for the Walt Disney empire?

OBJECTIVES STMG
- Study the link between working conditions and staff behaviour
- Identify motivation factors at work

1 A variety of careers and job opportunities

HELP!

DEFINITION ETLV
Corporate Social Responsibility (CSR) is a management concept that includes social and environmental concerns in business.

www.lienmini.fr/htr7-u1006

A. Watch the video and pick out information.

B. Pick out the employees' occupations in the Disney Company, and elements about their past and personal stories explaining why they work here. Identify their level of job satisfaction. Take notes in the table below.

	Occupation	Elements about their past or personal stories	Level of job satisfaction
Julie			
Carmen			
PJ			
Mark			
J.J.			
Agnes			
Denny			
Zeb			

C. Focus on the employees' personal and professional achievements with the Walt Disney Company. Identify the benefits of working for this company.

2 The pressure of the etiquette

A. Watch the video and pick out the four Disney etiquette rules which strike you the most.

....

....

B. Share your choice and your opinion in groups, then debate.

www.lienmini.fr/htr7-u1007

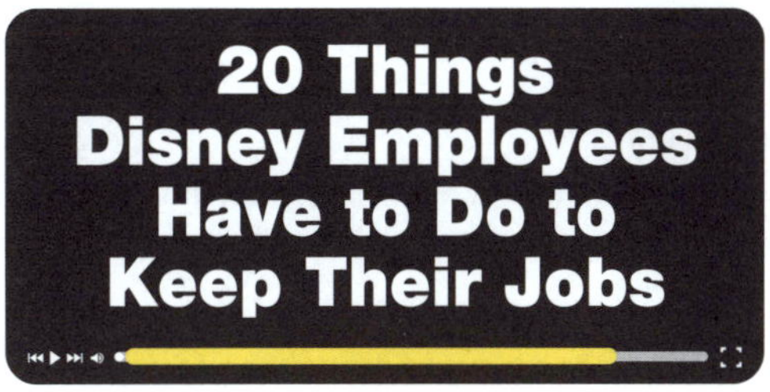

0'00 to 4'40

3 The happiest place on Earth?

Disneyland employees in Anaheim, California are paid so little, one in ten employees has experienced homelessness recently and two-thirds of park workers don't have enough food to eat three meals a day. Most Disneyland employees struggle to make ends meet[1]: 74 percent (and 80 percent of those with children) say they can't afford basic expenses[2] every month. 85% are paid less than $15 an hour. Many employees report limiting themselves to just one meal each day. In the decade from 2007-2016, Disneyland's attendance[3] grew 21%, ticket prices grew 59%, and revenue grew 98%. Theme parks are the biggest source of profit for the Walt Disney Company, but the value of workers' pay has dropped[4] 15 percent since 2000.

1 *joindre les deux bouts* • **2** *dépenses* • **3** number of visitors • **4** *chuter*

Exhibit 5: Average Hourly Wage[1] of Disneyland Resort Employees in 2017 Dollars

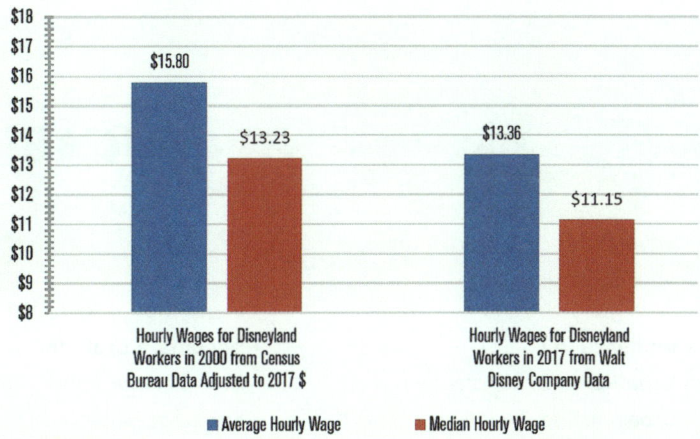

1 wage = salary

"Working for the Mouse", A survey of Disneyland Resort Employees, February 2018

A. Look at the chart, then read the text about Disneyland employees.

B. Highlight the issues faced by Disneyland employees (use the text and the chart).

C. Underline the facts showing the positive evolutions for the company between 2007 and 2016.

D. Use your findings to comment on the text.

....

....

....

....

YOUR PROJECT BAC

Imagine the first episode of a Disneyland employee's 2-minute podcast called "My 1st month working for the Mouse." You will present the company, talk about the pros and cons of working for it, and share your experience as an employee.
Go on Disney's corporate website, section "Careers" to choose the career area that best interests you for the podcast.

RULE THE GRAMMAR!

LE *PRESENT PERFECT*

• Formation

Auxiliaire *have* au présent + participe passé du verbe

Rappel : Participe passé = base verbale (verbe sans *to*) + *-ed* **ou** 3e colonne des verbes irréguliers

• Emploi

Le *present perfect* est avant tout un temps du présent.
Attention : Il n'est pas l'équivalent du passé composé français, même si sa structure y ressemble.

– Pour exprimer le résultat, ou le bilan, dans le présent, d'actions ou d'événements passés :
*Disney **has bought** Marvel.* => *Disney now owns Marvel.*
*Disney **has released** the latest Star Wars film.* => *The film can now be watched in cinemas.*
Remarque : Avec l'adverbe *just*, on peut renvoyer à une action dans un passé récent.
*Disney **has** just **released** a new princess film.*

– Pour exprimer la continuité d'actions ou d'événement débutés dans le passé et qui se poursuivent dans le présent :
*Wendy **has worked** for Disney since 2005.* => *She still works for the company.*

VOCABULARY

Disney's Empire

The media

- **ad**vertising /'ædvətaɪzɪŋ/ (n.)
- ad = adv**er**tisement /əd'vɜːtɪsmənt/ (n.)
- **au**dience (n.)
- br**oa**dcast /'brɔːdkɑːst/ (v.)
- br**oa**dcasting /'brɔːdkɑːstɪŋ/ (n.)
- entert**ai**nment **in**dustry
- **me**dia /'miːdiə/ **em**pire /'empaɪə/ (n.)
- str**ea**ming pl**at**form (n.)

Your words: ....

The business world

- acqui**si**tion /ækwɪ'zɪʃən/ (n.)
- **be**nefits = **pro**fit (n.)
- brand **i**mage /'ɪmɪdʒ/ (n.)
- **ca**pitalist (adj.)
- Chief Ex**e**cutive **O**fficer (CE**O**) (n.)
- **co**mpany = corpor**a**tion = firm /fɜːm/ (n.)
- deal (n.)
- entrepre**neur** /ɒntrəprə'nɜː/ (n.)
- ex**pand** = spread (v.)
- **fran**chise /'fræntʃaɪz/ (n.)
- **in**fluence (n.)
- **mar**keting **stra**tegy (n.)
- **mo**dernise (v.)
- mon**o**poly (n.)
- prom**o**te (v.)
- stra**te**gic /strə'tiːdʒɪk/ de**ci**sion (n.)
- take **lea**dership = take **o**ver (v.)

Your words: ....

At work

- employ**ee** (n.)
- empl**oy**er (n.)
- pay (v.)
- **sa**lary = wage /weɪdʒ/ (n.)
- work **e**tiquette (n.)
- **wor**ker (n.)
- **wor**king con**di**tions (n.)
- **work**place (n.)

Your words: ....

The gender issue

- **ar**chetype /'ɑːkɪtaɪp/ (n.)
- bold = au**da**cious (adj.)
- emanci**pa**tion (n.)
- emp**o**wering (adj.)
- **fe**minist ≠ **se**xist (adj.)
- **gen**der cli**ché** (n.)
- inspi**ra**tion (n.)
- out**da**ted = old-**fa**shioned (adj.)
- **ste**reotype /'steriətaɪp/ (n.)
- sub**mi**ssive (adj.)

Your words: ....

LANGUAGE LAB

1 Put the verbs in brackets in the present perfect.

A. The Walt Disney company (*buy*) a new franchise.

B. Mickey Mouse always (*be*) the company's mascot.

C. Disney (*change*) the representation of its female characters to keep up with society.

D. Artists often (*denounce*) Disney's influence.

2 Cross the odd word out. Explain your choice briefly.

A. profit – gain – debt – benefit – earnings

B. expansion – stagnation – development – extension – spread

C. progressive – modern – outdated – reformist – tolerant

D. omnipresent – widespread – universal – limited – everywhere

3 Put the verbs in the appropriate tense (preterite, or present perfect).

A. Bob Iger (*resign*) as Disney's CEO in February 2020.

B. In 2012, The Walt Disney Company (*acquire*) Lucasfilm.

C. Disney just (*release*) its latest princess film.

D. The company (*expand*) a lot over the past few years.

4 Complete the sentences using the right term related to work and business.

brand image • etiquette rules • competitors • growth • consumer products

A. The employees of the theme parks have to follow a lot of ....

B. Disney's .... is based on Mickey Mouse.

C. The company's effective storytelling contributes to the sale of ....

D. With its new acquisitions, Disney is ready to fight ....

E. The rapid .... of Disney+ could be detrimental to Netflix.

5 Unit's checkout

Sum up in 30-50 words the cartoonist's intention.

Help: Snoop Dogg was recently turned into a Disney character.

OPEN YOUR EARS!

La prononciation des mots en *-ion* MP3 N°13

Lisez les mots suivants en accentuant sur la syllabe qui précède la terminaison *-ion*. Vérifiez à l'écoute.

competition • emancipation • acquisition • emotion • evolution • representation • inspiration • exhibition • corporation • submission • decision

AXE 5

UNIT 11

TO CARE AND TO CURE

In real life or in fiction, what makes healthcare workers our new heroes?

YOUR PROJECTS

LV

Create the three main characters of a new medical TV show.

ETLV STMG

Debate: Should hospitals be run like companies?

ETLV ST2S

Present the idea for your latest article, "Carers need care too" to your chief editor.

Au menu de cette unité :

DÉCOUVERTES CULTURELLES

- Les séries américaines *Grey's Anatomy*, *House M.D.* et *The Good Doctor*
- Le *National Health Service* au Royaume-Uni
- Des artistes américains, anglais, canadiens inspirés par la pandémie de la Covid-19
- La gestion des hôpitaux (États-Unis, Royaume-Uni) ETLV STMG
- Le bien-être du personnel médical ETLV ST2S

OUTILS LINGUISTIQUES

- Les propositions relatives
- Le génitif
- Le lexique du milieu hospitalier et des conditions de travail, des qualités et des sentiments des soignants
- La prononciation de la lettre *u*

GET READY!

WORD CHALLENGE

Use as many of these words as possible throughout the unit.
Tick ✓ the box when you have used the word.

- ☐ be depicted as = described as (v.)
- ☐ care (v. / n.)
- ☐ career (n.)
- ☐ committed (adj.)
- ☐ dedicated (adj.)
- ☐ emergency room (ER) (n.)
- ☐ fictional (adj.)
- ☐ heal = cure /kjʊə/ (v.)
- ☐ healthcare worker = carer /ˈkeərə/ (n.)
- ☐ hospital staff (n.)
- ☐ injury = wound /wuːnd/ (n.)
- ☐ nurse (n.)
- ☐ operating room (OR) (n.)
- ☐ pandemic (n.)
- ☐ pay rise (n.)
- ☐ physician (US) = doctor (n.)
- ☐ realistic ≠ unrealistic (adj.)
- ☐ scrubs (n.): *blouses stériles*
- ☐ surgeon /ˈsɜːdʒən/ (n.)
- ☐ surgical mask / gloves (n.)
- ☐ take sth for granted
- ☐ undervalued (adj.)
- ☐ working conditions (n.)
- ☐ wounded /ˈwuːndɪd/ = injured (adj.)

BEFORE CLASS!

A. Watch the video and take notes.

B. Read the *Cultural fact* to learn more about the NHS.

C. Take notes to talk about the photo below. How is it related to the video?

D. Put all your information together and prepare a one-minute presentation of the documents.

www.lienmini.fr/htr7-u1101

Cultural fact
Founded in 1948, the National Health Service (NHS) refers to the medical and healthcare services funded by the British government. The NHS provides free access to basic care for patients. It is funded by taxes.

Graffiti on a wall in Pontefract, West Yorkshire

1 Glamour, Blood and Romance

Is the image of hospital staff in TV shows faithful to reality?

1 Famous fictional doctors

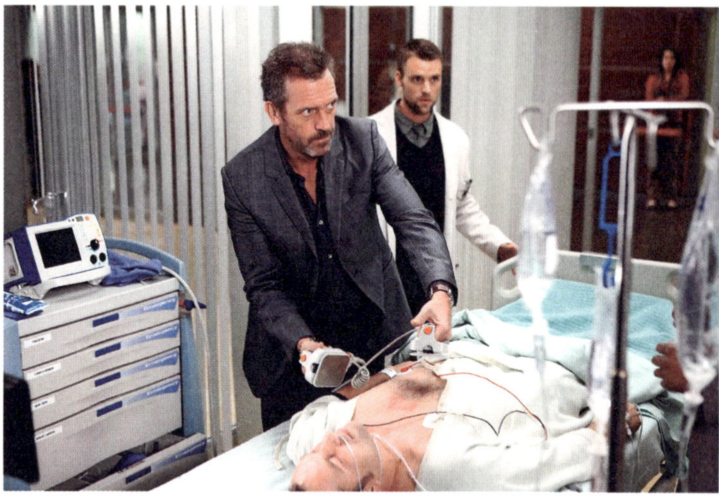

A. Look at the pictures above. Can you name these shows? How are the characters represented?

B. Do you think these representations are similar to what happens in real life? Explain.

2 Behind the scenes

www.lienmini.fr/htr7-u1102

0'24 to 2'52

A. Watch the video. Who's who? Match the following items.

a. Real doctor's name •	• Manish Dayal
b. Fictional character's name •	• Dr Mike
c. Actor's name •	• Devon Pravesh

B. The actor prepares for his role by looking up .... or watching ....

C. What does the actor admire in real doctors? Tick the correct answers.

- ☐ Their style
- ☐ Their dedication
- ☐ Their relationship with patients
- ☐ Their commitment
- ☐ Their salary
- ☐ Their knowledge
- ☐ How they put theory into practice
- ☐ Their diplomas

D. What is accurate and realistic in the set? ....

E. What is inaccurate and what would it mean in real life? ....

HELP!

Nouns
- a TV set = where the scenes are filmed
- commitment: *engagement*
- nurse station: *poste des infirmières*

Adjectives
- accurate /ˈækjʊrət/ = exact

3 Fact or fiction? Guessing time!

A. Read the following statements describing the healthcare world in the TV show *Grey's Anatomy*. Guess what is fiction and what is a fact in real life.

a. Surgeons spend time with patients and look after them personally.
Fact ☐ Fiction ☐

b. While operating on patients, doctors talk about their daily lives and hobbies.
Fact ☐ Fiction ☐

c. Medical residents are in competition with each other to become the best doctors.
Fact ☐ Fiction ☐

d. Nurses have a secondary role in patient care and are not allowed to do much.
Fact ☐ Fiction ☐

B. Now read the text below and highlight the correct answers to the previous statements.

C. Would you say that your vision of the healthcare world is influenced by TV shows?

Monster spoke with Andrew Holtz, a former CNN medical correspondent and author of The Real Grey's Anatomy, *which gives a behind-the-scenes look at the real lives of surgical residents he shadowed at Oregon Health & Science University (OHSU). Here's a side-by-side comparison.*

Grey's Anatomy: Surgeons get into really intense, close relationships with patients regularly.

Real life: Residents and physicians actually spend more time away from the patients in rooms with computers and lab test results. [...] Nurses are the ones who develop the close relationships with patients. "An awful lot of what you see on the show is what nurses do in terms of patient care."

Grey's Anatomy: Doctors discuss their personal lives while working on an unconscious patient.

Real life: Actually, yes. OK, maybe they aren't talking about who slept with who, but that conference they attended last week or the concert they saw last night? Yeah. But the second something changes, all conversation stops.

Grey's Anatomy: The residents are constantly competing for surgeries.

Real life: "There is a lot of stress, but I saw, for the most part, that people tended to support each other. [...] I saw a lot more collaboration and mutual support."

Grey's Anatomy: Nurses play a small role in the hospital.

Real life: Holtz says this is one of the biggest myths on *Grey's Anatomy* and other TV medical shows. "Nurses are absolutely essential to health care. What you see on TV is mostly nursing care. Giving patients injections, making sure they have their medicine, taking their blood pressure and doing hands-on things with the patient in the hospital room, that's almost all nursing care."

Monster, "9 ways your job is nothing like *Grey's Anatomy*"

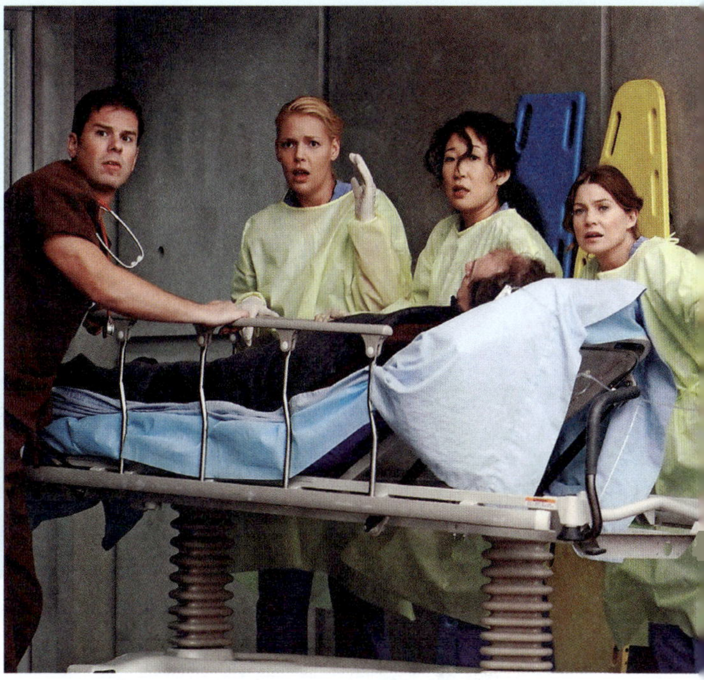

2 The New Superheroes

What role does art play in our perception of healthcare workers?

1 Inspiring artists

A. The following artworks were all created during the Covid-19 pandemic.
Pick your favourite one, comment on it and justify your choice.

HELP!

Nouns
- attribute
- carer
- chest
- emblem
- front line
- medical staff
- stethoscope
- trenches (pl.)

Adjectives
- injured = wounded /ˈwuːndɪd/

Expressions
- run towards
- the threat /θret/ of the pandemic

1

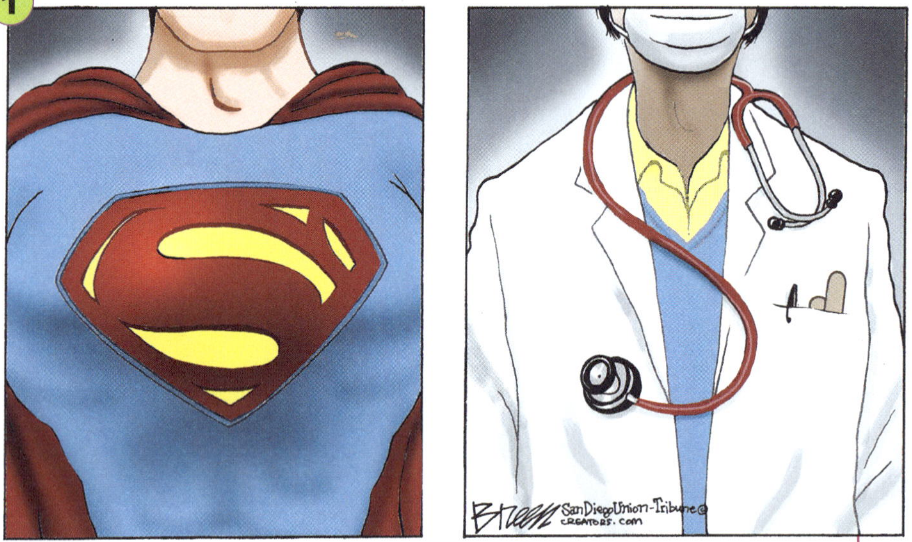

American cartoonist Steve Breen

Document 1: ....

2

American cartoonist Steve Benson

Document 2: ....

Document 3: ....

....

B. Give a title to your chosen artwork.

....

C. How do these artworks influence your view of the carers' work during the pandemic?

....

3

Game Changer, a Banksy artwork given by the artist to the Southampton Hospital, May 2020

2 New superheroes in comics

A. Canadian artists Jay Owen and David Watkins dedicated a website and a comic book to healthcare workers. Watch the video and pick out Jay Owen's reasons for creating the website.

....

B. Pick out the medical heroes' superpowers, according to David Watkins.

....

C. How has this comics inspired Kim Watkins in her job? How did her pupils react?

....

www.lienmini.fr/htr7-u1103

YOUR TURN! 3 Create a poster

As a comics illustrator, create a poster to illustrate your vision of carers during the Covid-19 pandemic.
Find a slogan to show your appreciation. You may use an illustration from the Internet or make a photomontage.

3 Hospital Staff's Real Feelings

Did healthcare workers feel like heroes during the pandemic?

1 Two nurses share their views

www.lienmini.fr/htr7-u1104

A. Listen to the testimonies of Jessica Bamford and Matthew Tovey and circle what they talk about in this interview.

a. Their personal experience during the pandemic.

b. Their professional experience of Covid-19.

c. The government's decision not to give nurses a pay rise.

d. Their decision to quit their jobs.

B. Tick the words or expressions you hear.

- ☐ horrendous (*terrible*)
- ☐ undervalued
- ☐ overlooked
- ☐ sacrifices
- ☐ stressful
- ☐ putting their lives at risk
- ☐ terrible
- ☐ disrespected
- ☐ a massive blow (*choc*)
- ☐ anxiety-provoking
- ☐ excluded
- ☐ we should be recognised

C. True or False? Justify orally.

Both nurses had to isolate from their families. T ☐ F ☐

D. Now fill in the grid below.

	Jessica Bamford	Matthew Tovey
Feelings about the pandemic		
Opinions about the government's decision		

HELP!

Noun
- blow: *choc*

Adjectives
- horrendous = dreadful: *terrible*
- overlooked = neglected
- recognised: *reconnu(e) (pour son travail)*
- undervalued = unappreciated

Verbs & Expressions
- bond: *se rapprocher*
- put one's life at risk
- succumb /sə'kʌm/ = die

2 Admiration or salary?

Are nurses treated as heroes by their employers? Use the picture and caption below to justify your answer.

HELP!

Noun
- pay rise

Adjective
- rewarded

Verbs
- applaud
- overlook
- protest
- undervalue

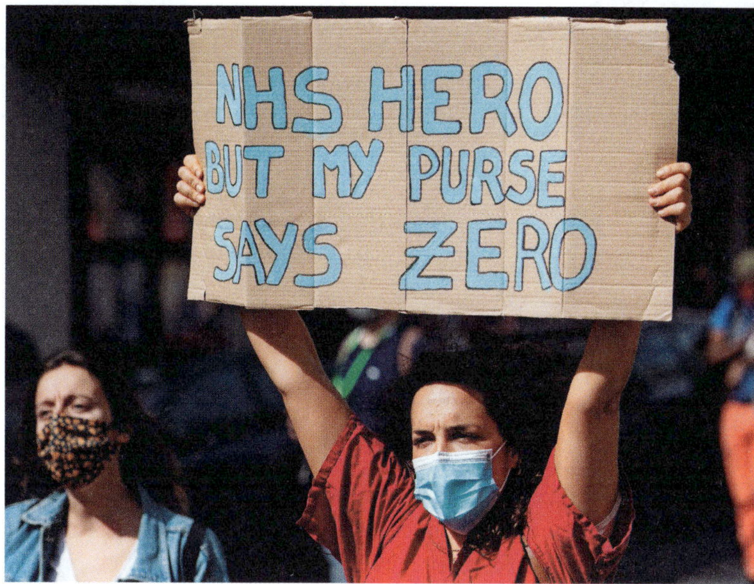

NHS workers protest in August 2020 after learning they would not get the pay rise promised by the British government.

3 Reluctant[1] heroes

It may surprise you to know that many of us in healthcare are uncomfortable being called heroes. We never **signed up** to be superheroes, and before COVID-19, it was unusual to hear people refer to us as such. As an oncologist who has spent his entire career utilizing radiation to treat cancer (I haven't given anyone superpowers yet, despite my patients' joking **inquiries**), I'm used to hearing **statements** about my job like "Doing that must be so hard," or "What made you choose that as a career?" or "I could never do that!" But up until a few weeks ago, I had never been called a "hero." [...]

Health care workers aren't heroes. But if we were, our superpowers would come from the people we so **faithfully** and lovingly serve. The "S" on our not so muscular **chests** stands for "Science," not Super. The masks we wear hide our faces, but not our proud identities. Our only protective armor is effective social distancing, both within and outside of hospitals. So, if you feel the need to say thank you, we graciously and humbly **bow our heads** to you because it means the world to us. But please, don't call us superheroes. Instead, help us by fighting this invisible enemy so that someday we can leave behind the life of Spider-Man and go back to being plain old Peter Parker.

1 *réticents*

KevinMD.com, June 2020

A. Write the words in bold letters (in the text) next to their definitions / explanations below.

a. Incline one's head respectfully: ....

b. Loyally: ....

c. What people ask about: ....

d. Consented, agreed to: ....

e. What people say: ....

f. The part of anatomy that is situated between one's arms: ....

B. How do healthcare workers feel about being called heroes? Highlight the answer in the text.

C. What changed recently in this doctor's job?

....

....

....

D. Underline superhero symbols and what they could mean for carers.

YOUR PROJECT BAC

Groupwork. As a screenwriter for a new British medical show, *Heartbeat*, you have been asked to create the three main characters of the series. Imagine their names, jobs, motivations for choosing their jobs, personality traits and some struggles they will have to face during season 1. Pick your actors and actresses.
Present your characters to your classmates. The class will vote for the three best characters!

4 It's Everyone's Business

ETLV STMG

Should hospitals be run like companies?

OBJECTIVES STMG

- Identify criteria that allow to distinguish the different categories of organisations
- Spot and analyse public organisations' strategic choices

1 The American viewpoint

In the wealthiest country in the world, the Covid-19 pandemic has exposed the core of a healthcare system that is structurally incapable of dealing with the pandemic. Federal and local governments, health insurers and employers have pledged to help Americans pay their way through this crisis, but to do so requires a dramatic overhaul of a system which has for decades prioritized cost over care. [...]

The pandemic crisis is being further exacerbated by the system's devotion to profits over people. Medical workers are being furloughed and losing jobs because of the pandemic – including those on the frontlines – as their employers seek[1] to cut costs.

Alteon Health, a private-equity backed company which employs about 1,700 emergency medicine doctors and other physicians, said it would temporarily stop providing benefits[2] including paid time off, according to the health website STAT.

While intensive care units and emergency rooms are billing[3] sky-high figures, there has been a pause on non-essential care that has, in turn, cut medical system profits.

Without high-margin treatments such as physical therapy, cosmetic surgery and orthopedic procedures, medical systems are struggling to pay salaries and cover administrative costs.

1 try to • **2** profits • **3** *facturent*

The Guardian, April 2020

A. Match each word with its translation or definition.

a. core •	• *restructuration*
b. pledged •	• essence, heart
c. overhaul •	• promised
d. furloughed •	• *mis au chômage technique*

B. Tick the better translation for each expression.

a. private-equity backed company:

☐ *entreprise financée par des capitaux privés*

☐ *entreprise qui tourne le dos aux capitaux privés*

b. paid time off: ☐ *chômage* ☐ *congés payés*

C. True or False? Highlight the justification in the text.

a. American hospitals are focused on making profits. T ☐ F ☐

b. As a consequence, hospital staff benefits from the situation. T ☐ F ☐

c. Medical systems function thanks to emergency operations. T ☐ F ☐

HELP!

DEFINITION ETLV

A **public organisation** serves the **general interest**. Its purpose is to provide **public services**.

2 The British point of view

A. Watch the video. Tick the right answer.

a. ☐ The NHS is funded by the patients', bills and works like a company.

b. ☐ The NHS is funded through tax and offers government jobs.

B. It is defined as: ☐ a risk-taking ☐ a risk-sharing system.

C. What is controversial about it?

www.lienmini.fr/htr7-u1105

2'22 to 3'56

YOUR PROJECT

Debate: Should hospitals be run like companies?

5 Taking Care of Carers

ETLV ST2S

How does doctors' health impact out-of-hours service?

OBJECTIVE ST2S

➤ Characterise the role of caregivers in the out-of-hours service and the healthcare system

American doctors need help

A. Observe the poster. What are the health problems faced by healthcare workers from mainland US, Alaska and Hawaii? Complete the caption. Use the following words.

unhealthy lifestyle that leads to obesity – loss of motivation and desire to change careers – feeling of increasing pressure – sleep deprivation due to stress.

B. Comment on the sources of these problems.

....

....

....

....

....

....

....

....

....

....

....

....

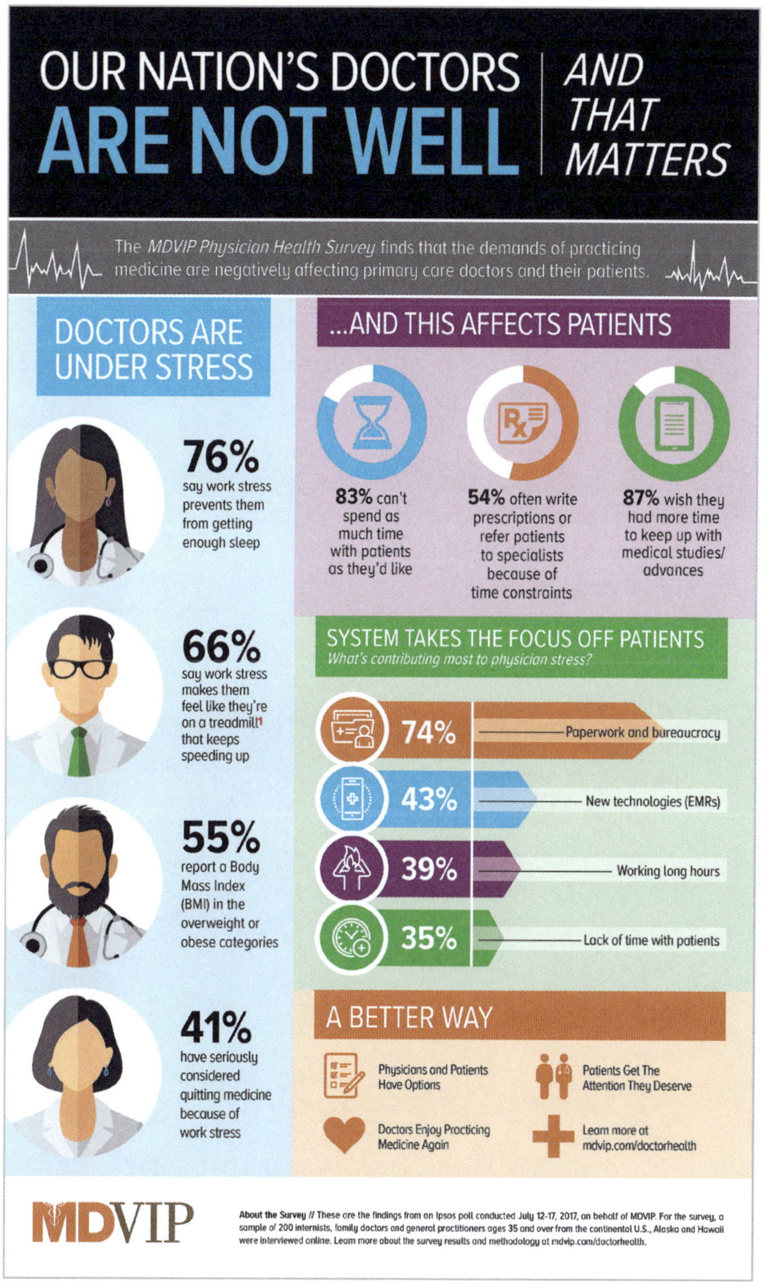

1 *tapis de course*

HELP!

DEFINITION ETLV

Out-of-hours service: agreements to provide equal access to healthcare services at all times and all hours (in hospitals and doctors' surgeries) within a given area.

YOUR PROJECT BAC

As a reporter for *Care Management Matters*, pitch the idea for your latest article, "Carers need care too" to your chief editor. Use what you have learnt and the document above.

RULE THE GRAMMAR!

1. LES PROPOSITIONS RELATIVES

Elles apportent des informations sur un nom et sont introduites par un pronom relatif.

- Quand les pronoms relatifs <u>sujet</u> renvoient à des humains, on utilise ***who***.
  <u>The nurses</u> who are working in the emergency room have stressful work conditions.

- Lorsqu'ils renvoient à des non-humains ou à des animaux, on utilisera ***that*** ou ***which***.
  <u>This hospital</u> that is mentioned in a famous American TV show, is now closed.
  <u>The careers</u> which interest me the most are all in the medical field.

2. LE GÉNITIF

Le génitif marque un lien de possession entre deux éléments. Le possesseur vient toujours en premier.

- On forme le génitif avec 's si le nom référant au possesseur est au singulier.
  I have just found <u>Dr Mike</u>'s stethoscope.

- On ajoute simplement une apostrophe s'il est au pluriel.
  I am waiting for you at the <u>nurses</u>' station.

VOCABULARY

Healthcare

The hospital

- carer /'keərə/ = caregiver (n.)
- emergency room = ER (n.)
- healthcare worker (n.)
- hospital staff (n.)
- nurse (n.)
- nurse station (n.)
- operating room = OR (n.)
- patient /'peɪʃənt/ (n.)
- physician = doctor (n.)
- scrubs (n.): *blouses stériles*
- stethoscope /'steθəskəʊp/ (n.)
- surgeon /'sɜːdʒən/ (n.)
- surgical mask / gloves (n.)

Your words: ....

Working conditions

- care (v. / n.)
- career (n.)
- commitment (n.): *engagement*
- front line (n.)
- heal = cure /kjʊə/ (v.)
- injury = wound /wuːnd/ (n.)
- pandemic (n.)
- pay rise (n.)
- protest (n.)
- protest (v.)
- rewarded (adj.)

Your words: ....

Qualities

- be depicted = described as (v.)
- caring (adj.)
- close /kləʊs/ to (adj.): *proche de*
- committed (adj.)
- courageous /kə'reɪdʒəs/ = brave (adj.)
- dedicated (adj.)
- selfless = altruistic (adj.)

Your words: ....

Feelings

- admire /əd'maɪə/ (v.)
- admiring /əd'maɪərɪŋ/ (adj.)
- appreciated ≠ unappreciated (adj.)
- overlooked = neglected (adj.)
- recognised (adj.)
- respected ≠ disrespected (adj.)
- stressed (adj.)
- take sth for granted
- the threat of the pandemic
- valued ≠ undervalued (adj.)

Your words: ....

MP3
www.lienmini.fr/htr7-u1106

LANGUAGE LAB

1 Fill in the blanks with the words below.

carers • careers • commitment • close

A. Fictional TV shows make us think that surgeons are always …………………… to patients.

B. The NHS video focuses on nursing …………………… .

C. The OR doctor's …………………… is remarkable!

D. …………………… must have altruistic personalities.

2 Give the synonyms (=) or antonyms (≠) of these words.

A. appreciated ≠ ……………………

B. selfless = ……………………

C. impressed = ……………………

D. undervalued ≠ ……………………

Then, make a sentence for each one.

A. ……………………

B. ……………………

C. ……………………

D. ……………………

3 Complete the sentences using the correct relative pronoun.

A. In the operating room, …………………… you can see over there, I performed my first operation.

B. My favourite fictional character, …………………… is a talented nurse, is always overlooked.

C. This pay rise …………………… had been promised by the government was never given.

D. The motivation …………………… she mentioned first was to care for patients.

E. Do you know Doctor Who, …………………… is one of the most famous British fictional characters?

4 Put the elements below in the correct order.

A. scrubs / a doctor / a stethoscope / costume / could / and / superhero / 's / be

……………………

B. commitment / inspiring / the real-life / ' / is / doctors

……………………

C. a surgeon / was / my sister / to become / it / 's / dream

……………………

5 Unit's checkout

Describe the cartoon. Use relative pronouns and the genitive. You may start your sentences with: *The man who... The tee-shirt's emblem is...*

……………………

OPEN YOUR EARS!

La prononciation de la lettre u MP3 N°14

Écoutez les mots suivants, puis notez le numéro correspondant à la prononciation de la lettre *u*.

1 *human* • 2 *but* • 3 *surgeon* • 4 *put* • 5 *cure* • 6 *valued* • 7 *unrealistic* • 8 *injury* • 9 *business* • 10 *nurse* • 11 *flu* (la grippe)

/ɜː/ (bird): …………… *\/juː/ (new):* …………… */ʊ/ (should):* …………… */ɪ/ (fill):* ……………

/uː/ (moon): …………… */ə/ (doctor):* …………… */ʊə/ (sure):* …………… */ʌ/ (come):* ……………

AXE 5

UNIT 12

UNDER SURVEILLANCE

Are we being watched for our own good only?

YOUR PROJECTS

LV
As a town councillor for the city of London present your views on surveillance.

ETLV ST2S
As residents in London, debate the possible use of AI in different areas of the city life.

Au menu de cette unité :

DÉCOUVERTES CULTURELLES

- Un extrait d'une nouvelle visionnaire de Ray Bradbury
- Les robots et caméras de surveillance à Singapour et à Londres
- Les drones en Australie et aux États-Unis
- Les problèmes de discrimination liés à l'intelligence artificielle ETLV ST2S

OUTILS LINGUISTIQUES

- La voix passive
- Le prétérit
- Le lexique de la surveillance (objectifs et problèmes), de la technologie, de la dystopie
- L'intonation montante et descendante

GET READY!

WORD CHALLENGE

Use as many of these words as possible throughout the unit.
Tick ✓ the box when you have used the word.

- ☐ achieve /ə'tʃi:v/ = accomplish /ə'kʌmplɪʃ/ (v.)
- ☐ AI /eɪ'aɪ/ = Artificial Intelligence
- ☐ be under close /kləʊs/ surveillance /sə'veɪləns/
- ☐ be under watch = be surveilled /sə'veɪld/ = be monitored
- ☐ biased /'baɪəst/ = partial (adj.)
- ☐ CCTV = closed-circuit /'sɜ:kɪt/ television (n.)
- ☐ digital /'dɪdʒɪtəl/ surveillance (n.)
- ☐ dystopian /dɪs'təʊpiən/ (adj.)
- ☐ foreboding = fear (n.)
- ☐ health /helθ/ (n.)
- ☐ infectious /ɪn'fekʃəs/ disease /dɪ'zi:z/
- ☐ keep fit = maintain health (v.)
- ☐ lockdown (n.): *confinement*
- ☐ monitoring technology (n.)
- ☐ Orwellian /ɔ:'welɪən/ (adj.) = from George Orwell
- ☐ patrol /pə'trəʊl/ (v.)
- ☐ privacy UK: /'prɪvəsi/ US: /'praɪvəsi/ (n.)
- ☐ prophetic = visionary (adj.)
- ☐ recording /rɪ'kɔ:dɪŋ/ (n.)
- ☐ robot /'rəʊbɒt/ (n.)
- ☐ safety (n.)
- ☐ spot = detect (v.)
- ☐ trial /'traɪəl/ = test (n.)
- ☐ warn /wɔ:n/ (v.): *avertir*

BEFORE CLASS!

A. Watch the video and circle the best title.

a. Thieves, beware of the robot dog!
b. A robot dog to help fight a virus.
c. Robodog the new policeman.
d. A robot dog to guide tourists.

www.lienmini.fr/htr7-u1201

B. What does the robot remind you of?

....

C. Say what the robot dog is for. Then justify its use.

....
....
....
....

D. Tick the right answers and justify.

On seeing the robot some passers-by are...

a. ☐ amused ☐ curious

....

b. ☐ frightened ☐ indifferent

....

c. ☐ overjoyed ☐ a bit worried

....

E. Get ready to share the information with the class.

1 A Dystopian World

Could fiction predict reality?

1 George Orwell, a visionary

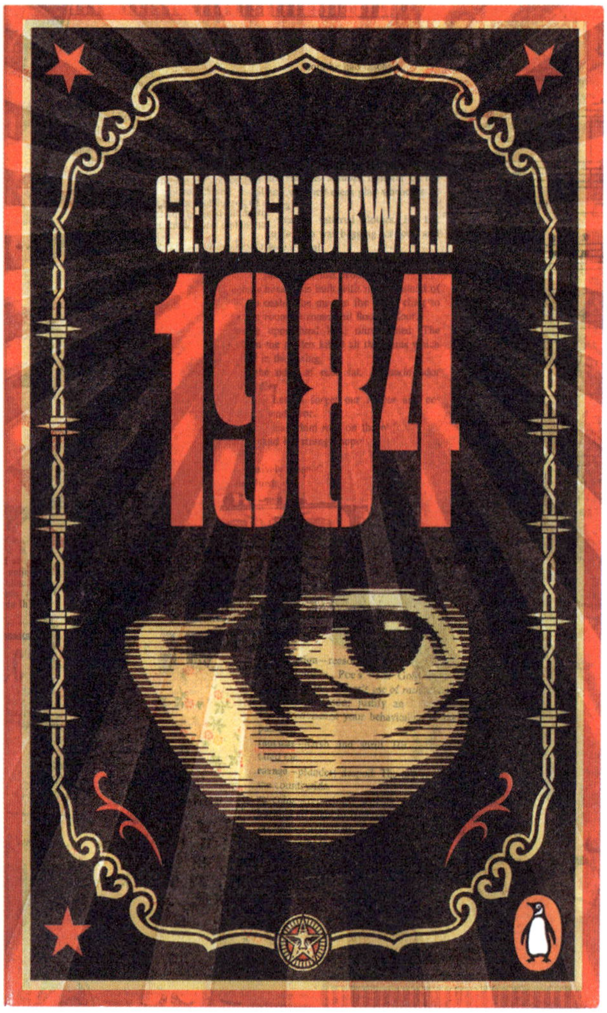

Cultural fact

In 1948, English novelist George Orwell (1903-1950) wrote an iconic, political satire: *1984*. Published in 1949, it depicts a society where the government controls every detail of the people's lives. The expression "Big Brother is watching you" appears at the beginning of the first chapter of the novel. It has since become a political slogan and has been used on various posters.

A. Describe the book cover briefly (colours, symbolic elements…). What do you think of it?

B. Does this image correspond to your idea of what surveillance is about? Why (not)?

HELP!

Nouns
- close-up /'kləʊsʌp/: *gros plan*
- foreboding = fear

Adjectives
- creepy = scary
- prophetic = visionary
- spine-chilling = terrifying

Verbs & Expressions
- be filled with horror
- display = show
- make sb's blood run cold
- stare at = look fixedly

2 Night walk, night watch

2053. Every evening Leonard Mead goes for long walks by himself in deserted streets. He is the only pedestrian near his home: in his town, nobody takes walks anymore...

To enter out into that silence that was the city at eight o'clock of a misty[1] evening in November, to put your feet upon that buckling[2] concrete walk, to step over grassy seams and make your way, hands in pockets, through the silences, that was what Mr. Leonard Mead most dearly loved to do. [...]

He was within a block of his destination when the lone car turned a corner quite suddenly and flashed a fierce[3] white cone of light upon him. [...].

A metallic voice called to him:
"Stand still. Stay where you are! Don't move!" He halted. [...]
"Your name?" said the police car in a metallic whisper[4]. He couldn't see the men in it for the bright light in his eyes.

"Leonard Mead," he said. [...]
"What are you doing out?"
"Walking," said Leonard Mead.
"Walking!"
"Just walking," he said simply, but his face felt cold.
"Walking, just walking, walking?"
"Yes, sir."
"Walking where? For what?"
"Walking for air. Walking to see."
"Your address!"
"Eleven South Saint James Street." [...]
The back door of the police car sprang wide.
"Get in."
"Wait a minute, I haven't done anything!"
"Get in."
"I protest!"
"Mr. Mead."
He walked like a man suddenly drunk. As he passed the front window of the car he looked in. As he had expected, there was no-one in the front seat, no-one in the car at all.
"Get in."
He put his hand to the door and peered[5] into the back seat, which was a little cell, a little black jail with bars. It smelled of riveted[6] steel[7]. It smelled of harsh antiseptic; it smelled too clean and hard and metallic. There was nothing soft there. [...]

"Where are you taking me?" [...]
"To the Psychiatric Centre for Research on Regressive Tendencies."
He got in. The door shut with a soft thud[8]. [...]

They passed one house on one street a moment later, one house in an entire city of houses that were dark, but this one particular house had all its electric lights brightly lit, every window a loud yellow illumination, square and warm in the cool darkness. "That's my house," said Leonard Mead. No one answered him. The car moved down the empty river bed streets and off away, leaving the empty streets with the empty sidewalks, and no sound and no motion all the rest of the chill November night.

1 lightly foggy • **2** *qui se déforme* • **3** *violent* • **4** very soft talk • **5** looked curiously • **6** fixed • **7** *acier* • **8** *bruit sourd*

The Pedestrian,
by Ray Bradbury, 1951

A. Read the text. Tick the adjectives corresponding to the characters' attitudes and the atmosphere.

a. The pedestrian:	☐ rebellious	☐ obedient (*obéissant*)	☐ challenging	☐ arrogant	☐ indifferent
b. The voice:	☐ threatening	☐ bossy (*autoritaire*)	☐ friendly	☐ neutral	☐ smooth
c. The atmosphere:	☐ noisy	☐ silent	☐ oppressive	☐ joyful	☐ depressing

B. Highlight the expressions associated with surveillance and underline the expressions associated with dehumanisation.

C. What can you deduce? Tick true or false. Justify orally.

a. Leonard Mead was under watch. T ☐ F ☐

b. Two police cars were patrolling. T ☐ F ☐

c. Three policemen arrested him. T ☐ F ☐

d. The police car is a robot. T ☐ F ☐

e. Another man was sent to hospital. T ☐ F ☐

D. Sum up what you have understood.

....

....

....

....

YOUR TURN!

3 Become actors

Pairwork. **Act out the scene. Respect the atmosphere of the passage.**

2 London Eyes

Should we be worried by ever more CCTV cameras?

1 You are being watched

www.lienmini.fr/htr7-u1202

A. Watch the trailer. Pick out the key sentence you hear in the soundtrack.

B. Tick the right answers, then draw a conclusion.
The key sentence suggests that:

a. ☐ Shaun is followed by the police.
b. ☐ Shaun repairs CCTVs.
c. ☐ CCTV is operating everywhere.
d. ☐ the series is about surveillance.

C. Watch again the end of the trailer. Note down the words on the screen. What do they mean?

D. Look at the images on the screen by the end of the trailer. What are they?

a. ☐ photomontages made by the police
b. ☐ screenshots from CCTV

2 The new top of the charts?

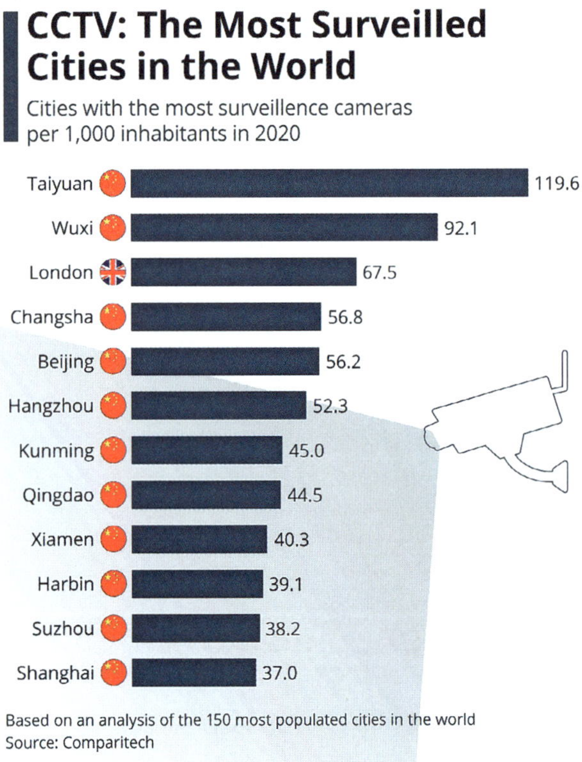

A. Look at the chart. Comment on the figures.

B. Highlight the conclusions you can draw from this document as regards fiction and reality.

a. Fiction probably inspires reality.
b. Reality and fiction are one and the same thing.
c. Reality might be inspired by fiction.
d. Reality is sometimes worse than fiction.
e. Fiction and reality are completely different.

HELP!

Nouns
- hood /hʊd/: *capuche*
- phrase /freɪz/ = expression
- screenshot = image captured /'kæptʃəd/ from a computer screen

Adjectives
- biased /'baɪəst/ = partial /'pɑ:ʃəl/
- weird /wɪəd/ = strange

Verbs & Expressions
- account /ə'kaʊnt/ for = explain
- crawl /krɔ:l/ = move on all fours: *ramper*
- deceive /dɪ'si:v/ = misguide
- monitor /'mɒnɪtə/ = observe

3 London, capital of CCTV

It is all quiet on a mid-morning weekday at the CCTV monitoring centre of Southwark Council, in London, when I pay a visit.

Dozens of monitors display largely mundane[1] activities – people cycling in a park, waiting for buses, coming in and out of shops.

The manager here is Sarah Pope, and there is no doubt that she is fiercely proud of her job. What gives her a real sense of satisfaction is "getting the first glimpse[2] of a suspect... which can then guide the police investigation in the right direction," she says.

Southwark shows how CCTV cameras – that fully adhere to the UK code of conduct – are used to help catch criminals and keep people safe. However, such surveillance systems do have their critics around the world – people who complain about a loss of privacy and an infringement[3] of civil liberties.

Manufacturing of CCTV cameras and facial recognition technologies is a booming industry, feeding a seemingly[4] insatiable appetite. In the UK alone, there is one CCTV camera for every 11 people.

1 everyday • **2** see briefly • **3** *atteinte* • **4** apparently

BBC, November 2019

A. **Describe the poster. Pay attention to the catchphrase. What can you deduce?**

B. **Read the text and highlight what the CCTV monitoring centre records.**

C. **Underline the reason why there is CCTV.**

D. **Pick out the expressions referring to the people's reactions about the use of CCTV.**

a. Dissatisfaction and fear:

b. Pride:

c. Gratification:

E. **Sum up what you have understood.**

YOUR TURN!

4 Debate CCTV

Groupwork. **How do you react to the use of CCTV cameras? You must decide if you agree, disagree or have mixed feelings. Then, join your group, make a list of your ideas and be ready to expose your views.**

3 Of Drones and Men

Are drones made to control or to protect?

1 Police drones

A. Read the comic strip. Are all the drones used in the same context?

B. By whom are the drones operated? Where from?

C. Pay attention to the last picture. What does the cartoonist denounce?

Brian McFadden, American cartoonist, 2012

2 Protective drones?

A. Watch the report. Pick out words or expressions about the places mentioned.

B. What are the two messages delivered by the drone?

C. Identify the goal of this particular use of drones.

www.lienmini.fr/htr7-u1203

0'00 to 0'51

HELP!

Nouns
- crackdown = repression
- HQ /eɪtʃ'kju:/ = headquarters
- intelligence /ɪn'telɪdʒəns/ = information
- lockdown: *confinement*
- pandemic /pæn'demɪk/
- range = reach
- rules = regulations
- weapon /'wepən/: *arme*

Adjectives
- critical = essential /ɪ'senʃəl/
- tough /tʌf/ = difficult = hard

Expression
- aka /eɪkeɪ'eɪ/ = also known as

3 Australian Big Brother

Software being developed at the University of South Australia in conjunction with Canadian drone manufacturer Draganfly could see drones used to monitor the health of people, including spotting sneezes[1] and tracking whether they have a fever. It is just one way technology could be used to track and slow the spread of a virus like COVID-19.

But experts warn that new surveillance technologies must include privacy safeguards before they are adopted.

Professor Javaan Chahl, who holds positions with the University of South Australia and the Department of Defence, is developing software for the pandemic drone. [...] "All such technologies carry a risk with them," he said. "I might think it's a very bad idea to use drones to chase people around who might be sick. But perhaps others might have different ideas. And it's very hard to restrain them from using it like that once the genie is out of the bottle."

Police in the US city of Westport, an hour north of New York, were trialling[2] the software along with Draganfly, but pulled out[3] last week over privacy concerns.

"There's a lot of discussion going on at the moment about how we manage that privacy so that you don't take away people's freedom, or start imposing on them unnecessarily," Professor Chahl said. "But you do want to watch for the presence of this infectious disease. So there's a lot of challenges."

Artificial intelligence expert Professor Toby Walsh urged a cautious approach towards adopting technologies like the pandemic drone. "I think the devil is in the detail: how it's rolled out[4], what safeguards are put in place," he said. "There's every reason that this technology could be a useful tool in our armoury[5] with rolling back the restrictions and allowing people to go about somewhat more normal lives. But, equally, there are concerns that you'd have about people's privacy and about whether when normality has returned, that we are not finding ourselves in a big brother surveillance state."

1 *éternuements* • **2** were testing • **3** *se retirer* • **4** *déployer* • **5** *arsenal*

ABC News, April 2020

A. Read the article and say why people could be under surveillance.

....

....

....

B. The people and their occupations. Write who does what.

a. Works for the University of South Australia: ....

b. Tested the software that is being developed at the University of South Australia: ....

c. Works for the Department of Defence: ....

d. Is an AI expert: ....

e. Is developing software for the pandemic drone: ....

C. Highlight what Javaan Chahl thinks about the use of drones, underline Toby Walsh's opinion and circle the police position.

D. Be ready to sum up what you have understood.

....

....

....

YOUR PROJECT

You have been invited to a local radio as a town councillor for the city of London to present your views on surveillance. Explain in 3 minutes why you are willing (or not) to use modern technologies for security reasons.

4 AI and Social Inequalities

ETLV ST2S

Does AI serve social good?

OBJECTIVE ST2S

➤ Specify what impacts Artificial Intelligence can have on social inequalities and social cohesion within a territory

1 Algorithms in the UK

Have you ever had a dream in which you are about to sit your final exams and you suddenly realise you did not do any prep and are going to fail? I have that anxiety dream a lot [...], despite having left school a million years ago. And I am not the only one: it is a surprisingly common phenomenon.

While that dream is disturbing, it is nothing compared with the nightmare British students have just lived through. The pandemic meant school-leavers did not get to sit their Highers or A-levels[1]; instead, algorithms determined their grades – and their futures. A lot of kids from poorer backgrounds had their final results dramatically downgraded from teachers' predictions; pupils at private schools, meanwhile, were treated remarkably well by the algorithms. After enormous controversy, the Scottish and UK governments performed U-turns[2], saying exam results would be based on teacher-assessed grades[3].

This is not the first time the UK government has suffered embarrassment by algorithm. Earlier this year, the Home Office[4] decided to scrap[5] a "racist algorithm" for visa applicants that was accused of creating "speedy boarding for white people" while making things harder for everyone else. And a security thinktank[6] warned last year that predictive policing algorithms could amplify human bias and make it more likely that young black men would get disproportionately stopped and searched compared with people from other demographics.

Mysterious algorithms control increasingly large parts of our lives. They recommend what we should watch next on YouTube; they help employers recruit staff; they decide if you deserve a loan[7]; they help landlords[8] calculate rent. You and I may have aged beyond school exams, but it does not matter how old you are – these days, it is almost guaranteed that an opaque algorithm is grading and influencing your every move. If that does not give you nightmares, I am not sure what will.

1 *passer un diplôme du supérieur ou le baccalauréat* • **2** *un virage à 180 degrés* • **3** *notes données par les professeurs* • **4** *ministère de l'Intérieur* • **5** *abandon* • **6** *groupe de réflexion* • **7** *prêt bancaire* • **8** *propriétaires*

The Guardian, August 2020

A. Read the text and highlight the reason why AI marked the pupils.

B. Underline the unfair consequences resulting from AI.

C. Quote the passage saying that the governments had to change their decision to use AI to grade students.

D. What was the final decision? Cross out the false statement.

a. Both AI and teachers evaluated students.

b. Teachers were the only ones to evaluate students.

E. Circle the passage showing that the British government used AI to discriminate against people.

F. Quote four ideas showing that algorithms control our lives more and more.

G. What conclusions is drawn from this text?

2 AI: a Unesco warning

www.lienmini.fr/htr7-u1204

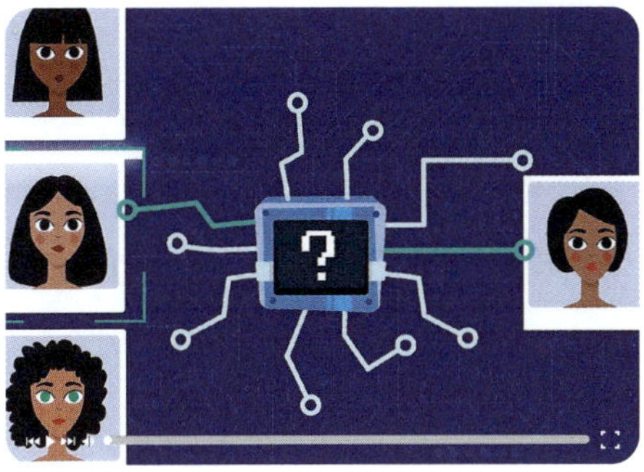

A. Before watching the video, tick the words you think you may hear.

☐ assimilate	☐ ethical norms	☐ personal data
☐ facial recognition	☐ privacy	☐ private life
☐ darker skin tones	☐ protected	☐ detects
☐ inequality	☐ protecting	☐ discrimination
☐ lighter skin tones	☐ eliminate	☐ males
☐ enforcing	☐ online shopping	☐ secrecy
☐ equality	☐ online tracking	☐ surveillance

B. Watch the video and highlight the words (from the list above) that you have heard.

C. Recap the video. Use as many words as you can from the list to explain what you have understood.

3 What is behind AI?

A. Look at the still. What do you notice? Make hypotheses about the probable reason why the person did that.

B. Watch the video. What is the issue raised? Highlight the false statements. Justify orally.

Facial recognition at MIT…

a. … is extremely effective.

b. … didn't recognise the woman.

c. … didn't work as she was wearing a white mask.

d. … worked when the woman wore a white mask.

C. The reasons for the problem. Tick the right answer.

The data provided for technology come from:

a. ☐ a very small, homogeneous group of people who may have unconscious biases.

b. ☐ too many people whose ideas about technology are contradictory.

c. ☐ only white men who do not agree at all on the possible uses of technology.

www.lienmini.fr/htr7-u1205

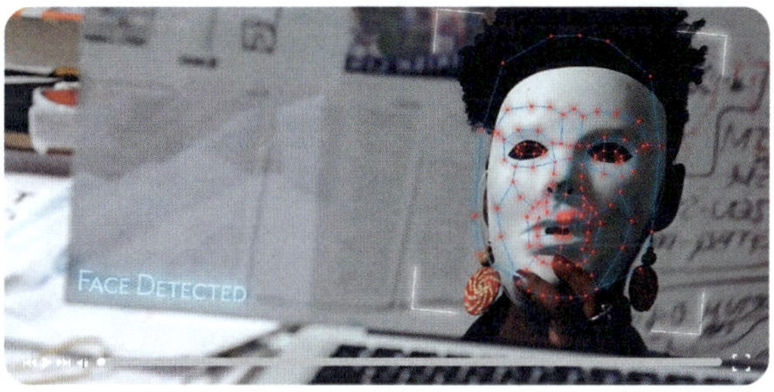

D. Why can AI become dangerous for people's lives? How could AI be accepted?

YOUR PROJECT BAC

As city residents in London, debate the possible use of AI in different areas of the city life and its impact on the social cohesion on the territory. Prepare your arguments for or against it. Focus on the way it is created, the reasons why it is used and its ethics – or absence of ethics – and see how AI affects social cohesion in a positive or a negative way. Then, debate, being as convincing as possible.

HELP!

Nouns
- coexistence
- commitment = involvement
- local activities
- social cohesion = social harmony

Adjectives
- committed = involved
- inclusive

Verbs
- contribute (to)
- gather information
- interact
- lessen = reduce
- share

DEFINITION ETLV

Social inequalities are unequal opportunities for social positions within a group. They can result from other people's stereotypes or prejudices.

RULE THE GRAMMAR!

1. LA VOIX PASSIVE

• Emploi

La voix passive permet de mettre en avant la personne ou la chose qui subit l'action.

• Formation

Be conjugué au même temps que le verbe à la forme active + participe passé (*by* + agent) (voir aussi page 86).

Leonard Mead was arrested by a robot car.

2. LE PRÉTÉRIT

• Emploi

Le prétérit s'emploie pour évoquer des actions ou des événement passés et terminés. Il est souvent accompagné d'un marqueur de temps (*yesterday, three years ago, when they met*...).

• Formation

On distingue les verbes réguliers (terminaison en *-ed*) des verbes irréguliers.

Forme affirmative : sujet + verbe conjugué (+ complément)

*They **asked** him to check the CCTV two days ago. He **found** nothing wrong.*

Forme interrogative : mot interrogatif en *wh-* + auxiliaire *did* + sujet + BV (+ complément)

*Why **did** algorithms **mark** the British pupils in 2020?*

Forme négative : sujet + auxiliaire *did* + *not* + BV (+ complément)

*We **did not know** that we were under watch.*

VOCABULARY

Surveillance /sə'veɪləns/

Purpose

- health /helθ/
- infectious /ɪn'fekʃəs/ (adj.)
- keep fit = maintain health (v.)
- intelligence /ɪn'telɪdʒəns/ = information (n.)
- lockdown: *confinement* (n.)
- monitor /'mɒnɪtə/ = observe (v.)
- pandemic /pæn'demɪk/ (n.)
- patrol /pə'trəʊl/ (v.)
- safety (n.)
- spot = detect (v.)
- trial /'traɪəl/ = test (n.)
- warn /wɔ:n/ (v.)

Your words: ....

Technology

- achieve /ə'tʃi:v/ = accomplish /ə'kʌmplɪʃ/ (v.)
- AI /eɪ'aɪ/ = Artificial Intelligence (n.)
- CCTV = closed-circuit /'sɜ:kɪt/ television (n.)
- close-up /'kləʊsʌp/ (n.): *gros plan*
- digital /'dɪdʒɪtəl/ (adj.): *numérique*
- drone (n.)
- facial recognition /'feɪʃəl rekəg'nɪʃən/ (n.)

Your words: ....

In fiction

- Big Brother
- dystopian /dɪs'təʊpiən/ (adj.)
- make sb's blood run cold (v.)
- Orwellian /ɔ:'welɪən/ (adj.) = from George Orwell
- prophetic = visionary (adj.)
- spine-chilling = terrifying (adj.)

Your words: ....

Issues

- be under close surveillance
- be under watch / monitored / surveilled /sə'veɪld/
- biased /'baɪəst/ = partial /'pɑ:ʃəl/ (adj.)
- crackdown = repression (n.)
- ethical ≠ unethical (adj.)
- privacy (UK) /'prɪvəsi/ (US) /'praɪvəsi/ (n.)
- rules = regulations (n.)
- social inequalities /'səʊʃəl ɪni'kwɒlɪtiz/

Your words: ....

MP3
www.lienmini.fr/htr7-u1206

1 Fill in the blanks with the words below.

privacy • ethical • information • AI • visionary

A. The .... they collected was carefully analysed.

B. The .... aspect of those novels warned us in many ways.

C. Is it .... to monitor people in the streets?

D. With all those drones there is an increasing invasion of ....

E. Is racial profiling the result of too much .... ?

2 Are the sentences in the active form or the passive form?

A. Some novelists had warned us about the possible excesses of technology. ☐ active ☐ passive

B. The stills were sent to the central office for a deeper analysis. ☐ active ☐ passive

C. Online tracking is more and more frequent. ☐ active ☐ passive

D. Two women with darker skin tones have been discriminated against. ☐ active ☐ passive

3 Turn the verbs into the preterite.

A. In the end they (*make*) the decision to put CCTV cameras.

....

....

B. She (*trust not*) facial recognition so she (*investigate*) into the system.

....

....

C. When you (*read*) *The Pedestrian*? I (*read*) it last summer.

....

....

D. The local authorities (*buy*) two drones during the pandemic.

....

....

4 Turn the sentences into the passive form.

A. They will explain to him how a robot dog works. → He ....
....

B. We should not always trust AI. → AI ....
....

C. George Orwell wrote *1984* in 1948. → *1984* ....
....

D. They must check the CCTV. → The CCTV ....
....

5 Unit's checkout

Observe this photo. Imagine a slogan denouncing or supporting video surveillance. Use the passive.

....

....

OPEN YOUR EARS!

L'intonation montante et descendante

Lisez les phrases en suivant les indications données. Vérifiez à l'écoute.

1. L'intonation est **montante** dans les questions fermées (yes/no questions) et les énumérations. **MP3 N°15**
   Are they being watched? They use CCTV in London, Beijing, Shanghai...
   ↗ (watched) ↗ (London) ↗ (Beijing) ↗ (Shanghai)

2. L'intonation est **descendante** dans les phrases affirmatives, négatives, les questions ouvertes (*wh-* questions) et les exclamations. **MP3 N°16**
   The schools in the UK were closed. Students did not sit exams.
   ↘ (closed) ↘ (exams)
   Why is AI so biased?
   ↘ (biased)
   That is a violation of our civil rights!
   ↘ (rights)

3. L'intonation est **montante** en 1re partie et **descendante** en 2e partie de phrase quand une question offre un choix. **MP3 N°17**
   Is London a big brother surveillance city or a protective city?
   ↗ (city) ↘ (city)

AXE 6

UNIT 13

WHOSE SPACE IS IT ANYWAY?

Can one nation or one company own outer space?

YOUR PROJECTS

LV

Take part in NASA's press conference on the necessity to use space for the benefit and well-being of humankind.

ETLV STMG

Debate on the advantages and drawbacks of using space for business and tourism.

Au menu de cette unité :

DÉCOUVERTES CULTURELLES

- Les lois et les traités sur la propriété et l'exploitation de l'espace
- L'exploitation des ressources spatiales
- Le tourisme et l'habitat dans l'espace
- La commercialisation de l'espace par des entreprises privées britanniques et américaines ETLV STMG

OUTILS LINGUISTIQUES

- *The* ou l'article zéro (Ø)
- L'émission d'hypothèses (*if…*)
- Le lexique de l'espace, de la conquête et de l'exploration spatiale, et de la commercialisation de l'espace
- La prononciation des lettres *ou*

GET READY!

WORD CHALLENGE

Use as many of these words as possible throughout the unit.
Tick ✓ the box when you have used the word.

- ☐ achievement = exploit /'eksplɔɪt/ (n.)
- ☐ breakthrough = major discovery (n.)
- ☐ challenging (adj.)
- ☐ conquest /'kɒnkwest/ (n.)
- ☐ conquer /'kɒŋkə/ (v.)
- ☐ expand (v.)
- ☐ frontier /'frʌntɪə/ (n.)
- ☐ journey /'dʒɜːni/ (n.)
- ☐ launchpad (n.): *rampe de lancement*
- ☐ lift off (v.): *décoller*
- ☐ manned crew / mission
- ☐ outer space
- ☐ pave the way for = prepare for
- ☐ push the boundaries /'baʊndəriz/
- ☐ resource /rɪ'zɔːs/ (n.)
- ☐ rocket (n.)
- ☐ settle (v.) / settlement (n.) / settler (n.)
- ☐ spaceflight (n.)
- ☐ spaceship = spacecraft (sg) = shuttle /'ʃʌtl/ (n.)
- ☐ space industry / race / tourism / travel
- ☐ uncharted / unexplored (adj.)
- ☐ (un)inhabitable (adj.)
- ☐ (zero) gravity

BEFORE CLASS!

A. Watch NASA's video and tick what you have seen.

- ☐ space crews
- ☐ a lunar module landing
- ☐ a shuttle crashing into the ocean
- ☐ sea explorers
- ☐ an ancient plane and a jet plane
- ☐ rockets lifting off
- ☐ a spacewalk
- ☐ NASA'S Rover on Mars
- ☐ the International Space Station
- ☐ an astronaut's interview
- ☐ a control room
- ☐ Mars
- ☐ space food
- ☐ a man walking on the Moon

www.lienmini.fr/htr7-u1301

B. What does the narrator refer to in the underlined elements?

a. "… helped build a castle in the sky that is <u>our lasting home in space</u>."

....

....

b. "… we have taken both <u>small steps</u> and <u>giant leaps</u> in that pursuit."

....

....

....

C. Use the following words and expressions to sum up the report orally.

space research and exploration – discover – technological progress – humankind – take small steps – take giant leaps

....

....

....

....

....

....

1 Extraterrestrial Real Estate

Can someone legally own a celestial body?

1 The 1967 Outer Space Treaty

Article I

– The exploration and use of outer space, including the moon and other celestial bodies, shall be carried out for the benefit and in the interests of all countries [...], and shall be the province of all mankind.

– Outer space, including the moon and other celestial bodies, shall be free for exploration and use by all States without discrimination of any kind, on a basis of equality and in accordance with international law, and there shall be free access to all areas of celestial bodies.

– There shall be freedom of scientific investigation in outer space, including the moon and other celestial bodies, and States shall facilitate and encourage international co-operation in such investigation.

Article II

– Outer space, including the moon and other celestial bodies, is not subject to national appropriation by claim of sovereignty, by means of use or occupation, or by any other means.

Treaty on principles governing the activities of states in the exploration and use of outer space, 27 January 1967

Cultural fact
"The Outer Space Treaty", a United Nations agreement was signed by 104 nations in 1967 when space exploration was only beginning, and the Cold War between the US and the USSR was raging. Originally the treaty's goal (still in use today) was to prevent future "space wars" and to stop nations from putting weapons of mass destruction into space.

A. Read articles I and II.

a. Highlight keywords related to global benefit, underline those related to free access, and circle those related to global ownership of outer space and other celestial bodies.

b. Rearrange the rules of the treaty according to what you think are the most important ones. Write keywords.

Example: 1st: space is the province of mankind

1st: ....

2nd: ....

3rd: ....

B. Read the *Cultural fact*. Say why such a treaty was signed at the time, and why it is still in use today.

....

....

....

....

....

....

2 The man who "owns" the Moon

www.lienmini.fr/htr7-u1302

4'43 to 6'05

A. Watch the video. Pick out information about:

a. What Dennis Hope did in 1980:

b. The price mentioned per acre (1 acre = 4,047 m²):

c. The benefits for him:

d. What is said about three former US presidents:

B. What is the space lawyer's view?

C. Write the last sentence of the report. What does it imply?

3 Whose Moon is it?

Tranquility base, the spot where humans first set foot on the moon, should be granted[1] special heritage status and protected against damage from future visitors and missions, according to the head of the European Space Agency.

The site where Neil Armstrong and Buzz Aldrin touched down 50 years ago on Saturday warrants[2] protection as it marks the historic moment when humans reached beyond Earth to another celestial body, said Prof Jan Wörner, the director general of ESA.

"The Apollo 11 landing site is world heritage for humanity," he told *the Guardian*. "This was humans, as they had in the past, going beyond what they had done before. When humans came out of their caves, they were going beyond. And this was another dimension of going beyond, to another body in our universe." [...]

But protecting lunar heritage may not be straightforward[3]. On Earth, the United Nations Educational, Scientific and Cultural Organisation (Unesco) decides what deserves world heritage status from nominations sent by countries that claim ownership of the sites. Different rules apply in space. The UN's outer space treaty, a keystone[4] of space law, states that all countries are free to explore and use space, but warns it "is not subject to national appropriation by claim of sovereignty". In other words, space is for all and owned by none.

Wörner is not put off and sees no need for troublesome regulations. "My hope is that humanity is smart enough not to go back to this type of earthly protection. Just protect it. That's enough. Just protect it and have everybody agree," he said. A no-go zone of 50 metres around Tranquility base should do the job, he added.

1 given • **2** *mériter* • **3** simple, easy • **4** foundation

***The Guardian*, July 2019**

A. Read the text and highlight the key ideas.

B. Tick what "special heritage status" (l. 2-3) would mean for the Moon.

a. ☐ The Moon will never be explored in the future.

b. ☐ The Moon may be explored in the future but will be protected under law.

c. ☐ The Moon may be exploited by every nation.

C. Circle the correct sentences, then justify orally.

a. The spot where Man landed on the Moon is not important at all.

b. The protection of the Moon will be a difficult process.

c. The protection of the Moon is made possible thanks to Unesco.

d. Space is nobody's property.

D. Using the previous questions, recap orally what you have learnt about the protection of the Moon.

2 Mining the Sky

Can humans exploit space resources?

1 Mining asteroids

www.lienmini.fr/htr7-u1303

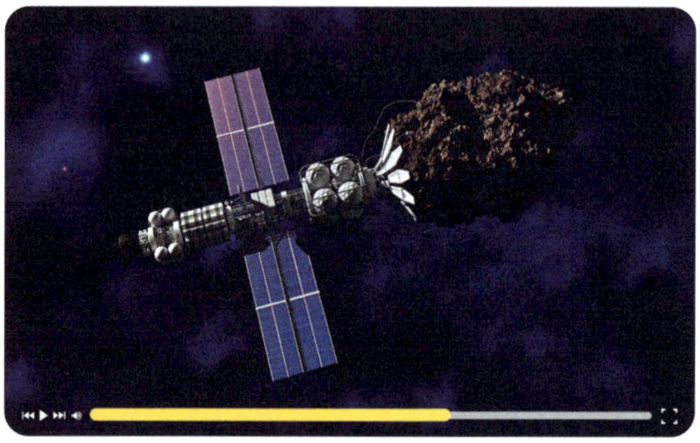

0'00 to 2'07

A. **Watch the video and cross out the false statements. Then correct them orally.**

a. All the metals that were found originate from Earth.

b. The metals found on Earth made possible the use of metal throughout history.

c. The metals found on Earth are in sufficient quantity.

d. The asteroid belt can provide men with all the metals they need for thousands of years.

B. **What do the following figures correspond to?**

a. 3.8 billion years ago: ....

b. 6,000: ....

c. $1.5 trillion: ....

C. **Recap orally what you have learnt about asteroid mining.**

2 A new Far West to conquer

Illustration by Allan Sanders, May 2019

A. **Describe this illustration orally.**

B. **List the elements that remind you of the Far West.**

....

C. **Why did the cartoonist choose to represent space mining like this? Write keywords and explain orally.**

....

HELP!

Nouns

- buttes /bju:ts/ = big sandstones hills that are found in Monument Valley, USA
- pioneer /paɪə'nɪə/
- spacesuit /'speɪssu:t/
- waggon /'wægən/: *chariot*

Verbs & Expressions

- claim land: *s'approprier une terre*
- hunt for resources
- turn a blind eye on sb / sth

3 Space miners

Through a variety of upcoming robotic and human activities on the surface and in orbit around the Moon, humans will better understand the universe and our home planet.

Renewed investment in lunar exploration (and beyond) will benefit basic research and applied science, but we need to tread carefully[1] in order to prevent the exploitation of extraterrestrial resources.

Our species tends to dream big, especially when it comes to space exploration. [...] Besides being a destination, the Moon is also a source of water, which could be electrolysed to produce oxygen and hydrogen for fuel, and possibly helium-3, a fuel source for clean nuclear energy; hence the Moon is a natural stepping stone[2] for space exploration. NASA is already planning a lunar Gateway – a spacecraft with living quarters, research laboratories and docking points[3] for spaceships – that will orbit the Moon and provide access to the lunar surface.

[...] NASA announced its collaboration with 11 US companies to develop prototypes for the Human Landing System as part of the Artemis Moon missions to return humans to the Moon by 2024. [...]

Is this the new Wild West though? We do not want to repeat the mistakes of the Earth's colonial past, after all. Therefore, now is the time to put in place safeguards[4] to protect the rest of the Solar System from the kind of gross mismanagement witnessed on Earth. Besides the Moon, other planets, minor planets and near-Earth asteroids will be visited in the name of research and exploration. These missions will be a huge boon[5] for science and technology [...]. The need to explore is inherently human, and every successful space mission brings delight to the international community. But let us learn from past mistakes and manage space resources sustainably.

1 behave carefully • **2** a bridge • **3** *points d'arrimage* • **4** *garde-fous* • **5** advantage

Nature, June 2019

A. Read the text. Highlight the words showing the benefits of space mining, and underline those showing that efforts are necessary not to repeat past mistakes.

B. Sum up the text orally with the help of question A.

C. Tick the sentences that illustrate the last idea of the article.

- ☐ Each nation should write its own rules to exploit space resources.
- ☐ Countries should monitor and regulate commercial space activities.
- ☐ Space resources should be owned by those who find them.
- ☐ Nations should clean up debris that result from asteroid or planet mining.
- ☐ Nations should cooperate and share space resources.

3 En Route to Space!

Are tourism and residence possible in space?

1 Going out of this world

A. Match the figures with what they correspond to:

75,000 feet •
3,000 miles •
6 miles •

• width (*largeur*) of some Martian canyons
• depth (*profondeur*) of some Martian canyons
• height (*hauteur*) of some Martian volcanoes

B. True or False? Justify orally.

a. There never was water on Mars. T ☐ F ☐

b. Microbes may still be found under the surface of the Red Planet. T ☐ F ☐

c. According to the narrator, a lot of astronauts would love to go to Mars. T ☐ F ☐

d. Life on Mars would be filled with dangers. T ☐ F ☐

C. Recap what you have learnt orally.

www.lienmini.fr/htr7-u1304

0'00 to 2'12

2 Space adventurers wanted!

A. Observe the poster and describe it, then read the text. Recap orally what you have learnt about Kepler-16b.

B. Would you like Kepler-16b to be your space destination? Use elements from the poster and the text to answer.

These visions of the future can become a reality. [...] Like Luke Skywalker's planet "Tatooine" in *Star Wars*, Kepler-16b orbits a pair of stars. Depicted here as a terrestrial planet, Kepler-16b might also be a gas giant like Saturn. Prospects for life on this unusual world aren't good, as it has a temperature similar to that of dry ice. But the discovery indicates that the movie's iconic double-sunset is anything but science fiction.

NASA, *"Visions of the Future"*

HELP!

Nouns

- 1 foot ≈ 30.48 cm
- 1 mile ≈ 1,609 metres
- landscape = scenery: *paysage*
- holiday resort
- Mars /mɑːz/
- MARSHA = **MARS HA**bitat
- pioneer /paɪəˈnɪə/
- TERA: a habitat for Earth

Adjectives

- barren = desolate /ˈdesələt/
- breathtaking = amazing = impressive
- desert /ˈdezət/
- hostile
- ideal /aɪˈdɪəl/

Verbs & Expressions

- gaze at sth: *contempler*
- (go) off the beaten track: *hors des sentiers battus*

3 Vacation guide to the solar system

From the humble ground of your home planet, you can look up at the night sky and see a future of adventure, relaxation, and romance. Every point of light is a possible vacation spot. Where would you like to go?

Your trip will bring you millions or even billions of miles from home. [...] Each journey[1] is different, and we can't predict what yours will hold, but we can promise you will never be the same: Your body, your outlook[2] on life, and your understanding of the universe will be permanently altered.

The places you visit will be both strange and familiar. [...] There might not be a ground to stand on. As you scale[3] a towering volcano on another planet, gaze up at the stars from the bottom of a deep crater, or sail through skies filled with strangely colored clouds, the worries you faced in life on Earth will melt away. [...]

The Moon is followed by Mercury, Venus, and Mars, before we venture to the giant planets of the outer solar system – Jupiter, Saturn, Uranus, and Neptune. [...]

When you're sailing the methane lakes of Titan, rappelling[4] the cliffs[5] of Mars's Mariner Valley, or diving the subglacial seas of distant Europa, you'll finally understand what it means to be an alien. We were built for Earth, after all, and nothing will remind you of your humanness more than an extended vacation to the vast void of outer space.

1 trip • **2** view • **3** climb up • **4** climb down • **5** *falaises*

***Olivia Koski, Jana Grcevich,** Vacation Guide to the Solar System: Science for the Savvy Space Traveler!*, 2017

A. Read the text and highlight the passages that focus on the good sides of space travel.

B. Would you be ready to travel to space? Why (not)?

4 NASA's Mars challenge

A. Watch the video. Write keywords about NASA's challenge.

a. The challenge: ....

....

b. The contestants: ....

....

c. The method to build the settlement on Mars: ....

....

www.lienmini.fr/htr7-u1305

0'00 to 1'46 — 7'26 to 8'40

B. Tick the obstacles that may not make this project viable (several answers). Justify orally.

a. Temperatures:

- ☐ Too hot
- ☐ Too cold
- ☐ Too hot and too cold
- ☐ – 70°C at night

b. Atmosphere:

- ☐ Very thick
- ☐ Very thin
- ☐ No atmosphere
- ☐ Cannot retain heat

c. Protection against solar and cosmic radiations: ☐ Yes ☐ No ☐ Almost no protection

C. Recap the "TERA" project orally.

YOUR PROJECT

Goupwork: NASA is holding a press conference on the necessity to use space for the benefit and well-being of humankind.
<u>Student A</u> is NASA's spokesperson. He / She defends the project.
<u>Student B</u> is a citizen who needs to be convinced that space research is not a waste of time or money.
<u>Student C</u> is the presenter who needs to be convinced that space tourism is safe and secure.

4 Private Companies on the Launchpad

ETLV STMG *Should private companies invest in space?*

OBJECTIVES STMG

- Show that innovation creates value
- Identify a competitive advantage

1 Building in outer space

A. Watch the video. Then tick the correct statements.

The industrialisation of space:

a. ☐ will bring great economic booms.

b. ☐ is seen as a waste of time and money.

c. ☐ offers a whole new environment to innovate with new products.

d. ☐ is made to make space a living place for all.

e. ☐ will enable to make things that could not be made on Earth.

B. Quote a product innovation that private companies are thinking of building in space and one promising application.

....

....

C. Quote keywords showing that Elon Musk, Richard Branson and Jeff Bezos make strategic decisions to conquer space.

....

....

D. What was American president Ronald Reagan's idea about space? Quote keywords.

....

E. What happened in July 2019?

....

....

....

www.lienmini.fr/htr7-u1306

0'00 to 3'05

F. Tick the correct answers and justify orally.
Studying products in micro-gravity could:

a. ☐ unlock new innovation opportunities.

b. ☐ lower the price of these products.

c. ☐ serve medical research.

d. ☐ help developing countries to access modern technology.

G. Explain how innovation creates value for a firm.

....

....

....

....

....

....

HELP!

Nouns
- **CEO** (Chief Executive Officer): *PDG*
- economic boom
- outer space
- opportunity
- rocket capsule /'rɒkɪt 'kæpsju:l/
- space conquest
- stunning = remarkable = amazing
- suborbital ride
- weightlessness = zero gravity

Verbs & Expressions
- carry out a research project
- do business with
- (go) bankrupt: *(faire) faillite*
- innovate

DEFINITIONS ETLV

- Innovation is a **key success factor** for an organisation that creates value.
- A **strategic decision** is made by top managers in the long term, is irreversible and requires numerous resources.

2 Who's Who in space tourism

A. Read the text about the three companies that aim to send people to space, and gather information about their respective project. Then choose which company you would like to travel with. Justify your choice orally.

B. Do you think that these companies use technology and space research in an ethical way? Why (not)?

Later this year Jeff Bezos, the first person to have led a business from nothing to a trillion-dollar valuation, will step down from his job as head of Amazon. But as you'd expect from a tech multibillionaire, his eyes are on a potentially bigger prize: outer space. Bezos will be dedicating more time to a space race between entrepreneur rivals that hopes to push the frontiers of society – and commerce – beyond planet Earth.

Having completed its 14th mission last month – successfully carrying a dummy[1], "Mannequin Skywalker", into space – Bezos's space company, Blue Origin, believes relatively cheap travel for humans is not far off. That would finally deliver a return on the $1bn (£730m) of Amazon stock Bezos has to sell annually to fund it. [...]

Rival billionaire Elon Musk's SpaceX is arguably ahead of Blue Origin. Despite an uncrewed test flight last week ending in a fiery crash, SpaceX is already able to reuse its Falcon 9 rockets. Musk (no stranger to making and sometimes breaking bold promises) aims to fly to Mars as soon as 2024. [...]

Sir Richard Branson predicted that Virgin Galactic, the space tourism company he founded, would first fly in space in 2009. Nonetheless, despite false starts and a fatal crash in 2014, analysts at UBS[2] say Virgin Galactic will in 2021 offer "the only way for consumers to gain entry into the [roughly] 560-member astronaut club in the next five years". [...]

Taking people to the moon and beyond is a key part of both Musk's and Bezos's visions, which can verge on the apocalyptic. Bezos talked in 2019 of a trillion humans populating the solar system, far beyond the resources of Earth; Musk has made clear his belief that a Mars colony could save humanity. That view is heavily criticised by some environmentalists, who argue we should focus on respecting the bounds of the planet we already inhabit.

1 *mannequin* • 2 a Swiss multinational bank

The Guardian, February 2021

Jeff Bezos's Blue Origin

Elon Musk's SpaceX

Richard Branson's Virgin Galactic

YOUR PROJECT BAC

Groupwork. Make an interview: Students A, B and C are spokespersons for Blue Origin, SpaceX or Virgin Galactic. Present your company at a press conference, focusing on the positive consequences for humankind.
Rest of the class: You are journalists. Interview the spokespersons.

RULE THE GRAMMAR!

1. *THE* OU L'ARTICLE ZÉRO (Ø)

• L'article défini *the* est employé pour désigner :
– des éléments / personnes uniques : ***the*** *space industry,* ***the*** *Earth,* ***the*** *Moon,* ***the*** *president…*
– des éléments précis au singulier ou au pluriel : ***the*** *rocket(s).*

• L'article zéro (Ø) est employé pour désigner :
– un ensemble / une notion toujours au singulier (indénombrable) : ***Ø*** *space,* ***Ø*** *research,* ***Ø*** *humankind…*
– des noms dénombrables au pluriel : ***Ø*** *scientists,* ***Ø*** *private companies,* ***Ø*** *astronauts…*
– des planètes aux noms de divinités : ***Ø*** *Mercury,* ***Ø*** *Venus,* ***Ø*** *Mars,* ***Ø*** *Jupiter…*

2. L'ÉMISSION D'HYPOTHÈSES (*IF…*)

• Probable : *If* + sujet + verbe au présent, sujet + ***will*** + BV
If the space mission ***succeeds****, we* ***will*** *colonise Mars.* => Il est possible que cela se produise.

• Improbable : *If* + sujet + verbe au prétérit, sujet + ***would*** + BV
If I ***went*** *to space, I* ***would*** *certainly enjoy zero gravity!* => Cela n'arrivera sans doute jamais.

• Non réalisée dans le passé : *If* + sujet + ***had*** + participe passé (*pluperfect*), sujet + ***would have*** + participe passé
If ***I had been*** *to space, I* ***would*** *have enjoyed zero gravity!* => Cela ne s'est pas produit.

VOCABULARY

Space

Outer space

- asteroid (n.)
- celestial body (n.)
- Earth (n.)
- Mars /mɑːz/ (n.)
- Martian /'mɑːʃən/ (n. / adj.)
- Moon (n.)
- orbit (n.)
- solar system (n.)
- weightlessness (n.) = zero gravity

Your words: ....

Space exploration

- achievement = exploit /'eksplɔɪt/ (n.)
- breakthrough = major discovery (n.)
- explore (v.)
- journey /'dʒɜːni/ (n.)
- landing (n.) ≠ lift-off (n.)
- launchpad (n.)
- lunar exploration
- spaceship = spacecraft (sg) (n.)
- shuttle /'ʃʌtl/ (n.)
- rocket (n.)
- spacesuit /'speɪssuːt/ (n.)
- uncharted = unexplored (adj.)
- (un)inhabitable (adj.)

Your words: ....

Space conquest

- agreement = treaty (n.)
- conquer /'kɒŋkə/ (v.)
- expand (v.)
- frontier /'frʌntɪə/ (n.)
- claim land: *s'approprier une terre*
- have legal value /'væljuː/
- own (v.) / ownership (n.)
- pioneer /paɪə'nɪə/ (n.)
- push the boundaries /'baʊndəriz/
- settle (v.) / settlement (n.) / settler (n.)

Your words: ....

Space business

- common good ≠ personal interest
- economic boom
- invest (v.)
- mining (n.)
- profitable (adj.)
- resource /rɪ'zɔːs/ (n.)

Your words: ....

MP3
www.lienmini.fr/htr7-u1307

1 Fill in the blanks with the words below.

uninhabitable • *journey* • *weightlessness* • *uncharted* • *pioneer*

A. Space tourism aims to explore .... territories.

B. In July 1969, Neil Armstrong was the first space .... to set foot on the Moon.

C. The .... to Mars takes about 9 months.

D. Tourism is impossible on such .... planets as Venus or Mercury.

E. Future space tourists will experience ....

2 Give the synonyms (=) or antonyms (≠) of these words.

A. landing ≠ ....

B. zero gravity = ...

C. exploit (n.) = ...

D. major discovery = ...

Then, make a sentence for each one.

A. ....

B. ....

C. ....

D. ....

3 Put the elements in brackets into the right form.

A. If space tourism (*be*) less expensive, I (*buy*) a ticket right away! (*hypothèse improbable*) ....

B. If I (*have*) time today, I (*watch*) the report on Blue Origin, SpaceX and Virgin Galactic. (*hypothèse probable*)

....

C. If the Rover Perseverance (*explode*) in February 2021, NASA (*not be able to*) send HD pictures of the Red Planet. (*hypothèse non réalisée*) ....

4 Fill in the blanks with *the* or Ø.

A. ...... life on ...... Red Planet is not possible. That is why ...... scientists want to build ...... pods (*capsules*) to allow ...... humans to live there.

B. ...... first human who will walk on ...... Mars is not born yet.

C. ...... space tourism will soon be possible, but only for ...... men and women who have enough money to pay for their trip.

5 Unit's checkout

Observe the cartoon and imagine what these two characters might say to each other. Use *the*, Ø, and *if*.

....

OPEN YOUR EARS!

La prononciation des lettres *ou* MP3 N°18

Écoutez les mots suivants, puis notez le numéro correspondant à la prononciation des lettres *ou*.

1 *journey* • 2 *source* • 3 *countries* • 4 *boundaries* • 5 *breakthrough* • 6 *outer* • 7 *resource* • 8 *tourism* • 9 *encourage* • 10 *ground* • 11 *announce*

/aʊ/ (how): .... /ɜː/ (world): .... /ʊə/ (poor): ....

/uː/ (food): .... /ɔː/ (door): .... /ʌ/ (but): ....

AXE 6

UNIT 14

FROM THE MINE TO "IT'S MINE!"

How can we consume new technologies more ethically and responsibly?

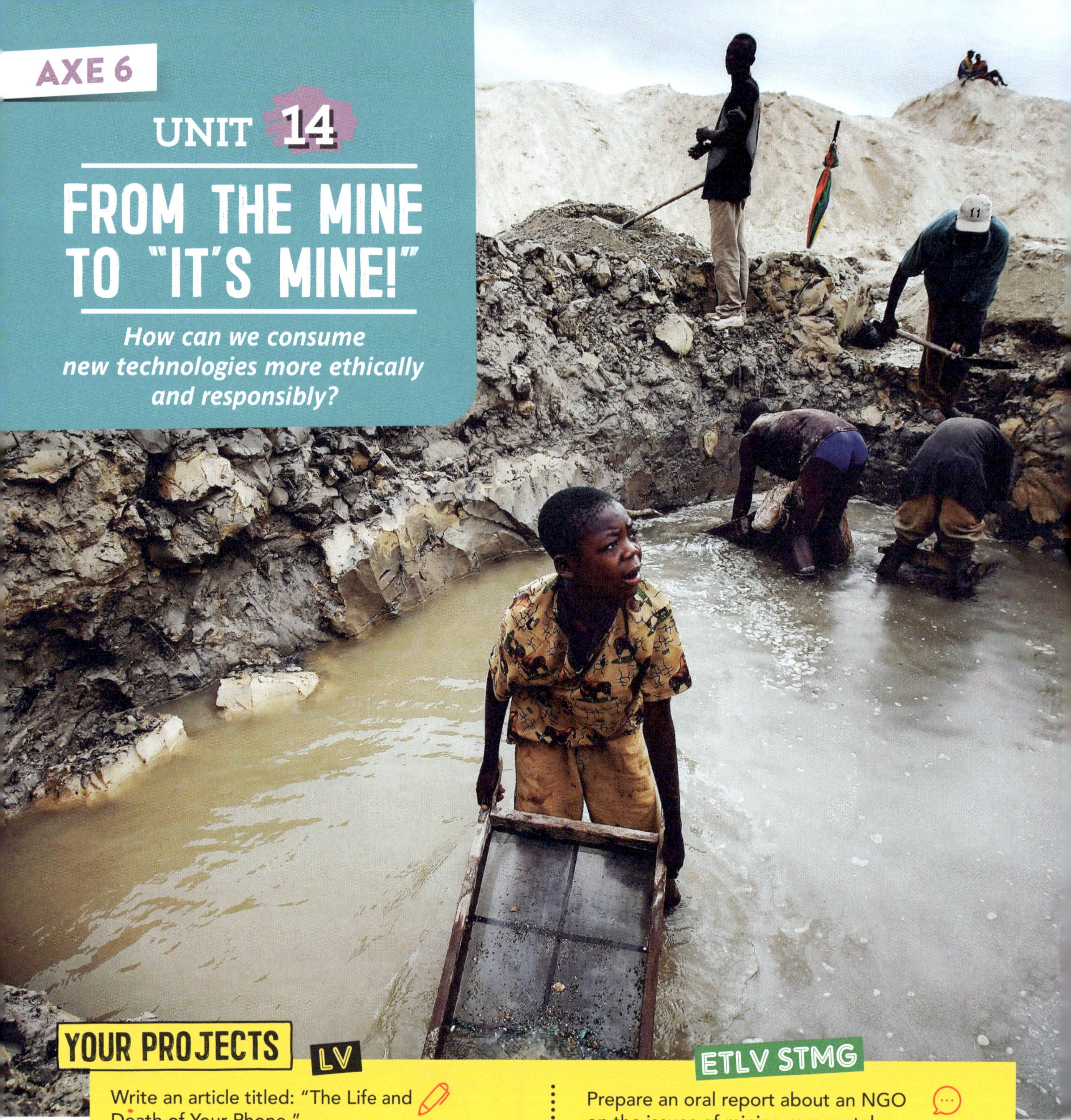

YOUR PROJECTS

LV

Write an article titled: "The Life and Death of Your Phone."

ETLV STMG

Prepare an oral report about an NGO on the issues of mining rare metals.

Au menu de cette unité :

DÉCOUVERTES CULTURELLES

- Les enjeux éthiques et environnementaux de l'exploitation des ressources minières
- Les solutions de recyclage du matériel électronique (Nigeria)
- Des entreprises éco-responsables (Dell, États-Unis ; MG, Royaume-Uni)
- Les ONG Amnesty International et PACT ETLV STMG

OUTILS LINGUISTIQUES

- La place des adjectifs
- Les adverbes
- Le lexique de la fabrication du matériel électronique, de la responsabilité éthique, des déchets numériques et de leur recyclage
- La prononciation de la lettre *i*

GET READY!

WORD CHALLENGE

Use as many of these words as possible throughout the unit.
Tick ✓ the box when you have used the word.

- ☐ acceptable ≠ unacceptable (adj.)
- ☐ accountability (n.)
- ☐ child labour (n.)
- ☐ chip (n.): *puce électronique*
- ☐ denounce /dɪˈnaʊns/ (v.)
- ☐ dismantle = take apart (v.)
- ☐ discard = throw away (v.)
- ☐ e-waste = electronic waste (n.)
- ☐ earn /ɜːn/ a living
- ☐ electronic device /dɪˈvaɪs/ (n.)
- ☐ ethical ≠ unethical (adj.)
- ☐ factory (n.)
- ☐ garbage dump = landfill (n.): *décharge publique*
- ☐ handle = manipulate (v.)
- ☐ human rights (n.)
- ☐ involvement (n.)
- ☐ point a finger at
- ☐ protest against (v.)
- ☐ raise awareness
- ☐ rare /reə/ metals (n.)
- ☐ raw materials (n.)
- ☐ sue /suː/ = bring to justice (v.)
- ☐ supply chain (n.)
- ☐ take into account (v.)
- ☐ underage ≠ of age (adj.)
- ☐ warn (v.)

BEFORE CLASS!

A. Watch the video and take notes.

www.lienmini.fr/htr7-u1401

B. Tick all the components mentioned. Then match them to the parts of the phone in which they are used.

- ☐ Lithium
- ☐ Copper
- ☐ Zinc
- ☐ Cobalt
- ☐ Indium
- ☐ Uranium
- ☐ Gold
- ☐ Silver
- ☐ Silicon

- Touchscreen
- Battery
- Electrical wiring
- Transistor in electronic chip

C. Say what the following figures correspond to:

a. 2.5 billion: ....

b. 118: ....

c. 75: ....

d. 10%: ....

D. Get ready to talk about this video in class!

1 The Human Cost of Cobalt

What ethical issues are raised by our use of electronics?

1 Dirty cobalt, shiny phone

40,000 children in the southern part of the Democratic Republic of the Congo [...] are forced to mine cobalt with their bare hands[1] to create mobile phone batteries.

But there is toxic dust in those mines, and those children are almost always given nothing to protect themselves from it. Inhaling cobalt dust can cause fatal lung diseases, chronic rashes[2], vomiting, and convulsions. If the children want to keep these jobs they need to survive, they have no other choice but to work in these horrendous conditions.

At the beginning of 2019, there were more than 5.1 billion unique mobile phone users in the world. But very little is disclosed[3] about how mobile phones are made, particularly the suffering that takes place at the beginning of the supply chain. [...] The human rights issues surrounding cobalt especially are so dubious[4] that the metal is often referred to as "the blood diamond of batteries."

1 without protection • **2** irritated skin • **3** *très peu de choses sont révélées* • **4** questionable

***OneZero*, October 2019**

A. **Read the text, then:**

a. underline what cobalt is used for;

b. highlight the problems it causes and who the main victims of these problems are;

c. circle what consumers are unaware of.

B. **Explain the issues with cobalt in your own words.**

2 A second chance

A. **Watch Ziki's story and take notes.**

B. **Write keywords about Ziki and his living conditions while working in the mine. Recap orally.**

C. **How did citizen involvement change his life and the lives of his siblings (brothers and sisters)?**

www.lienmini.fr/htr7-u1402

3 Corporate accountability

A young boy carries cobalt on his back in a mine, Democratic Republic of Congo.

Some of the biggest technology firms in the United States have been accused in a lawsuit of complicity in the death and maiming of hundreds, if not thousands of African children who mine cobalt, a mineral vital to the production of the lithium-ion batteries in everything from smartphones to electric cars.

CBS News, December 2019

A. In the text, find the words that mean:

a. *un procès*: ....

b. *mutilation*: ....

B. In your own words, explain why these companies are brought to justice.

....

4 A complex issue

All major electronics brands publicly state they will not tolerate human rights abuses in their supply chains. But it's easy to say this; verifying it is another matter. The reality is that supply chains are so complicated that very few companies are able to verify the information they receive from their suppliers – and some companies aren't even trying. [...]

It's clear that boycotting minerals from the DRC[1] will simply cut off the income of workers who need it most. What we really need are companies to directly engage with initiatives in countries like the DRC to encourage more responsible mining practices.

1 Democratic Republic of Congo

OneZero, October 2019

A. Match the words with their translations.

a. brand •	• *chaîne logistique*
b. state (v.) •	• *déclare*
c. supply chain •	• *marque*
d. supplier (n.) •	• *revenus*
e. income •	• *fournisseur*

B. Highlight the reason why it is difficult for companies to be held responsible.

C. Why is boycotting a problem more than a solution?

....

D. Say what companies can actually do to make things better.

....

YOUR TURN! 5 Plead your case BAC

Write an introductory speech to address the jury about the use of child labour in cobalt mining. Read it to your fellow lawyers and vote for the best one!

2 The E-Waste Problem

What happens to all our discarded electronics?

1 What is electronic waste?

1. *un tas*

Describe this cartoon and explain its meaning.
Read the *Cultural fact* for help.

Cultural fact
When stepping on the Moon for the first time in history, American astronaut Neil Armstrong said: "That's one small step for a man, one giant leap for mankind."

2 A source of income

www.lienmini.fr/htr7-u1403

HELP!

Nouns
- dump site: *décharge publique*
- handlers = people who manipulate e-waste
- income: *revenus*
- raw materials: *matières premières*

Adjectives
- hazardous = dangerous

Verbs
- dismantle = take apart
- handle = manipulate
- throw away = discard: *jeter*

A. Watch the video. Say where the report takes place and what it deals with.

B. Tick the problems caused by the unsafe handling of e-waste.

- ☐ Pollution of the environment by heavy metals and toxic chemicals
- ☐ Radioactivity
- ☐ Health risks for handlers

C. Say why some people in illegal dump sites hand e-waste anyway.

D. True or False? Tick the correct answer.

Most of the electronic devices donated by rich countries do not work. T ☐ F ☐

E. What does it say about these countries' ethics?

F. Explain orally how E-Terra works.

3 Upcycling and recycling

Agbogbloshie dump, Accra, Ghana

E-waste is now the world's fastest-growing waste stream. Indeed, we generated the equivalent of 4,500 Eiffel Towers of electronic waste in a single year. And yet just 20% of gets collected and recycled.

With 100 times more gold in a tonne of e-waste than in a tonne of gold ore[1], alongside other scarce[2] and valuable materials such as platinum, cobalt and rare earth elements, a safe and efficient recycling industry has huge economic potential.

According to the International Labour Organization, up to 100,000 people work in the informal e-waste recycling sector in Nigeria, and over half a million tonnes of discarded[3] appliances are processed in the country every year. Yet waste that is considered to have no economic value is often dumped or burned – releasing pollutants like heavy metals and toxic chemicals into the air, water and soil.

This new scheme led by the Nigerian government brings together players from international organizations, the private sector and civil society. [...] The initiative will develop systems for the disposal of non-usable and toxic waste, aiming to[4] collect, treat and dispose of more than 270 tonnes of e-waste contaminated with persistent organic pollutants and 30 tonnes of waste containing mercury.

The project also aims to have an impact beyond Nigeria through the development of a practical circular electronics model for Africa and beyond, by sharing best practices, promoting regional and global dialogue, and engaging global manufacturers.

1 *minerai* • **2** rare • **3** thrown away • **4** with the objective of

World Economic Forum, June 2019

A. Read the text and highlight the figures related to e-waste. Share your reaction with the class.

B. "A safe and efficient recycling industry has huge economic potential." (l. 8) Underline elements from the text that illustrate this quote.

C. In your own words, explain why Nigeria could become an example for other countries.

....

....

....

....

....

HELP!

Nouns
- **recycling** = an industrial process that allows the dismantled parts of an object to be reused
- **upcycling** = giving a new life and a new use to an old object by using your creativity (eg.: turn an old shoe into a flowerpot)

YOUR TURN! 4 Investigate e-waste

Have you ever heard of e-waste recycling solutions in your city? What happens to your electronic devices when they stop working? Investigate and share your findings with the class.

3 Green or Greenwashing?

Do companies take their environmental responsibilities seriously?

1 Going green

Dell is launching new efforts to shrink[1] its carbon footprint and cut down on e-waste. [...] When it comes to stemming[2] the greenhouse gases that lead to climate change, Dell will source 100 percent of its electricity from renewable sources by 2040. [...] Dell isn't just switching to renewable sources; it's also trying to use less energy. It plans to make its products more energy efficient and cut the emissions generated directly from its operations and its electricity usage in half by 2030.

[...] By 2030, the company plans to reuse or recycle an equivalent product for every device that a customer buys. It is also pledging[3] that, by then, at least half of all the materials used in its products will be "recycled or renewable," and 100 percent of its packaging will be recycled or renewable.

"We believe that this is a business critical[4] initiative," Christine Fraser, Dell's chief responsibility officer, tells [us]. "The imperative is really what our customers and our team members expect of us."

1 reduce • **2** limiting • **3** promising • **4** very important, essential

The Verge, November 2019

A. In the text, find the words that mean:

a. *empreinte carbone*: ....

b. *gaz à effet de serre*: ....

c. *renouvelable*: ....

d. *emballage*: ....

B. Highlight the elements that show how Dell intends to become a greener company.

C. Focus on the last sentence. What is Dell's motivation in going greener?

....

....

....

....

HELP!

Noun
- claim: *affirmation*

Adjectives
- eco-conscious = who cares about ecology
- misleading: *trompeur(-euse)*
- mistrustful = suspicious
- trustful
- unproven: *non prouvé(e)*

2 Greenwashing

A. Observe the cartoon. Read the sentence and define "greenwashing" in your own words.

....

....

B. How does the character make you feel?

....

....

....

....

C. What is the cartoonist's message?
Tick the right answer(s).

a. ☐ Unethical companies will do anything to sell their products.

b. ☐ Greenwashing is an ethical and positive action.

c. ☐ Customers will trust anyone if there is enough green in the message.

3 My "green" car: the British case

A. Watch video 1 and pick out the selling arguments for this electric car.

B. Do you think electric cars could be the green solution for the future? Why (not)?

C. Now watch video 2 and fill in the table below.

Advantages of buying an electric car

Drawbacks of buying an electric car

D. Say if this video has changed your mind, and why (not).

HELP!

Nouns
- charging point
- manufacturer: *fabricant*

Verbs
- increase ≠ decrease

1

www.lienmini.fr/htr7-u1404

2

www.lienmini.fr/htr7-u1405

YOUR PROJECT BAC

As a student at the Massachusetts Institute of Technology (MIT), write an article for the online university newspaper titled: "The Life and Death of Your Phone." Appeal to the students' responsibility in their personal choices of electronics.

4 Two NGOs Take Action

ETLV
STMG

How can NGOs make a difference in the fight against child labour?

OBJECTIVES STMG

- Link together individual and collective actions
- Give the characteristics of an organisation (type, purpose, scope)

1 Discover Amnesty International

A. Do some research and give the characteristics of Amnesty International. Fill in the grid below.

Type of organisation	....
Purpose	....
Scope	....

B. Comment on the campaign poster and say how it is related to this unit.

C. Watch the video and explain how Amnesty International works.

HELP!

DEFINITIONS ETLV

- **NGO**: Non-Governmental Organisation
- The **purpose** of an organisation is its goal.
- The **scope** of an organisation is where it sells its products or offers its services. It can be local, national, regional, international, etc.

2 Discover PACT

A. Log on to the PACT World website, section "Our stories". Read the article: "In the Democratic Republic of Congo, meet three young people leaving child mining behind". Say how it is related to what you have learnt.

B. Visit the section "About us" and give the characteristics of PACT. Fill in the following grid.

Name of the organisation	....
Type of organisation	....
Number of employees	....
Purpose	....
How they are financed	....
Scope	....
Write down some of the current campaigns and issues	....

YOUR PROJECT BAC

As a journalist for CBS News, you have to prepare a report about an NGO that raises awareness on the issues of mining rare metals for technological innovations. Read through the two pages and pick either Amnesty International or Pact. Answer the questions related to your chosen NGO and then prepare a two-minute video presentation of the NGO!

RULE THE GRAMMAR!

1. LA PLACE DES ADJECTIFS

En anglais, les adjectifs sont toujours invariables.

• **Les adjectifs épithètes** qualifient un nom et se placent **avant celui-ci** :

*In **unethical** mines, **underage** children work for two dollars a day.*

Lorsqu'il y a plusieurs adjectifs épithètes, on les place en général du plus subjectif au plus objectif :

*This **shiny new** phone can be dismantled for parts when it stops working.*

• **Les adjectifs attributs** se placent **après un verbe d'état** (*be, seem, become*…) :

*Smartphones are **useful** but few components are **recyclable**.*

2. LES ADVERBES

Les adverbes apportent des précisions sur des adjectifs ou des verbes.
Pour transformer un adjectif en adverbe de manière, on ajoute le suffixe ***-ly***.
Pour les adjectifs se terminant en ***-ble***, on remplace simplement le ***-e*** par un ***-y***.

*It is essential to consume **responsibly, sustainably** and **ethically**.*

VOCABULARY

Electronics

Manufacture

- chip (n.): *puce électronique*
- component (n.)
- electronic device (n.)
- earn /ɜːn/ a living
- factory (n.)
- income (n.)
- mining /'maɪnɪŋ/ (n.): *extraction minière*
- rare metals (n.)
- raw materials (n.)
- supplier /sə'plaɪə/ (n.): *fournisseur*
- supply chain (n.)

Your words: ……………………

Responsibility

- acceptable ≠ unacceptable (adj.)
- accountability (n.)
- child labour (n.)
- denounce (v.) = point a finger at
- ethical ≠ unethical (adj.)
- human rights (n.)
- protest against (v.)
- raise awareness
- sue (v.) = bring to justice
- warn (v.)

Your words: ……………………

The environment

- carbon footprint (n.)
- consume (v.)
- eco-conscious (adj.)
- greenhouse gases (n.)
- greenwashing (n.)
- lethal /'liːθəl/ = deadly (adj.)
- packaging (n.): *emballage*
- pollute (v.)
- renewable (adj.)
- responsibly (adv.)
- sustainability (n.) / sustainable (adj.)
- toxic (adj.)

Your words: ……………………

Recycling

- discard = throw away (v.)
- dismantle = take apart (v.)
- e-waste (n.)
- garbage dump = dump site (n.): *décharge publique*
- handle = manipulate (v.)
- hazardous = dangerous (adj.)
- recyle (v.)
- upcycle (v.): *donner une nouvelle vie à…*
- set up / launch (a programme) (v.)

Your words: ……………………

MP3
www.lienmini.fr/htr7-u1407a

LANGUAGE LAB

1 Cross the odd word out.

A. hazardous – safe – toxic – dangerous

B. upcycle – discard – dump – throw away

C. handle – dismantle – renewable – manipulate

D. responsibility – sustainability – responsibly – renewability

Justify your choice.

A. ....

B. ....

C. ....

D. ....

OPEN YOUR EARS!

La prononciation de la lettre *i* MP3 N°19

Écoutez les mots, puis notez le numéro correspondant à la prononciation de la lettre *i*.

1 dirty • 2 dismantle • 3 mine • 4 firm • 5 ethical • 6 discard • 7 wiring • 8 rights • 9 chip • 10 supplier

/aɪ/ (my): ....

/ɪ/ (tip): ....

/ɜː/ (bird): ....

/aɪə/ (fire): ....

2 Translate the following sentences.

A. *Les métaux rares de nos téléphones portables sont recyclables.* ....

B. *Il est dangereux de démonter sans protection un vieil appareil électronique.* ....

C. *J'adore ton magnifique ordinateur noir et gris.* ....

D. *Cette entreprise est poursuivie en justice parce qu'elle utilise le travail des enfants.* ....

3 Turn the following adjectives into adverbs and make a sentence with each.

A. Eco-conscious: ....

B. Ethical: ....

C. Unacceptable: ....

D. Responsible: ....

4 Find the adjectives that match the following definitions.

A. A synonym for sustainable: ....

B. Something that cannot be accepted: ....

C. A synonym for dangerous: ....

D. A synonym for responsible: ....

5 Unit's checkout

Use the photo below to write slogans that encourage people to consume responsibly.

....

AXE 7

UNIT 15

HEALTHY FOOD FOR EVERYONE

How can we fight food inequalities?

YOUR PROJECTS

LV — Discuss to agree on the best project to promote a healthy diet for all.

ETLV STMG — Present a brand or a shop which promotes healthy food.

ETLV ST2S — Create a tutorial to advise the population to adopt better food habits.

Au menu de cette unité :

DÉCOUVERTES CULTURELLES

- L'obésité en Angleterre
- Les acteurs publics et privés anglais impliqués dans la lutte contre l'obésité
- Des programmes de prévention contre l'obésité en Angleterre
- Les stratégies des marques alimentaires ETLV STMG
- Des campagnes de sensibilisation dans le monde anglophone ETLV ST2S

OUTILS LINGUISTIQUES

- Le conseil et l'obligation
- Le lexique de l'insécurité alimentaire et de ses conséquences, d'une alimentation saine et des bonnes habitudes alimentaires
- L'accentuation des mots composés

GET READY!

WORD CHALLENGE

Use as many of these words as possible throughout the unit.
Tick ✓ the box when you have used the word.

- ☐ advert / advertising (n.)
- ☐ advertise /'ædvətaɪz/ (v.)
- ☐ balanced (adj.)
- ☐ calorific (adj.)
- ☐ diabetes /daɪə'bi:ti:z/ (n.)
- ☐ diet /'daɪət/ (n.)
- ☐ disease /dɪ'zi:z/ = illness (n.)
- ☐ eat one's fill: *manger à sa faim*
- ☐ experience hunger (v.)
- ☐ feed (v.)
- ☐ (food) insecure (adj.)
- ☐ (food) insecurity (n.)
- ☐ health /helθ/ (n.)
- ☐ healthy (adj.)
- ☐ improve = enhance /ɪn'hɑ:ns/ (v.)
- ☐ intake (n.)
- ☐ junk food ≠ healthy food (n.)
- ☐ labelling (n.)
- ☐ nutrition (n.)
- ☐ nutritious /nju:'trɪʃəs/ (adj.)
- ☐ obese /əʊ'bi:s/ (adj.)
- ☐ obesity /əʊ'bi:səti/ (n.)
- ☐ overweight (adj.)
- ☐ skip meals (v.)
- ☐ tasty /'teɪsti/ (adj.)
- ☐ unaffordable /ʌnə'fɔ:dəbl/ (adj.)
- ☐ weight gain ≠ weight loss (n.)

BEFORE CLASS!

A. Watch the video. Cross out the idea that you do not hear in the video.

This project is important because...

a. The population is aging and growing.

b. The environment is not affected by our food production system.

c. The food and health systems are under pressure.

B. Complete the two consequences of poor nutrition on health.

a. ....

b. ....

c. cardiovascular diseases

C. Tick the correct answer.

The Institute:

- ☐ offers programmes to cure obese people.
- ☐ produces healthy food.
- ☐ fights to protect the environment.
- ☐ works on the interrelation between health, nutrition, food and the environment.

D. Who can make a change?

....

....

E. Be ready to introduce the programme of the Institute.

www.lienmini.fr/htr7-u1501

Institute for Food, Nutrition and Health, *Working together to find solutions across the food system*, University of Reading

1 Food Issues in the UK

How equal are the British in their access to quality food?

1 Food insecurity

8,400,000
people in the UK are estimated to be "food insecure"

WHAT IS FOOD INSECURITY?

MILD FOOD INSECURITY | MODERATE FOOD INSECURITY | SEVERE FOOD INSECURITY

- worrying about the ability to obtain food
- compromising quality and variety of food
- reducing quantities, skipping meals
- experiencing hunger

4,700,000
people in the UK are estimated to be "severely food insecure"

THE UK IS IN THE BOTTOM HALF
OF ALL EU COUNTRIES (2016)

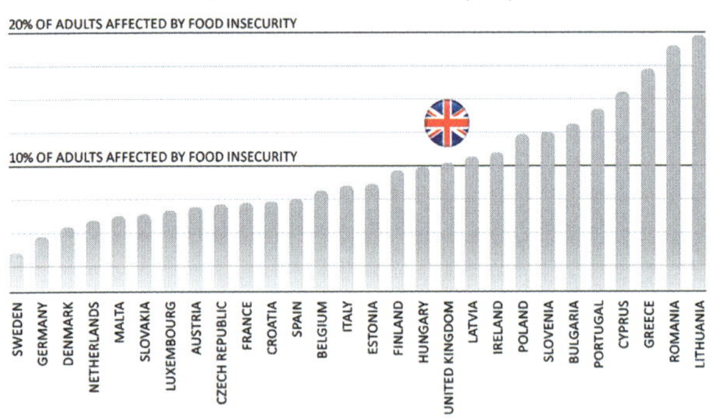

Sources: These data are from the UN Food and Agriculture Organisation's Voices of the Hungry project which included measures of food insecurity in the Gallup World Poll. The data has been gathered using the Food Insecurity Experience Scale and a nationally representative sample of 1,000. In 2014. The data are provisional as sample sizes are too small to get very precise estimates. The UK government should start to incorporate measurement of food insecurity into existing national survey instruments so we can track food insecurity in the UK.

"Holiday hunger" – when children go without the food normally provided to families during school term time – is an increasingly recognised issue. If children are not given the nutrition they need, there are long-term effects on their health. In the short term, children who are living in food-insecure families are more likely to suffer from education losses. Research from the US showed that after the summer holidays, children had lost an average of one month's worth of skills learned at school, and that poorer children may fare worst.

Children experiencing food insecurity are more likely to suffer from anxiety and stress, and hunger in childhood has been linked to depression and suicidal episodes in teenagers. Hunger is also linked to increased levels of chronic illnesses such as asthma. [...] The government advises that children need to eat a balanced diet. This is set out in the Eatwell guidelines developed by Public Health England. [...]

The evidence is clear: children not eating a healthy diet will not perform as well at school as those who are well nourished. They are more likely to suffer from mental health problems such as stress, and as they age they will be more likely to suffer from diseases such as cancer, diabetes, heart disease and obesity.

The Conversation, October 2020

A. Focus on the infographics. What is "food insecurity"?

B. Read the text.

a. Circle what "holiday hunger" is.

b. Highlight the two consequences of holiday hunger.

c. Give the result of the American research. Quote keywords.

d. Underline the consequences on children's health and explain them in your own words.

HELP!

Nouns
- anxiety /æŋˈzaɪɪti/
- deficiency /dɪˈfɪʃənsi/ = lack of hunger
- side effect: *effet secondaire*

Verbs & Expressions
- eat one's fill: *manger à sa faim*
- experience hunger
- lack: *manquer de*
- skip meals
- worry about

2 Obesity levels

A. Describe the situation of obesity in England (proportion of adults, men and women, different situations, evolution).

B. What do the figures show?

C. Guess why obesity is on the rise and its consequences. Write keywords only.

a. Reasons: ....

....

....

....

b. Consequences: ....

....

....

....

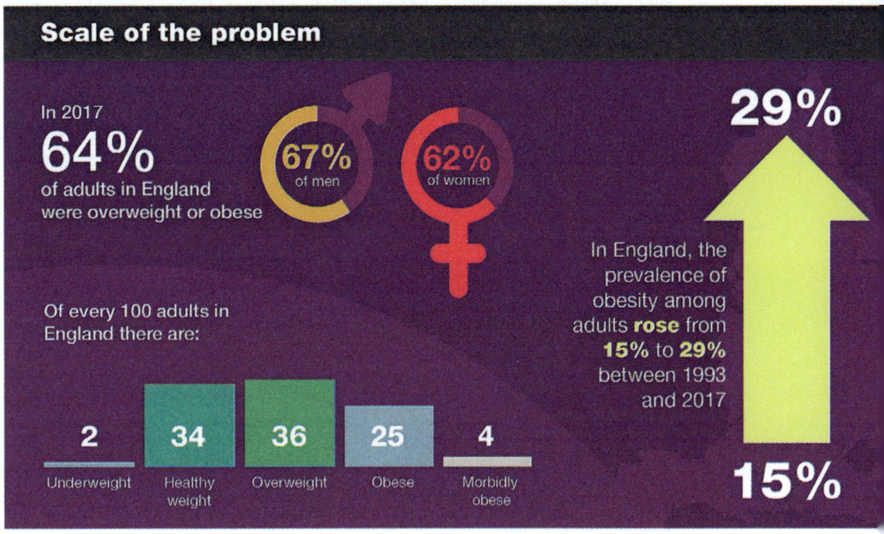

3 Why are more people obese today?

Obesity is a complex issue with many root causes, and one of the biggest influences is the world we live in. [...]

While we might think we're in complete control of what we eat, we're probably all being influenced more than we realise. It could be at work, in a restaurant or in a supermarket. When unhealthy options are the easiest, cheapest, or only thing available, weight gain becomes more likely. [...]

Over time food has become cheaper, larger, tastier and more calorific. At the same time food advertising and marketing has become more sophisticated. [...] Selling food and drink is a big business. Millions are spent every year on influencing us to eat more unhealthily. This makes it harder and harder to be healthy and is one of the main reasons that more people are obese now.

cancerresearchuk.org

A. Read the text. Tick the right answers.

a. Obesity is due to:
- ☐ people
- ☐ the world we live in
- ☐ stress
- ☐ genetics

b. We are (two answers):
- ☐ in control of our desires
- ☐ influenced by our environment
- ☐ attracted by quality food
- ☐ looking for easy and cheap options

B. Circle five adjectives that describe the evolution of food and its marketing.

C. List the two strategies to sell unhealthy food.

....

D. Recap what you have learnt.

HELP!

Nouns
- diet /ˈdaɪət/
- morbidity /mɔːˈbɪdɪtɪ/

Adjectives
- available /əˈveɪləbl/
- cheap
- ready-to-eat
- underprivileged /ʌndəˈprɪvɪlɪdʒd/ = deprived /dɪˈpraɪvd/

Verbs
- influence = put pressure on
- rise = increase

2 Fighting Food Inequalities

What are the initiatives to give equal access to healthy food?

1 The "Eat them to Defeat them" campaign

www.lienmini.fr/htr7-u1502

A. Watch the campaign once. Give its target audience and its message.

a. Target: ....

b. Message: ....

....

....

B. Give the message and the strategy used to convince the audience. Tick the right answers.

- ☐ The spot is made like an animal documentary, because children love animals.
- ☐ Parents have tried to fight the invasion of vegetables but they can't do it alone.
- ☐ The spot is made like a thriller movie because children like suspense.

C. Do you think the document is effective? Why (not)?

2 The Croydon Food Flagship programme

A. Watch the video. According to Rosie Boycott, the Croydon Food Flagship programme is about:

- ☐ one project per city ☐ many projects per city
- ☐ different projects in one borough (*district*), around schools, and communities
- ☐ work around fast food restaurants

B. Complete the following sentences and tick the correct answer.

a. For Rosie, the best success of the programme is to offer

....

b. List the four advantages (adj.) of meals at school:

....

c. For Rosie, quality food helps to fight:

- ☐ obesity and ill-health ☐ social inequalities
- ☐ bad school results

HELP!

Nouns	*Verbs*
• campaign • food habits • school meal	• benefit from • consume • /kən'sjuːm/ • put at risk • set up • support
Adjectives • free • sugary /'ʃʊgəri/ = sweet • terrific /tə'rɪfɪk/	

www.lienmini.fr/htr7-u1503

0'00 to 1'57

C. In Rockmount primary school:

Amber Vijayaratnam believes that if children are healthy and happy they will:

- ☐ fight obesity ☐ learn best
- ☐ not fall asleep in class ☐ stay concentrated

D. In Meridian high school:

Katie and Henry (several answers):

- ☐ are health and food ambassadors
- ☐ buy vegetables for their school
- ☐ weed (*désherber*) the garden once a week
- ☐ cook their own food
- ☐ deliver the food to their kitchen

3 Boris Johnson puts England on a diet

Watch the video. Tick the right answers or complete.

a. Say why Boris Johnson has recorded this video.

- ☐ He wants to motivate the English population to lose weight.
- ☐ He has always struggled to lose weight.
- ☐ He has survived Covid-19 and has understood the importance of staying fit.
- ☐ He still cannot resist junk food.
- ☐ He advises people to eat vegetables.

b. Losing weight makes you:

☐ healthier ☐ feel better ☐ feel lighter

c. To exercise you simply need (two ideas) ....

....

www.lienmini.fr/htr7-u1504

4 Junk food banned by legislation

Downing Street has unveiled plans to [...] ban [...] online junk food advertising – the toughest digital marketing restrictions in the world – in an attempt to tackle the growing obesity crisis. [...] The new rules, which go much further than proposals in the summer, would affect foods [...] too high in fat, salt and sugar. [...]

Matt Hancock, the health secretary, said: "I am determined to help parents, children and families in the UK make healthier choices about what they eat. We know children spend more time online. Parents want to be reassured they are not being exposed to adverts promoting unhealthy foods, which can affect habits for life." [...]

The consultation cited research finding that children were being exposed to increasing online junk food advertising. The government estimated that children aged under 16 were exposed to 15bn junk food adverts online in 2019, compared with an estimated 700m two years earlier.

If implemented, the ban would affect digital marketing, from ads on Facebook, to paid-search results on Google, text message promotions, and social media activity on Twitter and Instagram.

"This would be a world-leading policy to improve children's health," said Fran Bernhardt, coordinator of the Children's Food Campaign. "Online adverts have cast unhealthy food in the starring role for far too long. The current regulations are inadequate to protect children. Companies advertising healthier foods have nothing to fear."

The Guardian, November 2020

A. Focus on the plan of the English government, its objective and the food targeted. Underline keywords and summarise the information orally.

B. True or False? Tick the correct answer and justify orally.

a. The plan will help families to choose healthy food.

T ☐ F ☐

b. Being exposed to online adverts can have life-long consequences.

T ☐ F ☐

c. Fran Bernhardt thinks the measures don't go far enough.

T ☐ F ☐

C. Highlight examples of digital marketing that will be impacted by this plan.

HELP!

Nouns
- digital marketing = online advertising
- fitness
- policy = legislation

Adjectives
- fat
- salty /'sɔːlti/

Verbs
- ban = forbid
- go up and down (weight)
- implement = apply
- keep fit
- struggle against = fight

YOUR PROJECT

Goupwork: Discuss to agree on the best project to promote a healthy diet for all. Then present your choice and justify.

3 Giving Everyone a Role in Nutrition

ETLV STMG

How do brands and other actors improve the nation's health?

OBJECTIVES STMG

- Analyse environmental factors and identify the keys to success
- Analyse ways and modalities for communication implemented by an organisation

1 Reaching new consumers

"Consumers are grocery shopping with an ever-expanding perspective on overall health and well-being," said Krystal Register, FMI [Food Industry Association]'s director of health and well-being. "In addition to health, they want convenience, affordability, clear labeling, food safety, taste, and transparency. [...] We see consumers looking for more balance and less stress as they seek personalization in the grocery store." [...]

There are generational differences, too, Ms. Register said. Nutrition, moderation, and quality are important for older shoppers, while younger shoppers look to enjoy a deeper sense of connection to their food to include ethical considerations and the environment. [...]

More and more consumers continue to see food as a way of addressing a wide range of health conditions. They're scrutinizing labels as they shop, weighing a variety of diets and looking for local and organic products to enhance their well-being. [...] The top health benefits sought are weight loss, energy, digestive health and heart/cardiovascular health. Even as consumers identify which benefits they desire, they're revising opinions on which attributes will get them there. Fiber, whole grains, protein from plant sources, Omega-3 fatty acids and probiotics top IFIC's[1] current list.

1 International Food Information Council

foodbusinessnews.net, July 2020

A. **Highlight what the new consumers want.**

B. **Cross out the wrong sentences and justify orally.**

a. Nutrition and quality are important for younger shoppers.

b. Older shoppers value ethics and protection of the environment.

c. All consumers have health considerations when they shop.

d. They look for a diversity of diets and organic food.

C. **Underline the top health benefits.**

HELP!

Nouns
- **customer** /ˈkʌstəmə/
- **fiber** /ˈfaɪbə/
- **labelling** /ˈleɪbəlɪŋ/
- **protein** /ˈprəʊtiːn/
- **whole grains**
- **probiotic** /prəʊbaɪˈɒtɪk/

Adjectives
- **ethical** /ˈeθɪkl/
- **organic**
- **tasty**

Verbs
- **make choices**
- **scrutinise**

DEFINITION ETLV

A **stakeholder** is a person or a group of people who can affect or be affected by the decisions made by an organisation: employees, customers, suppliers, trade unions, State, partners, etc.

2 The Healthy High Streets Challenge

A. **Say what the Healthy High Streets Challenge is (place, actions).**

B. **Tick the right answers:**

a. The best ideas will receive (two answers):

☐ up to £2,000 ☐ £12,000 ☐ some expert advice

b. Identify the stakeholders Nil Guzelgun is working with (two answers):

☐ families ☐ local businesses ☐ politicians

c. For Jessica Attard ☐ families ☐ local businesses ☐ politicians play a crucial role in this change.

C. **Describe the example of Shahid Majeed's fast food (alternative idea, results).**

www.lienmini.fr/htr7-u1505

0'00 to 1'31 3'24 to 3'49

3 The Healthy Markets Initiative

A. Watch the video. Tick the correct answers (several possible answers for each question).

a. At school…

- ☐ 1 in 5 children is overweight or obese.
- ☐ 1 in 5 children has an increased risk of disease.
- ☐ 1 in 5 practises two sports activities a week.
- ☐ Overweight children face bullying and mental health challenges.
- ☐ Other children are protective with overweight children.

b. Say who / what is responsible:

☐ the parents ☐ the schools ☐ the government
☐ the food and drink industry ☐ our environment
☐ our personal tastes

B. Cross out the wrong sentences.

a. Every day we are bombarded with easy, cheap, unhealthy food.

b. Every day we are bombarded with organic, sugar free, healthy food.

c. Healthy alternatives are missing or unaffordable.

d. Healthy alternatives are available and cheap.

C. Tick the three solutions given in the video.

- ☐ Investors must stop investing in the making and marketing of unhealthy food.
- ☐ We must set up school programmes.
- ☐ We must take positive actions.
- ☐ We must develop a healthier food environment.

HELP!

Nouns
- bullying /ˈbʊlɪŋ/
- food industry
- mental health challenges

Adjectives
- missing
- targeted /ˈtɑːgɪtɪd/

Verbs & Expressions
- raise awareness /əˈweənɪs/
- shape = influence

DEFINITION ETLV

Commercial communication promotes a product through a **medium** in which it gives a message to its **target** (most of the time, customers).

www.lienmini.fr/htr7-u1506

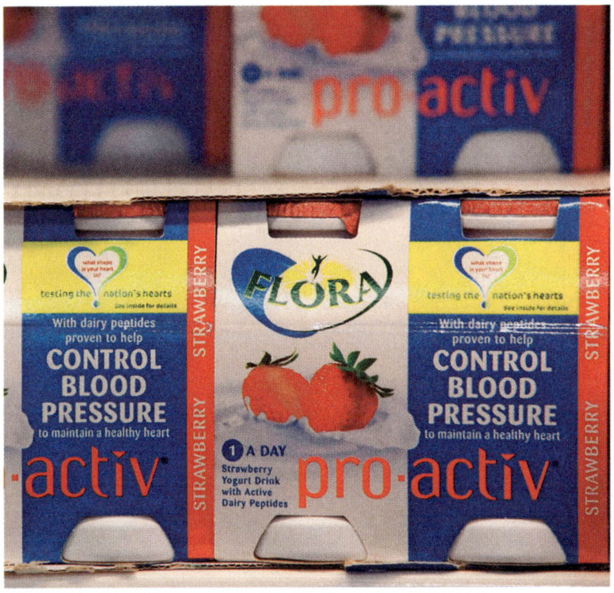

4 Advertising healthy food

A. Give the brand and the product advertised.

B. Analyse orally the communication strategy used: target, message and medium.

C. Would you buy this product? Why (not)?

YOUR PROJECT BAC

Present a shop or a brand involved in healthy food. Speak for 2'30. Include the story of the brand, its values, and a description of an advert.

4 Adopting a Healthy Lifestyle

ETLV ST2S

How can prevention campaigns promote healthy food?

OBJECTIVES ST2S

- Establish a relationship between a health initiative and an underlying health issue
- Characterise a means of action in public health

1 An Australian campaign

www.lienmini.fr/htr7-u1507

A. Watch the video. Say how people behave when they eat sweet food. Give examples.

B. What solutions do other people have to change their mood?

C. Do you find this campaign effective? Why (not)?

HELP!

Nouns
- breakdown
- distraction
- grade
- home-made (meals)
- (un)processed
- whole (food)

Adjectives
- ad-free
- harmful

Verbs
- track
- weaken

2 An app to track bad fat?

Foodcucate

It can be hard to figure out exactly what's in your food just by reading the nutrition labels alone. With the *Fooducate* app, you can find out if your food contains harmful ingredients, like added sugars, trans fats, or MSG[1]. Once you track what you eat, the app measures the calorie quality of the food and gives you a food grade. Healthy, unprocessed foods tend to have higher scores. But if the item has a low food grade, the app gives you suggestions for healthier alternatives. When you upgrade to the premium Pro version, you can get a breakdown of your intake of proteins, carbs, fiber, and more. You will also get advanced tools for diet-specific training [...]. In addition, you get an ad-free experience and tracking for certain metrics, like body measurements, blood pressure, and more.

1 salt

hellotech.com, 2020

A. Say what the document promotes: ....

B. Explain the choice of the app name.

....

C. Say in your own words how the app works.

....

....

....

D. Highlight what the premium Pro version offers.

E. Would you like to download and use such an app? Why (not)?

3 The British Eatwell Guide

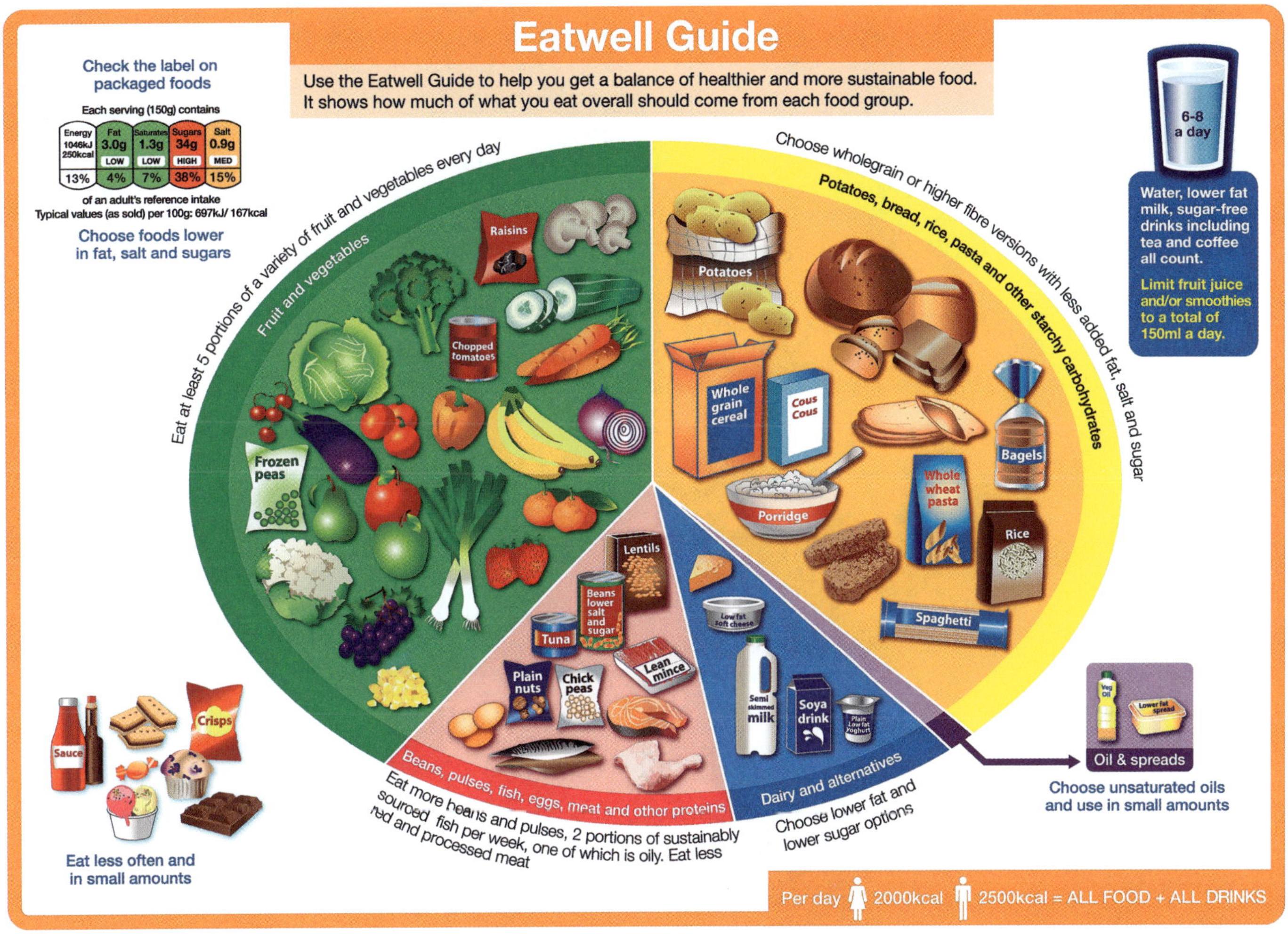

A. **Give the nature of the document and its goal.**

a. Nature: ....

....

....

b. Goal: ....

....

....

B. Pairwork. **Use the document as a prompt to give advice orally.**
Rather than + GN / V-ing … it is better to + V
We should + V
Instead of + V-ing, we'd better + V
It is highly recommended to + V

C. **Do you think that state-run projects are effective in the fight against obesity? Why (not)?**

HELP!

Nouns
- beans
- dairy products: *produits laitiers*
- nuts
- oil
- pulses: *légumineuses*

Adjectives
- starchy: *riche en féculents*
- sustainable /sə'steɪnəbl/: *durable*
- sugar-free

DEFINITION ETLV

Prevention refers to a set of measures, actions and means which aim to prevent health risks from arising, developing or worsening.

YOUR PROJECT BAC

Use what you have learnt to create a tutorial video to warn people against obesity and to give them advice.

RULE THE GRAMMAR!

LE CONSEIL ET L'OBLIGATION

On peut exprimer le conseil et l'obligation à l'aide de modaux ou d'expressions.

	Modaux	Expressions
Le conseil	sujet + *should* + BV *To be healthy* ***you should*** *eat more fruit.* => tu devrais / vous devriez…	sujet + *had better* (*'d better*) + BV : *To keep fit* ***you had better/you'd better*** *eat less sugar.* => Avec l'idée d'éviter un problème : tu ferais mieux / vous feriez mieux de…
L'obligation	Pour exprimer une obligation personnelle et morale : sujet + *must* + BV ***Parents must*** *cook home-made meals to their children.* => *This is what is expected from them.*	Pour exprimer une obligation extérieure et imposée : sujet + *have to* + BV ***Following legislation schools have to*** *offer balanced meals to the children.* => *The law makes it an obligation.*

VOCABULARY

Food and health

Food insecurity

- calorific (adj.) (n.)
- experience hunger (v.)
- fat (adj. / n.)
- fatty (adj.)
- (food) insecure (adj.)
- junk food (n.)
- labelling (n.)
- poor /pʊə/ (adj.)
- processed = ready-to-eat (adj.)
- salty /'sɔ:lti/ (adj.)
- skip meals
- sugary /'ʃʊgəri/ = sweet (adj.)
- unaffordable /ʌnə'fɔ:dəbl/ = expensive (adj.)
- underprivileged /ʌndə'prɪvɪlɪdʒd/ = deprived /dɪ'praɪvd/

Your words: ....

Consequences

- anxiety /æŋ'zaɪɪti/ (n.)
- diabetes /daɪə'bi:ti:z/ (n.)
- disease /dɪ'zi:z/ = illness (n.)
- harmful (adj.)
- ill-health /ɪl 'helθ/ (n.)
- mental health challenges (n.)
- obese /əʊ'bi:s/ (adj.)
- obesity /əʊ'bi:səti/ (n.)
- overweight (adj.)
- weight gain / loss (n.)

Your words: ....

Good nutrition

- advert = ad (n.)
- advertising campaign (n.)
- advertise /'ædvətaɪz/ (v.)
- ban = forbid (v.)
- commercial (n.) /kə'mɜ:ʃəl/
- implement = apply (v.)
- improve = enhance /ɪn'hɑ:ns/ (v.)
- labelling (n.)
- policy = legislation (n.)
- raise awareness /ə'weənɪs/ (v.)
- set up / launch (a programme) (v.)

Your words: ....

Good food habits

- balanced (adj.)
- fiber /'faɪbə/ (n.)
- fitness (n.)
- keep fit / healthy
- nutritious /nju:'trɪʃəs/ (adj.)
- organic (adj.)
- protein /'prəʊti:n/ (n.)
- sugar-free (adj.)
- sustainable /sə'steɪnəbl/ (adj.)

Your words: ....

MP3
www.lienmini.fr/htr7-u1508

LANGUAGE LAB

1 Complete each sentence with the words below.
ban • anxiety • diabetes • health • labelling • heart diseases • junk food • bullying

A. Fatty and sugary food, also called .... has harmful consequences on your ....

B. Unhealthy food has medical consequences such as .... and ....

C. Obesity can have mental health and social consequences like .... and ....

D. Food issues can be fought through legislation like a .... on digital marketing or clear .... on products.

2 Complete with the most appropriate structure: *should* + V or *had better* + V.

A. If you don't want to gain weight, you .... junk food. (*not eat*)

B. To stay fit, he .... sport. (*practise*)

C. To have a healthy heart, we .... five fruit and vegetables per day. (*eat*)

D. To spare our children health problems later, we .... more healthy food campaigns. (*launch*)

3 Highlight the right proposition (*must* or *have to*). Be ready to justify orally.

A. By law, food companies *must* / *have to* label their products to inform customers about the food quality.

B. In his video, Boris Johnson says people *must* / *have to* practise sport to lose weight.

C. With Downing Street's plan, the food industry *must* / *has to* remove online advertising for junk food.

D. Younger consumers feel that they *must* / *have to* buy ethically and sustainably.

E. Younger consumers also know that they *must* / *have to* buy organic products for their well-being.

4 Replace the underlined adjective in each sentence with one adjective from the mind map.

A. Fruit and vegetables are often <u>expensive</u> for poor families.
→ Fruit and vegetables are often .... for poor families.

B. <u>Poor</u> families are the most food insecure. → .... families are the most food insecure.

C. <u>Ready-to-eat</u> food is the most <u>dangerous</u> for our health.
→ .... food is the most .... for our health.

D. <u>Good</u> food is the secret to be <u>in good shape</u>. → .... food is the secret to be ....

5 Unit's checkout

Observe this picture. What would you advise the girl to do or not to do? What do you suggest that she should do?

....

....

....

....

....

....

....

OPEN YOUR EARS!

L'accentuation des mots composés

MP3 N°20

1. Écoutez les mots, soulignez la syllabe accentuée ou complétez.

junk food • food habits • food industry • underprivileged • ill-health • ill-balanced • overweight • ad-free weight loss • sugar-free • fat-free • food insecure • school meal • deep frozen (food) • light green (label)

2. Concluez (surlignez la bonne réponse).

• En général, les noms composés portent l'accent principal sur le premier mot / le deuxième mot.
• En général, les adjectifs composés ou précédés d'une préposition portent l'accent principal sur le premier mot / le deuxième mot.
• Les mots composés d'un adjectif et d'un nom portent l'accent sur le nom / l'adjectif, sauf les mots composés se terminant par ....

AXE 8

UNIT 16

INDIGENOUS PRIDE

How can Natives fight for the preservation of their land and culture?

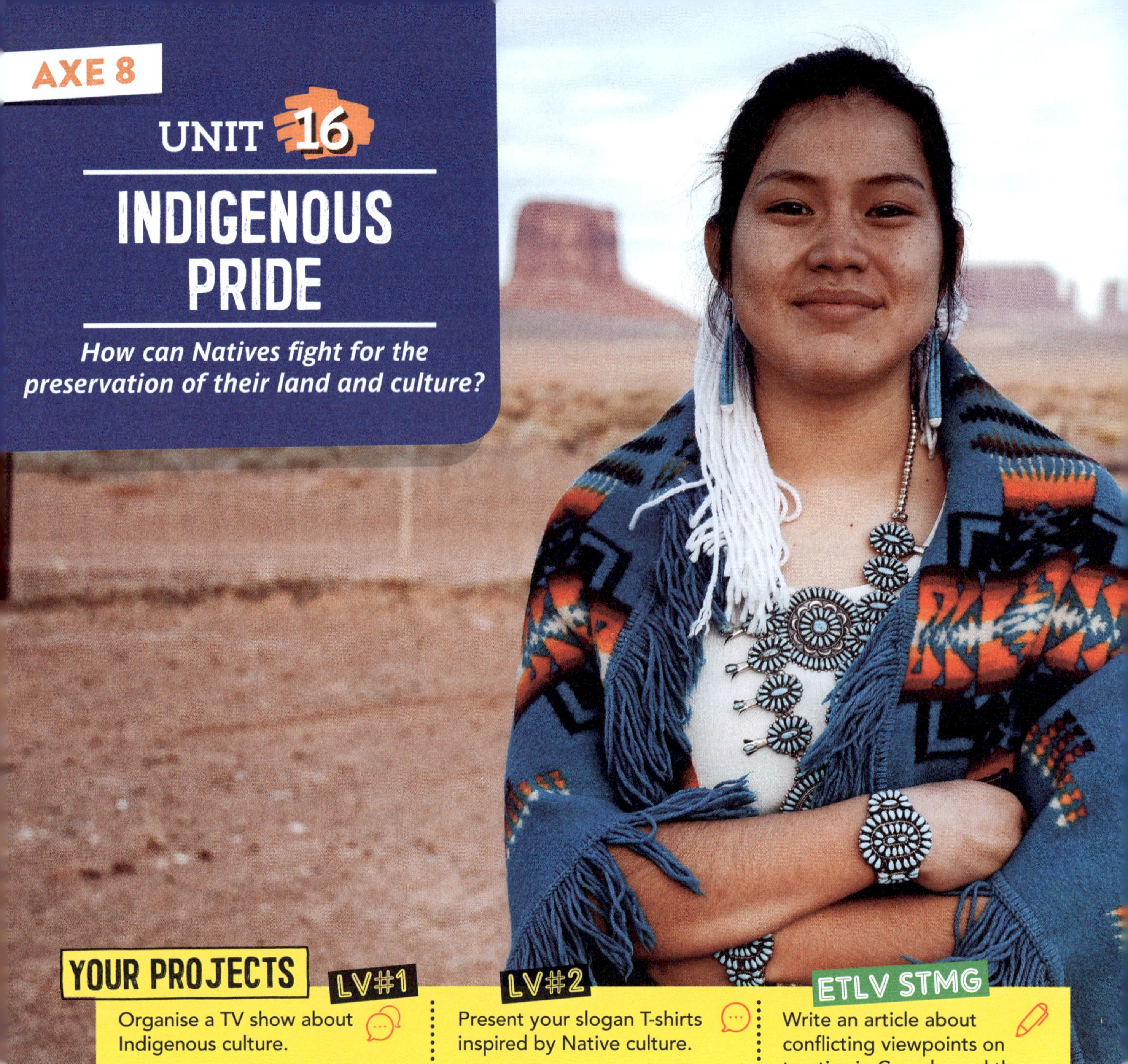

YOUR PROJECTS

LV#1
Organise a TV show about Indigenous culture.

LV#2
Present your slogan T-shirts inspired by Native culture.

ETLV STMG
Write an article about conflicting viewpoints on treaties in Canada, and the solutions that are found to reach a consensus.

Au menu de cette unité :

DÉCOUVERTES CULTURELLES

- La bataille des Sioux contre l'oléoduc dans le Dakota du Nord
- La défense des vestiges amérindiens au Nouveau-Mexique
- Deb Haaland, première Amérindienne secrétaire à l'Intérieur
- La terre sacrée des Aborigènes d'Australie (le cas d'Uluru)
- La préservation de la mémoire à travers la mode
- La terre des Inuits, le respect des traités ETLV STMG

OUTILS LINGUISTIQUES

- Le *present perfect*
- Le prétérit
- Le lexique du patrimoine des peuples premiers, de la protestation et de la défense des droits
- Le lexique des problèmes environnementaux et de leurs solutions, du compromis et de la négociation
- La prononciation de la lettre *a*

GET READY!

WORD CHALLENGE

Use as many of these words as possible throughout the unit.
Tick ✓ the box when you have used the word.

- ☐ activist (n.)
- ☐ agreement = pact = treaty (n.)
- ☐ claim (n. / v.)
- ☐ cultural /'kʌltʃərəl/ (adj.)
- ☐ cultural appropriation (n.)
- ☐ demonstration (n.)
- ☐ environment (n.)
- ☐ environmental (adj.)
- ☐ fight / struggle against (v.)
- ☐ fight for / stand up for one's rights (v.)
- ☐ heritage /'herɪtɪdʒ/ (n.)
- ☐ Indigenous /ɪn'dɪdʒɪnəs/ (adj.)
- ☐ make a difference
- ☐ make history
- ☐ Native /'neɪtɪv/ (adj.)
- ☐ oil drilling (n.)
- ☐ pipeline /'paɪplaɪn/ (n.)
- ☐ prejudice: *prejugé* (n.)
- ☐ preserve (v.)
- ☐ protest (v.)
- ☐ protest march (n.)
- ☐ right the wrongs
- ☐ take to the streets = demonstrate (v.)
- ☐ territory /'terətərɪ/ (n.)

BEFORE CLASS!

A. **Watch the video. Make a list of as many names, nouns and adjectives heard in the video as you can.**

Some first names	Some tribes names	Nouns	Adjectives
....	....	....	....
....	....	....	....
....	....	....	....
....	....	....	....
....	....	....	....
....	....	....	....

B. **Explain why they are proud of being Native Americans.**

....
....
....
....
....

C. **Focus on the last picture. Complete what the narrator says and explain what he means.**

"Native Americans call themselves ....
The one thing ...."

....
....
....

www.lienmini.fr/htr7-u1601

1 Native Americans, Protectors of Their Land

How did a protest become the greatest Native American movement in modern history?

1 Fighting for their land

A. Before watching: observe the photo and guess why these people are protesting.

B. Watch the video, then tick the correct answers.

a. The Sioux refuse the construction of… ☐ 2 ☐ 4 oil pipelines.

b. They are marching because they want to protect their water and their lands. T ☐ F ☐

c. The Dakota access pipeline will travel under the…
☐ Colorado ☐ Missouri River.

d. Tom Goldtooth considers it blood oil because it contaminates their water. T ☐ F ☐

e. Wayne Frederick thinks that the government should ask for their consent because they are a sovereign entity. T ☐ F ☐

www.lienmini.fr/htr7-u1602

0'00 to 2'00

2 The Standing Rock case

A. Read text 1. Highlight the words / expressions related to civil rights and change for Native Americans.

B. Read text 2. Highlight the sentences that mention the outcome of the fight and the reasons that led to the decision.

C. Explain what the oil pipeline protest in North Dakota was about, and give your opinion about their victory.

HELP!

Nouns
- demonstration: *manifestation*

Adjectives
- sacred /'seɪkrɪd/ = precious /'preʃəs/
- victorious

Verbs & Expressions
- fight for / stand up for one's rights
- preserve = protect
- take to the streets = demonstrate

Text 1

The world has been electrified by protests against the Dakota access pipeline. Is this a new civil rights movement where environmental and human rights meet? [...] What's happening at Standing Rock is extraordinary and possibly transformative for native rights, Sioux history, and the intersection of the climate movement with indigenous communities.

The Guardian, September 2016

Text 2

After four years locked in legal struggle over the construction of the controversial[1] 1,172 mile-long, Dakota Access Pipeline, the Standing Rock and Cheyenne River Sioux tribes won a major victory on Monday when a federal court ordered the pipeline to cease[2] its operations by August 5. Judge James E. Boasberg, from the US District Court of the District of Columbia, ruled[3] that the US Army Corps of Engineers – tasked with awarding the permits for construction – failed[4] to fully assess[5] the environmental risks posed by a segment of the pipeline. The tribes argued the segment, which runs under Lake Oahe, a large reservoir half a mile from Standing Rock Reservation land, has both despoiled[6] sacred land and contaminated their water supply.

"Fearing severe environmental consequences," the ruling states, "American Indian Tribes on nearby reservations have sought for several years to invalidate federal permits allowing the Dakota Access Pipeline to carry oil under the lake. Today they finally achieve that goal."

1 polémique • 2 cesser • 3 prononcer un jugement • 4 échouer à • 5 évaluer • 6 déposséder, spolier

Mother Jones, 6 July 2020

3 Protecting sacred sites from fracking

New Mexico's Navajos are facing a new threat[1]: fracking[2].

Today, the US Bureau of Land Management is considering a plan, known as the Mancos-Gallup Amendment, which could lease[3] land in the region for some 3,000 new wells – many of which would be for fracking oil and gas. The plan would expand drilling into some of northern New Mexico's last available public lands, threatening the desecration of sacred Native artefacts near Chaco Canyon [...].

Fighting the amendment is something of a last stand for Native and environmental activists who have seen the oil and gas industry proliferate in recent decades. They say at least 90% of public lands in northern New Mexico are already leased for oil and gas drilling.

Under the Trump administration, the amount of US lands up for lease to oil and gas companies has soared – 461m acres across the country [...].

The new proposal would encroach[4] further upon the Chaco culture national historical park – a network of historic archaeological sites that today hold Unesco world heritage status and are of spiritual importance to Navajo and Puebloan people in the region.

"To a non-indigenous person, they [are] ruins. But to an indigenous Pueblo person, they're still active sites that are used in spiritual ways," said Julia Bernal, the environmental justice director at the Pueblo Action Alliance, an indigenous sustainability organization formed in the wake of Standing Rock. "The fight has constantly been, 'These are sacred sites.' But the non-indigenous power is like, 'Well prove to us these are sacred sites.' How can we prove that when it's our beliefs?" [...].

1 *menace* • 2 *fracturation hydraulique* • 3 *louer* • 4 *empiéter*

The Guardian, June 2020

A. Read the text and match each word (left) with its translation (right).

a. wells •	• *profanation*
b. available •	• *s'envoler (économie)*
c. desecration •	• *puits*
d. stand •	• *durabilité*
e. soared •	• *disponible*
f. sustainability •	• *bataille*

B. Highlight the plan of the US Bureau Management.

C. Underline the reasons for fighting.

D. Recap orally what you have learnt.

YOUR TURN! 4 Act out

A Navajo chief has been invited to the US Senate to speak out against fracking on Navajo land.
List five arguments against fracking on Indian territory and act out the speech.

HELP!

Nouns
- desecration: *profanation*
- greed: *avidité*
- resources /rɪˈzɔːsɪz/

Adjectives
- ancestral
- sacred /ˈseɪkrɪd/

Verbs & Expressions
- claim (land): *s'approprier*
- endanger
- fight for / against
- harm: *nuire*
- stand up for one's rights = defend one's rights
- thirst for: *soif de*

❷ Lands of Memory, Territories for the Future

How do Native Americans see their role for the future?

1 Committing for the Earth

Poster by Jared Yazzie, Navajo artist

A. Comment on this poster. What roles do Native Americans imagine for their future generations?

B. From what you have learnt, would you say they already have this role? Justify orally.

HELP!

- at the top / at the bottom
- in the background / in the foreground
- hold a baby
- traditional costume and necklace
- look ahead

2 The Earth guardians

A. Watch and say what activist Xiuhtezcatl /ʃuw'teskatl/ Martinez talks about.

- ☐ Being elected as a political leader to save the Earth.
- ☐ You as the future generation, taking action to save the Earth.
- ☐ This cool postcard that links to an animated video.

www.lienmini.fr/htr7-u1603

B. How does this video relate to the poster above? Write a few keywords and get ready to explain orally.

C. This activist sees the climate crisis only as a problem. T ☐ F ☐

Justify:

3 Deb Haaland: a new political era

A. **Before watching, look at the still. Guess why it is entitled a "new political era".**

B. **Watch the video and focus on the following elements.**

a. Deb Haaland's feelings and background:

b. Her grandparents:

c. The horrific ideology of a former minister:

d. Her father:

e. Joe Biden's goal:

f. Climate change:

www.lienmini.fr/htr7-u1604

4 "I'll be fierce for all of us"

In an interview days before her nomination, Haaland told *The Guardian* that as secretary of the interior[1] she would "move climate change priorities, tribal consultation and a green economic recovery forward".

It's a big job with high expectations after four years of racist rhetoric and destructive environmental rollbacks by the Trump administration, which showed contempt for the climate or environment [...]. "I'll be fierce for all of us, for our planet, and all of our protected land," said Haaland in her acceptance speech. [...]

Indigenous communities in the US, and globally, are disproportionately vulnerable to the impact of the climate crisis such as rising sea levels and droughts, and environmental hazards resulting from polluting industries. As secretary of the interior, Haaland will play a key role in undoing Trump's rollbacks and will also be a key lieutenant in Biden's new climate team.

This is not the first time Haaland has made history. In 2018, she became one of the first two Native women in Congress, alongside Sharice Davids of Kansas. In January, a record-breaking six Native Americans – four Democrats and two Republicans – will be sworn in.

1 *Le département de l'Intérieur gère les ressources naturelles fédérales et le bureau des affaires amérindiennes.*

The Guardian, December 2020

A. Read the text and find the following words (in the order of the text).

a. *faire avancer :*

b. *reprise économique :*

c. *retours en arrière :*

d. *mépris :*

e. *féroce :*

f. *sécheresses :*

g. *dangers :*

h. *être assermentés :*

B. Highlight information about the Trump administration.

C. Underline information about Deb Haaland's role and Indigenous communities.

D. Explain orally why she represents a new political era. Use the following elements: *make history, make a difference, voice (v.), symbolise.*

3 Australia: An Ongoing Fight

How can profit-making and respecting sacred Aboriginal sites be balanced?

1 Protecting an Indigenous heritage

Mining giant Rio Tinto must rebuild a 46,000-year-old Aboriginal cave system it blew up[1] in May, an Australian parliamentary inquiry has said.

The Juukan Gorge caves in Western Australia were destroyed as part of an iron ore[2] exploration project.

In a report released on Wednesday, the inquiry blasted Rio Tinto's "inexcusable" act, and said they should compensate the traditional owners.

Rio Tinto repeated its apology and pledged to change its practices.

Earlier this year several senior figures at the company, including Chief Executive Jean-Sébastien Jacques, resigned over the incident, following a backlash from shareholders and the public.

Before their destruction, the Juukan Gorge caves in Pilbara had shown evidence of continuous human habitation since the last Ice Age.

They were seen as one of Australia's most significant archaeological research sites, but they also had more than eight million tonnes of high-grade iron ore, with an estimated value of £75m (A$132m; $96m).

Following an outcry over their destruction Rio Tinto held an inquiry, after which it cut bonuses for directors and began attempts at repairing relations with Aboriginal communities.

A parliamentary inquiry was also established to investigate Rio Tinto's behaviour and assess the damage caused to the Puutu Kunti Kurrama and Pinikura (PKKP) people – the traditional owners of the land where the caves were based.

In its report – titled *Never Again* – the inquiry concluded Rio Tinto "knew the value of what they were destroying but blew it up anyway".

It made seven recommendations, including a moratorium on all mining in the local area, and changes to heritage protection laws.

The PKKP Aboriginal Corporation has welcomed the verdict and said it hopes it will "prompt a fundamental reset of the [mining] sector".

In a statement, Rio Tinto said it was "working very hard to progress a remedy" with the PKKP, and the caves' destruction "does not reflect the values that [we] aspire to".

1 *faire exploser* • **2** *minerai*

BBC, December 2020

A. Read the text and match each word with its synonym or meaning.

a. blasted	•	•	negative reaction
b. backlash	•	•	blew up
c. shareholders	•	•	protest
d. outcry	•	•	evaluate
e. assess	•	•	*actionnaires*

B. Highlight words and expressions linked to why some sites are considered Indigenous heritage.

C. Underline what caused the initial problem and why the mining company did it.

D. Circle how the Indigenous tribes, the public and the investigators reacted.

E. Pick out the consequences for the company.

....

....

....

....

F. Using what you have learnt, sum up the article in your own words.

2 Climbing ban on Uluru

A. **Watch the video, then tick the correct answers.**

a. This report is about the last time tourists can climb Uluru.

T ☐ F ☐

Justify with a quote: ....

....

b. Before, park rangers were concerned because:

☐ tourists climbed day and night

☐ tourists needed rescue

☐ some climbers lost their lives

c. Traditional owners wanted to close the climb because:

☐ it desecrated their land ☐ it caused safety problems

☐ it did not bring enough money

d. What finally led to the decision to close the climb?

☐ Only 1 in 5 visitors climbed it. ☐ Uluru was given back to Anangu elders in 1985.

www.lienmini.fr/htr7-u1605

B. **Pick out the reasons why they are happy about the decision.**

Traditional owners are happy because...	Park rangers are happy because...
....	....
....	....
....	....

3 Sacred territory

Comment on this cartoon and say how it illustrates "territory and memory".

HELP!

- underground ≠ above ground
- belong to = be a part of
- it aims at showing...
- it conveys the message that...
- compromise /ˈkɒmprəmaɪz/
- agreement

By Australian cartoonist Glen Le Lievre

YOUR TURN! 4 Report!

Prepare a one-minute news report for the Australian national radio programme entitled: "Indigenous heritage and resource exploitation: a compromise is possible."

4 Indigenous Fashion

How does fashion help to preserve Indigenous memory?

1 Native American fashion

www.lienmini.fr/htr7-u1606

0'17 to 2'02 | 3'20 to 5'00 | 5'33 to 8'09

A. Groupwork. Watch your group's extract and take notes.

Designers / Clothes (Group 1: 0'17 to 2'02)	
Values / traditions (Group 2: 3'20 to 5'00)	
Prejudice (Group 3: 5'33 to 8'09)	

B. Share the information with the class. Sum up Jessica Metcalfe's conception of Indigenous fashion.

2 Sage Paul: a Canadian designer

Paul, 34, is the founder and artistic director of the first-ever Indigenous Fashion Week Toronto (IFWTO) [...] The showcase will feature Indigenous-made textiles, fabric and crafts, and has a broader mission of challenging mainstream perceptions of Indigenous people and culture, which are often stereotyped and commodified[1]. [...]

Once she moved [...] into the Canadian fashion world, Paul felt pressure to become a stereotype of what an Indigenous designer "should" be. It's this homogenization – or, as she calls it, the effort to "Pan-Indian us" – that she wants to combat with IFWTO. "I want to see Indigenous people leading how [they're] represented," says Paul. "I don't want other people talking for us, and I don't want other people telling us how we're supposed to look."

1 *transformé en objet, marchandisé*

Locallove.ca, May 2018

A. Read the text and highlight the main elements about Sage Paul and her mission.

B. According to her, how do people generally see Indigenous fashion? Underline the answer in the text.

3 Meet Sage Paul

www.lienmini.fr/htr7-u1607

A. Watch the video and tick the right answers.

a. ☐ She grew up surrounded with textiles and fashion.

b. ☐ She learnt with her grandmother and her community.

c. ☐ They made their own clothing and designs.

d. ☐ Painting was part of her culture.

e. ☐ There are a few Indigenous designers in Canada and the world.

f. ☐ She wants Fashion Week in Toronto to be by and for the community first.

B. Memory game: close your book and give as much information as you can about Sage Paul.

4 Aboriginal fashion: Grace Lillian Lee

Grace Lillian Lee: I'm so proud of you, Shonae, for curating[1] the Piinpi exhibition[2]. It's so important for our people. [...] I think Indigenous fashion is the future of Australian fashion. It's time for First Nations people to reclaim it.

Shonae Hobson: There's definitely a lot that non-Indigenous people and designers can learn from Indigenous people, especially in terms of sustainability.

Grace Lillian Lee: [...] Fashion is very tangible and relatable[3] and accessible. I like to call it a soft entry into reconciliation and healing[4] our people – not only our mob, but also Australians who want to learn and feel more connected to our Country. It is an act of preservation of our cultural knowledge [...].

1 *ici, organiser* • 2 an exhibition of contemporary First Nations fashion design in Australia • 3 *à quoi l'on peut s'identifier* • 4 righting the wrongs done to Aboriginals

The Guardian, November 2020

"Body Armour", a dress created by Grace Lillian Lee in 2018.

A. Read the text. What does Grace Lillian Lee think of the exhibition? Highlight the answer.

B. Underline the expressions showing that fashion is essential to her.

YOUR PROJECTS

#1. For the History channel, organise a TV show about Indigenous culture (a journalist, historians, Native fashion designers, environmental activists, CEOs of oil / gas companies, etc.).

OR

#2. As a sustainable fashion designer, you are inspired by Native cultures. You want to create a collection of slogan T-shirts to celebrate Indigenous land and memory. Write three messages and present your ideas to your colleagues.

5 Preventing and Solving Conflicts

ETLV
STMG

How were Native lands lost to American and Canadian private interests?

OBJECTIVE STMG

➤ Identify sources of conflicts and points of consensus

1 Chief Dana Tizya-Tramm's speech

www.lienmini.fr/htr7-u1608

A. Watch the video, then tick the correct answers.

a. What endangers Native Alaskans? ☐ oil drillings ☐ climate change

b. The permafrost is: ☐ polluted ☐ melting ☐ well-preserved

c. There is a project to develop the exploitation of oil and gas that is a source of conflict. T ☐ F ☐

B. Pick out elements showing that the Natives depend on their land, and on us.

....

....

....

2 A conflict in Kaktovik, Alaska

Bears have become a popular attraction for visitors to Kaktovik, a 250-person Native Alaskan village surrounded by the Arctic National Wildlife Refuge (ANWR), the U.S.'s largest wildlife park covering 19.6 million acres (7.9 million hectares). This has generated steady work for indigenous Inupiaq hunters-turned-guides. [...] "The polar bears are in abundance here on the shore[1] because their habitat has gone away – because the world is burning too much fossil fuel," guide Robert Thompson told [us] after a day of polar bear guiding.

The link between fossil fuels and a warming Arctic is the key reason Thompson opposes oil drilling in a 1.5 million acre coastal plain of the ANWR. [...] Thompson is on one side of a bitter fight that has divided this remote village and sparked debate over who are the true custodians[2] of Native Alaskan land. [...] A small 2016 poll[3] conducted by the village found 52 percent of surveyed residents supported oil and gas drilling in ANWR, while 32 percent opposed it and 16 percent were neutral. [...]

The Gwich'in Athabascan people of Alaska and Canada, who live and hunt in the southern part of ANWR, oppose oil development because it threatens the caribou herd that is central to their diet and culture. [...] Crawford Patkotak, an Inupiaq whaling captain [...], said that "we as Inupiaq people consider ourselves the first conservationists, but with the right balance. We believe that (oil development) can be done in a way that it doesn't harm the migration of the caribou."

1 *littoral* • 2 guardians • 3 *sondage*

Thomson Reuters Foundation, May 2019

A. Read the text. Highlight what brings resources to these Native Alaskans, and underline the elements of a potential conflict.

B. Draw a chart showing the percentages for the different opinions in this conflict. ....

C. Is a consensus possible? Which sentence answers this question? ....

HELP!

DEFINITIONS ETLV

- A **conflict** appears when individual or collective interests are in contradiction with each other.
- A **consensus** is a common decision made by all the stakeholders *(parties prenantes)*.

3 The real meaning of treaties

For Indigenous peoples, the sacred and binding[1] character of treaties is not found primarily in the documents' legalistic language. Instead, the true force of treaties is rooted in what was actually said, often in Indigenous languages, at the time of the negotiations. In addition, treaty deliberations were frequently accompanied by ceremonial conventions such as the smoking of sacred pipes (calumet) or an exchange of symbolically significant presents. [...] Accordingly, many Indigenous peoples look to their elders who are schooled in oral histories as the highest authorities on the spirit and intent of the treaties. [...]

In spite of the constitutional character of treaties, the non-Indigenous peoples who made and implemented[2] them tended to see them as self-serving deals rather than sacred pacts between independent nations. Historically, non-Indigenous treaty negotiators believed treaties were inexpensive and convenient ways to strip[3] Aboriginal title (i.e., ownership) from most of the lands in Canada so that resources could be used by settlers[4] [...] Even in modern times, the federal and provincial governments tend to interpret treaties in legalistic terms, contending that Indigenous peoples "ceded, surrendered, and yielded[5]" their ancestral rights and titles through treaties.

1 obligatory • **2** put into effect • **3** *retirer* • **4** *colons* • **5** gave up, abandoned

The Canadian Encyclopedia, September 2011

A. From what you know, what is generally the objective of treaties? ....

B. Read the text. Who thinks what?

Indigenous peoples •

Federal and provincial governments •

- Treaties are legal documents that must be respected to avoid conflicts.
- What you said is more important than what you signed.
- A ritual marks the agreement between two nations.
- Natives should not be treated as equals.
- The elders' advice must be listened to.

C. In the text, highlight the elements showing that the settlers knew they were unfair.

D. What happened to the lands taken from Native people in Canada? Explain in your own words.

4 Land claims: coming to real agreements

www.lienmini.fr/htr7-u1609

A. Watch the video, then tick the correct answer. Specific claims are made when Native people:

☐ want to get their land back ☐ were wronged by a treaty in the past

B. Say who signed the treaties and when they started.

....

....

C. Tick examples of situations where specific claims can be accepted.

☐ When the Native people already live on the land they claim.

☐ When money has been badly managed.

☐ When the land promised to the Natives has not been given.

D. How do the government and First Nations come to an agreement now?

....

....

YOUR PROJECT BAC

As a reporter for Reuters, write an article in which you explain the conflicting viewpoints on treaties of Indigenous peoples and the Canadian government, then the solutions that are found to reach a consensus.

RULE THE GRAMMAR!

1. LE *PRESENT PERFECT*

• Formation
Auxiliaire *have* au présent + participe passé du verbe (voir aussi pages 52 et 124).

• Emploi
Le ***present perfect*** est un **temps du présent**.

1. Il exprime le résultat ou le bilan dans le présent d'actions ou d'événements passés.
   *Bears **have become** a popular attraction for visitors to Kaktovik.* => *They are popular now.*
2. Il exprime la continuité d'actions ou d'événements débutés dans le passé, qui se poursuivent dans le présent. On traduit par un présent de l'indicatif en français.
   *Aborigines **have struggled** to preserve their sacred sites for decades.* => *They still struggle today.*

2. LE PRÉTÉRIT

• Formation
BV + *-ed* ou 2ᵉ colonne des verbes irréguliers (voir aussi page 148).

• Emploi
Le prétérit s'emploie pour évoquer des actions ou des événements passés et terminés. On trouve souvent un marqueur de temps dans la phrase.
*Bears **became** a popular attraction two years ago.*
*The President **gave** companies the right to use fracking on Indian Territory last year.*

VOCABULARY

Indigenous fights

Fighting for a cause

- activist (n.)
- conflict (n.)
- demonstrate (v.)
- fight (for / against) = struggle (v.)
- preconception = prejudice (n.): *préjugé*
- protest = march (v.)
- protest march (n.)
- strong-willed = determined /dɪ'tɜːmɪnd/ (adj.)
- take to the streets

Your words: ......

Environmental issues & solutions

- climate crisis /'klaɪmət 'kraɪsɪs/ (n.)
- desecration /desɪ'kreɪʃn/ (n.): *profanation*
- despoil /dɪ'spɔɪl/ (v.): *déposséder*
- endanger (v.)
- fracking (n.)
- greed (n.): *avidité*
- harm (v.): *nuire*
- oil drilling (n.): *exploitation pétrolière*
- oil leak (n.): *fuite de pétrole*
- pipeline /'paɪplaɪn/ (n.)
- preserve = protect (v.)
- sustainability (n.)
- sustainable (adj.)

Your words: ......

Indigenous heritage

- cultural /'kʌltʃərəl/ (adj.)
- heritage /'herɪtɪdʒ/ (n.)
- Indigenous /ɪn'dɪdʒɪnəs/ (adj.)
- Native (adj.)
- people(s) (n.): *peuple(s)*
- sacred /'seɪkrɪd/ (adj.)
- tribe /traɪb/ (n.)

Your words: ......

Compromise and negotiation

- claim (v.): *s'approprier*
- commitment (n.): *engagement*
- make a difference
- move forward
- put an end to sth
- treaty = agreement = pact (n.)
- right the wrongs: *réparer les torts*
- territory (n.)
- unite (v.) = come together

Your words: ......

MP3
www.lienmini.fr/AQ132htr7-u1610

LANGUAGE LAB

1 Replace the underlined expressions or words with synonyms.

A. <u>Determined</u> protestors decided to march against the oil pipeline. ....

B. It is true that White settlers had strong <u>prejudices</u> against Native tribes. ....

C. Let us <u>come together</u> and fight the climate crisis. ....

D. The Aborigines organised numerous <u>protests</u> against the mining companies. ....

2 Preterite or present perfect? Tick the right tense in each sentence.

A. The protest ☐ has started ☐ started three years ago.

B. Native Americans ☐ have been ☐ were discriminated against for centuries, and unfortunately they still are.

C. The oil company ☐ has halted ☐ halted plans to expand a mine. I hope it will last (*durer*).

D. They ☐ have fought ☐ fought the government for months, and it is not over.

3 Conjugate the verb in the preterite or the present perfect.

A. This man (*live*) on this reservation for years. I think that he will die there. ....

B. The explosion (*destroy*) a 46,000-year-old site yesterday. ....

C. Polar bears (*lose*) their natural habitat because of climate change. ....

D. This designer (*work*) on this new Indigenous collection since last summer. ....

4 Match elements from A, B, C and D to make three meaningful sentences.

A.	C.
Determined activists The desecrated land The treaty	put an end to a Native tribe for the Indigenous peoples
B.	**D.**
was signed by come together to was reclaimed by	the oil drilling conflict. to right the wrongs. a sustainable project.

....

5 Unit's checkout

Observe the cartoon and write a short dialogue between the man on the left and the Native American. Use the preterite and the present perfect.

....

OPEN YOUR EARS!

La prononciation de la lettre *a*

MP3 N°21

Écoutez les mots et notez le numéro correspondant à la prononciation de la lettre *a*.

1 Native • 2 Canadian (x2) • 3 Canada (x2) • 4 activist • 5 demonstration • 6 heritage • 7 sacred • 8 Senate • 9 necklace • 10 traditional

/eɪ/ (make): ....

/æ/ (fact): ....

/ə/ (winter): ....

/ɪ/ (hit): ....

POUR LES ÉVALUATIONS COMMUNES DU BACCALAURÉAT

COMPRÉHENSION

Compréhension de l'oral

En 1re et en Tle :
*La **CO** est évaluée à partir d'un document audio ou vidéo de 1 minute 30 maximum. Le document est écouté trois fois, les écoutes sont espacées d'une minute. Le titre du document et, éventuellement, les noms propres, sont fournis. Vous pouvez prendre des notes à tout moment.*
*Vous devez rendre compte du document **en français**, de manière libre ou guidée.*

Les trois écoutes du document

- Identifiez le nombre de locuteurs.
- Soyez attentif(ve) aux types de voix (homme, femme, jeune, âgée…) et au ton (émotions…).
- Notez les mots-clés (ceux que vous entendez le plus / le mieux), les dates, les chiffres…
- Lors des 2e et 3e écoutes, complétez vos notes mais ne rédigez pas et ne traduisez pas.
- Dans le cas d'une vidéo, aidez-vous des images pour comprendre le message oral.

Compréhension de l'écrit

En 1re et en Tle :
*La **CE** est évaluée à partir d'un ou deux documents, dont la longueur cumulée est comprise entre 2 300 et 4 000 signes (en 1re), et 2 500 et 4 300 signes (en Tle).*
*Vous devez rendre compte **en français ou en anglais**, selon la consigne indiquée, de manière libre ou guidée.*
En Tle, il peut vous être demandé de répondre en français ou en anglais à une question portant sur la compréhension de l'ensemble du dossier (constitué par les documents supports de l'évaluation de la compréhension de l'oral et de l'écrit).

Lire et comprendre

- Observez la source, le titre, et déduisez la nature du document (fiction, article, blog, poème…).
- Lisez les éventuelles questions de compréhension, elles vous aideront à anticiper le thème et à repérer des éléments de réponse.
- Lisez le(s) texte(s) attentivement une première fois.
- Faites bien attention aux signes de ponctuation et à la composition du texte (guillemets de dialogue, éléments valorisés visuellement, majuscules indiquant des noms propres ou des lieux…).
- Identifiez la structure du texte, repérez les mots de liaison. S'il y a plusieurs dates, notez-les et établissez une chronologie des faits au brouillon.
- Si le texte est long, annotez les paragraphes et donnez-leur un titre pour vous repérer plus facilement.
- Identifiez l'intention de l'auteur / le contexte (article de sensibilisation, témoignage pour émouvoir, billet journalistique d'opinion pour convaincre, récit fictif…).

Résumer / Rendre compte

Les épreuves de compréhension aboutissent à la production d'un **résumé en français** (compréhension de l'oral) ou d'un **compte rendu en français ou en anglais** (compréhension de l'écrit).

Votre résumé / compte rendu doit contenir :

- la nature du document (reportage, discours, interview radiophonique, extrait de roman, autobiographie, article de presse, extrait de blog, etc.) ;
- le but du document (informer, sensibiliser, dénoncer, promouvoir, etc.) ;
- le thème ;
- des informations sur les intervenants ou personnages (sexe, âge, métier, etc.) et sur les événements (chronologie des faits…), les points de vue (narrateur / personnages…).

Remarque : Lors de l'épreuve de compréhension de l'écrit, appuyez-vous sur les questions guidées pour structurer votre compte rendu. Si le sujet comporte deux textes, établissez des comparaisons : les textes sont-ils contradictoires ? complémentaires ?

- Utilisez des connecteurs logiques pour structurer votre résumé / compte rendu.

	🇫🇷	🇬🇧
Introduction et énumération	En premier lieu, tout d'abord, premièrement… Ensuite, puis, deuxièmement…	*To begin with, to start with, first of all, firstly… Secondly, then, next…*
Addition	En outre, par ailleurs, de même, de plus, également, de surcroît, d'une part… d'autre part…	*Also, not only… but also, besides, furthermore, moreover, what's more, on top of that… last but not least…*
But	Pour que, afin que, de façon à ce que…	*In order to, to this end, so as to, to…*
Cause	Parce que, car, puisque, du fait que, en raison de, dans la mesure où, étant donné que, grâce à / à cause de, en effet…	*Because of / thanks to, since, this is the reason why, due to, owing to…*
Conséquence	C'est pourquoi, par conséquent, donc, aussi, ainsi, si bien que, d'où, de ce fait, de sorte que…	*Therefore, consequently, so, as a result of, thus, that's why…*

Condition	À condition que, pourvu que, dans l'hypothèse où, probablement, en admettant que…	*Unless, otherwise, if, in case…*
Comparaison	Comme, de même (que), comme si…	*Like, as, in comparison, on the one hand… / on the other hand…*
Opposition	Mais, cependant, or, alors que, en revanche, tandis que, à l'inverse, au contraire, néanmoins, pourtant, quoique, en dépit de…	*But, contrary to, on the contrary, unlike, however, nevertheless, yet, in spite of / despite the fact that…*
Conclusion	Pour conclure, enfin, en somme…	*Finally, eventually, to finish, to conclude, to cut a long story short, to put in a nutshell, to sum up, all in all, all things considered…*

EXPRESSION

Expression écrite

En 1re et en Tle :
*Le sujet d'**EE**, à traiter **en anglais**, se fonde sur une ou deux questions, en lien avec la thématique générale des documents d'évaluation de la compréhension de l'oral et de l'écrit. Le sujet peut prendre appui sur un document iconographique.*

1/ Avant de commencer

On peut vous demander de commenter une citation, exprimer votre opinion sur un thème, répondre à une problématique, ou de l'écriture créative (un dialogue, une lettre, un article, une ou plusieurs entrées d'un journal intime…) : dans tous les cas, prenez le temps de bien lire le sujet pour éviter tout contresens.

2/ Rédiger un essai / un commentaire

- Notez vos idées au brouillon, sans rédiger. Associez à chaque idée un exemple.
- Notez tous les termes en lien avec le thème général et que vous voulez utiliser (vous les rayerez au fur et à mesure que vous les emploierez dans votre rédaction).
- Organisez vos idées dans un plan.
- Soignez l'introduction et la conclusion.
- Veillez à utiliser des connecteurs logiques pour structurer votre production (voir tableau ci-dessus).

3/ Rédiger un dialogue

- Au brouillon, notez les différentes personnes qui prendront part au dialogue : leurs noms et rôles dans l'histoire, leurs opinions, leurs sentiments…
- Dressez une liste de verbes pour rapporter les propos des personnages (*say, tell, reply, hesitate, add, agree, ask, answer, reply, cry, shout, smile, confess, whisper…*).
- Lors de la rédaction, prévoyez une introduction pour présenter le lieu de l'action, le moment et les personnages du dialogue.
- Mettez les propos des locuteurs entre guillemets (pas de tirets). Allez à la ligne à chaque fois qu'un personnage parle.
- Caractérisez la manière dont s'expriment les personnages, par un verbe (*he shouted* ≠ *he whispered*) ou par un adverbe (*he said proudly / cheerfully / kindly…*).
- Incluez des marques de la langue orale (pauses, interjections, formes contractées, *gap fillers, question tags…*) pour rendre plus vivants les échanges (*"Err… are you sure? Really?… Like, really sure?" / "You want to come, don't you?"*).

4/ Rédiger un article

- Donnez un titre, de préférence court et percutant.
- Soignez l'introduction : en deux ou trois phrases, votre lecteur doit savoir ce dont va parler l'article (= *Who, What, Where, When, Why*).
- Créez un paragraphe par idée. Associez à chaque idée ou argument un exemple, et sautez une ligne entre chaque paragraphe.
- Soignez votre conclusion.
- Signez d'un nom de journaliste imaginaire, incluez le nom du journal et la date de publication.

5/ Rédiger une lettre

- Identifiez bien la situation de communication posée par le sujet de l'épreuve, pour pouvoir adapter le ton et le vocabulaire que vous emploierez (vous n'écrirez pas de la même manière si vous vous adressez à un(e) proche ou à quelqu'un que vous ne connaissez pas).
- En haut de la page, incluez le nom du destinataire et la date.
- Rédigez des paragraphes distincts. Utilisez des connecteurs logiques (voir tableau ci-dessus).
- Si vous écrivez à quelqu'un qui ne vous connaît pas, présentez-vous brièvement dès le 1er paragraphe.
- Abordez le sujet de votre lettre rapidement (dès le 1er ou le 2e paragraphe).
- Dans le dernier paragraphe, terminez par une formule de remerciement.
- En bas de page, incluez une formule de politesse (pour un courrier formel : *Best regards / Yours sincerely / Yours faithfully* ; pour un(e) proche : *Love / Hugs from…*) et la signature.

Expression orale

En Tle :
*L'évaluation d'**EO/EOI** commence par une prise de parole en continu **en anglais**, à partir de ressources que vous proposerez (ETLV). Cette présentation est suivie d'un entretien avec le jury, composé de deux enseignants, l'un pour l'enseignement technologique, l'autre pour l'anglais.*

1/ Avant de commencer

- Préparez un schéma mental de ce que vous allez dire en première partie de l'épreuve, en tenant compte du temps dont vous disposez (5 minutes). Faites un essai en vous chronométrant, voire en vous filmant.

- Listez les mots et expressions que vous souhaitez utiliser en fonction de votre sujet. Vous pouvez noter des mots clés, sur une petite fiche, sans rédiger mais en faisant ressortir la trame de votre discours.
- Pour structurer votre discours, aidez-vous des expressions et connecteurs logiques (voir tableau p. 201).

2/ Lors de la présentation

- N'hésitez pas à exagérer l'accentuation : l'anglais est une langue très rythmée et accentuée, en faire trop vous aidera à bien prononcer.
- Soyez enthousiaste et poli(e). N'oubliez pas de saluer (*Goog morning Madam / Sir*) et de remercier à la fin (*Thank you*).

3/ Pendant l'entretien avec le jury

- Écoutez bien les questions du jury : elles vous guideront vers un approfondissement / un éclaircissement de votre discours. On ne vous tendra pas de piège, au contraire, on vous suggérera des pistes pour préciser ou compléter votre propos.
- Si vous n'êtes pas certain(e) d'avoir compris une question, dites-le en faisant répéter votre interlocuteur (*Could you please repeat?*). Vous ne devez pas rester avec un doute.
- Si, malgré cela, le doute persiste, tentez de reformuler la question vous-même (*If I understand (well), you're asking me… / Just to make sure I get your point, you want me to say if…*).

Enrichir son expression orale

Introduire votre sujet :

- First, to start with / begin with…
- I'm going to introduce / talk about my project which is about…
- I'm here to talk to you about…
- I chose to work on / to study / to check if…
- The issue / key question I chose to work on is…
- To begin with, I'd like to talk about…
- Have you ever wondered if…?
- My objective today is…
- I've always been interested in…, that's why…

Présenter votre méthode de travail :

- I gathered different information / documents from…
- I collected data about… on the Internet / thanks to a survey.
- I studied the impact of… on…
- I checked if…
- I undertook an experiment on…
- I compared… with… to deduce / conclude that…
- I made / produced a connected object for…
- I created a poster / a flyer / a newspaper article about…
- I used a software programme called…
- I used scientific / digital tools / methods, like…
- I controlled the results I got thanks to… and concluded that…

Exposer vos arguments :

- First / secondly / then…
- Most importantly…
- The main thing is…

Exprimer la cause et la conséquence :

- Therefore…
- Consequently…
- As a result…
- That's why…

Résumer :

- All in all…
- To sum it up…
- What can be / I understood from this document is that…
- What I mean / the author means is that…
- What you have to understand is that…
- If you see / know what I mean…
- To put it more simply…
- To make things easier…
- To make it easier to understand…
- What I mean is…

Reformuler :

- Let me rephrase this.
- To put it differently…
- It's as if I told you to…
- How shall I put this / explain this to you?
- Let me give you an example.
- As I see it…
- As the author puts it / writes / says…
- This sentence / word / expression means that…

Conclure :

- Finally / To conclude, I want to show that…
- My conclusion is that…
- Last but not least…
- To put it in a nutshell…
- To cut a long story short…
- Then, and finally, to conclude…

Interagir avec le jury :

- I agree with you…
- I see eye to eye with you…
- I share your point of view…
- This is exactly what I meant to say…
- That's very interesting…
- Well, I must say that you have a point!

LEXIQUE Anglais-Français

www.lienmini.fr/htr7-01
Lexique Français-Anglais

A

abuse (n.): maltraitance
accountability (n.): responsabilité, fait de rendre des comptes
achieve (v.): accomplir, réaliser
achievement (n.): exploit, réussite
acknowledge (v.): reconnaître (que)
activist (n.): militant(e)
address an issue (v.): s'occuper d'un problème
admiring (adj.): admiratif(ve)
advertisement, advert, ad (n.): publicité (support papier)
advertise (v.): faire de la publicité, faire la promotion de
advertising (n.): publicité, communication (campagne)
advertising campaign (n.): campagne de publicité
advice (n.): conseil(s)
affect (v.): toucher, influer sur
affordable (adj.): abordable, pas trop cher(ère)
agree (v.): être d'accord, accepter
agreement (n.): accord
Artificial Intelligence, AI (n.): intelligence artificielle
anxiety (n.): anxiété, angoisse
ancestor (n.): ancêtre, aïeul(e)
applicant (n.): candidat, postulant
apply (for a job) (v.): postuler (à un emploi)
artwork (n.): œuvre d'art
assault (n.): attaque, agression
assembly line (n.): chaîne de montage
audience (n.): public, audience
Augmented Reality, AR (n.): réalité augmentée
available (adj.): disponible
aware (adj.): conscient(e) de, vigilant(e)
awareness campaign (n.): campagne de sensibilisation

B

balanced (adj.): équilibré(e)
ban (n. / v.): interdiction, exclusion / interdire, exclure
be (wrongfully) accused of sth / V-ing (exp.): être accusé(e) (à tort) de qqch / d'avoir fait qqch
be acquitted (adj.): être acquitté(e)
be addicted to (adj.): être accro à
be allowed to (adj.): être autorisé(e) à
be brought to justice (adj.): être traduit(e) en justice
be charged with (adj.): être accusé(e) de
be depicted as (adj.): être dépeint(e) comme
be filled with horror (exp.): être empli(e) d'horreur / d'effroi
be laid off / fired (adj.): être renvoyé(e), licencié(e)
be prejudiced (against) (adj.): avoir des préjugés (contre)
be taken aback (adj.): être pris(e) de court
be under close surveillance (exp.): être sous étroite surveillance
be under watch / monitored / surveilled (exp.): être surveillé(e) / contrôlé(e)
believe (v.) **in oneself / sb / sth**: croire en soi / qqn / qqch
beneficial (to sb) (adj.): bénéfique (à qqn), avantageux(se)
benefit from (v.): bénéficier de, profiter de
benefits (n.): profit, bénéfice ; avantage
bias (n.): préjugé
biased (adj.): partial(e)
bold (adj.): audacieux(se) ; effronté(e)
booming (adj.): en plein essor, prospère
boost (v.): pousser, encourager, stimuler
brand (n.): marque
brand image (n.): image de marque
brave (adj.): courageux(se)
break the glass ceiling (exp.): briser le plafond de verre
breakthrough (n.): percée, découverte majeure
bridge the gap (exp.): combler un écart ; faire l'affaire
broadcast (v.): diffuser, retransmettre
broadcasting (n.): l'audiovisuel
bully (v.): brutaliser, harceler
burnout (n.): épuisement (professionnel)

C

campaign (v.): mener une campagne, faire campagne
canvas (n.): toile
carbon footprint (n.): empreinte carbone
care (n. / v.): soin / s'occuper de
career (n.): carrière
career path (n.): carrière professionnelle
carer, caregiver (n.): soignant(e) ; aidant(e)
caring (adj.): attentionné(e)
CCTV (closed-circuit television) (n.): vidéosurveillance
celebrate (v.): fêter
celebration (n.): fête
celestial body (n.): corps céleste
censorship (n.): censure
challenge (n. / v.): défi / défier ; poser un problème
charity (n.): association caritative
Chief Executive Officer (CEO) (n.): président-directeur général (PDG)
Chief Happiness Officer, Director of Happiness (n.): directeur général du bonheur, responsable du bien-être au travail
child labour (n.): travail des enfants
childcare (n.): garde d'enfants, crèche
chip (n.): puce électronique
Christianity (n.): christianisme
citizenship (n.): citoyenneté
civil rights (n.): droits civiques
Civil Rights Movement (n.): mouvement pour les droits civiques
claim (v.): réclamer
cliché (n.): cliché, préjugé
client (n.): client(e) (pour un service)
climate crisis (n.): crise climatique
clock in / clock out (v.): pointer (à l'entrée ou à la sortie du travail)
close to (adj.): proche de
close-up (n.): gros plan
coder (n.): codeur(euse)
collect (v.): récupérer ; encaisser
commercial (n.): publicité (support audiovisuel)
commitment (n.): engagement
committed (adj.): engagé(e)
commodity (n.): produit, marchandise
common good (n.): bien commun
community-based (adj.): communautaire
commute (n. / v.): trajet (n.) / faire la navette (entre son domicile et son travail)
company (n.): entreprise
component (n.): composant
conflict (n.): conflit
connection (n.): connexion
conquer (v.): conquérir, vaincre
consume (v.): consommer
consumer (n.): consommateur(trice)

consumer society (n.): société de consommation
contaminated (adj.): contaminé(e)
controversial (adj.): controversé(e), polémique
convey (v.): transmettre
cope (with) (v.): surmonter, faire face (à)
corporate ladder (n.): échelons d'une entreprise
corporate tax rate (n.): taux d'imposition des entreprises
corporate world (n.): monde de l'entreprise
counterfeit (n. / v.): contrefaçon / contrefaire, falsifier
court of justice (n.): tribunal
coworking (n.): cotravail, coworking
crackdown (n.): répression
create bonds (v.): créer des liens
crowdfunding (n.): financement participatif
crunch time (n.): moment décisif
cure (v.): guérir (qqn)
currency (n.): devise (financière)
customer (n.): client(e) (pour un produit)
customise (v.): personnaliser
cut oneself off from (v.): s'isoler de
cyberbullying (n.): cyberharcèlement

D

data (n. pl.): données
deadly (adj.): mortel(le)
deal (n.): accord, transaction
dedicate oneself to (v.): se dévouer à
dedicated (adj.): dévoué(e), consacré(e)
delete (v.): effacer, supprimer
demand equal rights (exp.): réclamer l'égalité des droits
demonstrate (v.): manifester
demonstration (n.): manifestation
denounce (v.): dénoncer
deprived (adj.): défavorisé(e)
desecration (n.): profanation
despoil (v.): déposséder
detrimental (to) (adj.): néfaste, préjudiciable (à)
developer (n.): développeur(se)
devote (time) to (v.): consacrer (du temps) à
diabetes (n.): diabète
digital (adj.): numérique
digital nomadism (n.): nomadisme numérique
digitally-created (adj.): généré(e) virtuellement
disability (n.): handicap
discard (v.): jeter
discriminate against (v.): faire de la discrimination contre
disease (n.): maladie
dismantle (v.): démonter
display (n. / v.): vitrine / exposer
do business with (exp.): faire affaire avec
doctor (n.): médecin
drinking water (n.): eau potable
dump site (n.): décharge publique
duty of remembrance (n.): devoir de mémoire
dystopia (n.): dystopie
dystopian (adj.): dystopique

E

e-sport event (n.): événement sportif en ligne
e-waste (n.): DEEE (déchets d'équipements électriques et électroniques)
earn (v.): gagner, toucher (argent, salaire)
earn a living (exp.): gagner sa vie
Earth (n.): la Terre
eco-conscious (adj.): sensible à l'environnement
eco-friendly (adj.): écologique, respectueux(se) de l'environnement
educate (v.): éduquer
educational (adj.): éducatif(ve)
efficient (adj.): efficace
electronic device (n.): appareil électronique
emergency room, ER (n.): salle des urgences
employ (v.): employer
employee (n.): employé(e)
employer (n.): employeur
empowering (adj.): émancipateur(trice)
endanger (v.): mettre en danger
endorsement (n.): approbation, soutien
enhance (v.): améliorer
entertaining (adj.): divertissant(e)
entertainment (n.): divertissement ; spectacle
entertainment industry (n.): industrie du divertissement
entrepreneur (n.): homme / femme d'affaires
equity (n.): égalité
ethical (adj.): éthique
ethics (n.): éthique, morale
exhausted (adj.): épuisé(e)
exhibition (n.): exposition
expand (v.): étendre, (se) répandre
expensive (adj.): cher(ère)
experience hunger (v.): ressentir la faim

F

facial recognition (n.): reconnaissance faciale
factory (n.): usine
fail (v.): échouer
fairly (adv.): équitablement
fake (adj.): faux, contrefait(e)
fat (adj. / n.): gras(se) / graisse
feminist (adj.): féministe
fiber (n.): fibres (alimentaires)
fight for / against (v.): lutter pour / contre
fill one's heart with (exp.): emplir son cœur de
firm (n.): entreprise
fitness (n.): forme physique
fix (v.): réparer
flexibility (n.): souplesse, flexibilité
flexible hours (n.): horaires flexibles
flexible schedule (n.): emploi du temps flexible
food insecurity (n.): précarité alimentaire
forbid (v.): interdire, empêcher
foreboding (n.): (mauvais) pressentiment
foreign (adj.): étranger(ère)
fracking (n.): fracturation hydraulique
franchise (n.): franchise
front line (n.): front, première ligne
frontier (n.): frontière
full-time (adj.): à temps plein

G

garbage dump (n.): décharge publique
gender (n.): genre
gender cliché (n.): cliché sexiste
gender pay gap (n.): inégalité de salaires entre hommes et femmes
gender-based discrimination (n.): discrimination en raison du genre

genuine (adj.): authentique
get a promotion / a raise (exp.): obtenir une promotion / une augmentation
get access to (v.): accéder à
give access (v.): donner accès
goal (n.): but
go hiking (v.): faire de la randonnée
go on a trip (v.): partir en voyage
go sightseeing (v.): faire du tourisme
greed (n.): convoitise
greenhouse gases (n.): gaz à effet de serre
greenwashing (n.): discours écologique de façade, écoblanchiment

H

handle (v.): manier, manipuler
hard power (adj. / n.): pouvoir de contrainte
harm (v.): nuire, faire du mal
harmful (adj.): dangereux(se), nuisible
harvest (v.): récolter
have access to (v.): accéder à
have legal value (exp.): avoir une valeur juridique
have the time of one's life (exp.): s'amuser comme jamais, s'éclater *(fam.)*
hazardous (adj.): dangereux(se)
head-up display (n.): affichage frontal / tête haute
heal (v.): soigner
health (n.): santé
healthcare worker (n.): personnel soignant
healthy (adj.): en bonne santé
heartbeat (n.): battement de cœur
heritage (n.): héritage, patrimoine
heritage site (n.): site classé (patrimonial)
hire (v.): recruter
hoax (n.): canular
holiday(s) (UK): vacances
hospital staff (n.): personnel hospitalier
hub (n.): plateforme, plaque tournante
human rights (n.): droits de l'homme
human waste (n.): déchets humains, excréments
humanitarian project (n.): projet humanitaire
hygiene (n.): hygiène

I

iconic (adj.): iconique, emblématique
ill-health (n.): mauvaise santé
illness (n.): maladie
implement (v.): mettre en œuvre
improve (v.): améliorer
in the open (adv.): à l'air libre
inclusiveness (n.): inclusion, non-discrimination
income (n.): revenu(s)
Indigenous (adj.): autochtone, local(e)
indoor plumbing (n.): sanitaire domestique, toilettes
inequity (n.): inégalité
infectious (adj.): infectieux(se), contagieux(se)
inhabitable (adj.): habitable
injury (n.): blessure
inspiring (adj.): inspirant(e), exaltant(e)
intelligence (n.): informations, renseignements (sur qqn)
interact (v.): interagir
invest (v.): investir
issue (n.): problème

J

journey (n.): voyage
junk food (n.): malbouffe
justice system (n.): système judiciaire

K

keep fit / healthy (exp.): se maintenir en forme

L

labelling (n.): étiquetage
landfill (n.): décharge
landing (n.): atterrissage
landscape, scenery (n.): paysage
launch (n. / v.): lancement / lancer
launchpad (n.): rampe de lancement
law (n.): loi ; droit
leader(ship) position (n.): position de leader / meneur
leather (n.): cuir
legislation (n.): loi
lethal (adj.): fatal(e), mortel(le)
life-changing (adj.): bouleversant(e), qui change la vie
lifelike (adj.): ressemblant(e), réaliste
lift-off (n.): décollage
lift off (v.): décoller
lift sb out of poverty (exp.): sortir qqn de la pauvreté
lockdown (n.): confinement
loneliness (n.): solitude
low income household (n.): foyer à bas revenus
lucrative (adj.): lucratif(ve), profitable

M

make a change (exp.): modifier, changer
make a difference (exp.): faire bouger les choses
make friends with sb (exp.): devenir ami(e) avec qqn
make sb's blood run cold (exp.): glacer le sang à qqn
manufacture (v. / n.): fabriquer / fabrication
marketing strategy (n.): stratégie marketing
mass production (n.): production de masse
maternity / paternity leave (n.): congé maternité / paternité
media empire (n.): empire médiatique
meet deadlines (exp.): tenir les délais
mental health challenge (n.): problème de santé mentale
mindset (n.): état d'esprit, mentalité
mining (n.): extraction minière
misinformation (n.): désinformation, fausse information
mislead (v.): induire en erreur, tromper
misogynist (n.): misogyne
misogynistic (adj.): misogyne, sexiste
monetise (v.): monétiser
monitor (v.): observer, surveiller
monopoly (n.): monopole
Moon (n.): la Lune
motivated (adj.): motivé(e)
move forward (v.): aller de l'avant

N

narrow-minded (adj.): étroit(e) d'esprit
Native (n. / adj.): autochtone / originaire (de)
nine-to-five job (n.): travail (à horaires) de bureau
non-profit (adj. / n.): non lucratif(ve) / bénévole
northern (adj.): du Nord
nurse (n.): infirmier(ère)
nurse station (n.): salle des infirmiers
nutritious (adj.): nutritif(ve)

O

obese (adj.): obèse
obesity (n.): obésité
office building (n.): immeuble de bureaux
oil drilling (n.): exploitation pétrolière
oil leak (n.): fuite de pétrole
old-fashioned (adj.): démodé(e)
online gaming (n.): jeu en ligne
open defecation: défécation en plein air
open-minded (adj.): ouvert(e) d'esprit
operating room, OR (n.): salle d'opération
orbit (n.): orbite
organic (adj.): bio(logique)
outdated (adj.): dépassé(e), obsolète
outdoors (adv.): à l'extérieur
overcome (v.): surmonter
overlooked (adj.): oublié(e), négligé(e)
overtourism (n.): tourisme de masse
overweight (adj.): en surpoids
overwork (n.): surcharge de travail
own (v.): posséder
ownership (n.): propriété

P

packaging (n.): emballage
paid time off (n): congé payé
pandemic (n.): pandémie
parade (n.): défilé
parental leave (n.): congé parental
part-time (adj.): à temps partiel
partnership (n.): partenariat
patrol (v.): patrouiller
pave the way for (exp.): ouvrir la voie à
pay rise (n.): augmentation de salaire
people(s) (n.): peuple(s)
personal interest (n.): intérêt personnel
physician (US) (n.): médecin
pioneer (n.): pionnier(ère)
pipeline (n.): oléoduc ; gazoduc
plant (n.): usine
point a finger at (exp.): pointer du doigt
policy (n.): législation, politique
pollute (v.): polluer
polluting (adj.): polluant(e)
portray (v.): représenter, décrire
power (n.): pouvoir
preconception (n.): stéréotype
prejudice (n.): préjugé
prejudiced (against) (adj.): avoir des préjugés (contre)
preserve (v.): protéger
pretend (v.): faire semblant
prevention (n.): prévention
privacy (n.): vie privée
prosecution (n.): poursuites judiciaires
processed (adj.): industriel(le), transformé(e)
processing waste (n.): traitement des déchets
product (n.): produit, marchandise
product placement (n.): placement de produit
productive (adj.): productif(ve)
productivity (n.): productivité
profitable (adj.): rentable
promote (v.): promouvoir
prophetic (adj.): prophétique, visionnaire
protein (n.): protéine
protest (n. / v.): protestation / protester
protest against (v): manifester contre
protest march (n.): manifestation
protest song (n.): chanson contestataire, engagée
provide (v.): fournir
purpose (n.): but
push the boundaries (exp.): repousser les limites
put an end to sth (exp.): faire cesser qqch
put sb under arrest (exp.): placer qqn en état d'arrestation

R

raise awareness (v.): éveiller les consciences
raise funds / money (v.): lever des fonds
rape (n. / v.): viol / violer
rare metal (n.): métal rare
raw materials (n.): matières premières
ready-to-eat (adj.): préparé(e), prêt(e)-à-manger
reclaim (v.): récupérer
recognise (v.): reconnaître
recognised (adj.): reconnu(e)
recycle (v.): recycler
regulation (n.): réglementation
release (n. / v.): sortie, parution / sortir (sur le marché / en salle)
reliable (adj.): fiable, digne de confiance
relocate (v.): déménager ; s'installer
remote / distant working (n.): télétravail
renewable (adj.): renouvelable
resale (n.): revente
resource (n.): ressource
respected (adj.): respecté(e)
responsibly (adv.): de façon responsable
rewarded (adj.): récompensé(e)
rewarding (adj.): gratifiant(e), enrichissant(e)
right the wrongs (exp.): réparer les torts
right to disconnect (n.): droit à la déconnexion
riot (n.): émeute
rocket (n.): fusée
role model (n.): modèle, exemple
rubber (n.): caoutchouc, gomme
rule (n.): règle

S

sacred (adj.): sacré(e)
safety (n.): sécurité
salary (n.): salaire
salty (adj.): salé(e)
sanitary (adj.): sanitaire, hygiénique
scientist (n.): scientifique
screen (v.): filtrer
scrubs (n.): blouses stériles
second-hand (adj.): d'occasion
segregation (n.): ségrégation, séparation
self-fulfilment (n.): épanouissement personnel
self-isolation (n.): auto-confinement
selfless (adj.): altruiste, généreux(se)
set up (a programme) (v.): mettre au point, installer (un programme)
settle (v.): s'installer ; régler ; se mettre d'accord

settlement (n.): installation, colonisation ; accord
settler (n.): colon
sewage (n.): eaux usées
sewer (n.): égout
sexism (n.): sexisme
shamrock (n.): trèfle
share (v.): partager
ship (v.): transporter ; expédier
shipment (n.): cargaison, marchandise
shorter hours (n.): diminution du temps de travail
shuttle (n.): navette
sick leave (n.): congé maladie
skill (n.): compétence, talent
skip meals (v.): sauter des repas
sneakerhead (n.): fan de chaussures de sport
social media / network (n.): réseau social
social inequalities (n.): inégalités sociales
socialise (v.): fréquenter des gens, avoir des relations
soft power (n. / adj.): pouvoir de convaincre, manière douce
solar system (n.): système solaire
sole (n.): semelle
southern (adj.): du Sud
sovereignty (n.): souveraineté
spaceship / spacecraft (n.): vaisseau spatial
spark sth (off) (v.): déclencher
spine-chilling (adj.): terrifiant(e), à glacer le sang
spot (v.): repérer
spread (v.): s'étendre, (se) répandre
stand trial (v.): comparaître en justice
stand up for (v.): défendre, se battre pour
stereotype (n.): stéréotype, cliché
strategic decision (n.): décision stratégique
street art (n.): art urbain
stressed (adj.): stressé(e), tendu(e)
strong-willed (adj.): résolu(e), déterminé(e)
struggle (n. / v.): combat, lutte / lutter
submissive (adj.): soumis(e), docile
subversive (adj.): subversif(ve)
succeed (v.): réussir
sue (v.): poursuivre en justice
sugar-free (adj.): sans sucre
sugary (adj.): sucré(e)
supplier (n.): fournisseur
supply chain (n.): chaîne logistique
support a cause (v.): soutenir une cause
surgeon (n.): chirurgien(ne)
surgical mask / gloves (n.): masque chirurgical / gants chirurgicaux
sustainability (n.): développement durable
sustainable (adj.): recyclable, durable
sweatshop (n.): atelier où l'on exploite la main-d'œuvre
sweet (adj.): doux(ce), sucré(e)

T

take a break (v.): faire une pause
take action (v.): agir, passer à l'action
take a trip (v.): partir en voyage
take leadership / take over (v.): prendre le pouvoir / le contrôle
take sth for granted (exp.): prendre qqch pour acquis
take to the streets (exp.): descendre dans la rue (pour manifester)
target (n. / v.): cible / cibler
team spirit (n.): esprit d'équipe
teleworking (n.): télétravail
territory (n.): territoire
threat (n.): menace
threaten (v.): menacer
three-dimensional, 3-D (adj.): en trois dimensions, en 3-D
thrive (v.): prospérer
toxic (adj.): toxique, nocif(ve)
torchbearer (n.): porte-flambeau, porte-drapeau *(fig.)*
trailblazer (n.): pionnier(ère), éclaireur(euse)
trauma (n.): traumatisme
travel by plane / by car / on boat / on foot (v.): voyager en avion / en voiture / en bateau / à pied
treaty (n.): traité
trial (n.): test ; procès
tribe (n.): tribu

U

unacceptable (adj.): inacceptable
unaffordable (adj.): inabordable, trop cher(ère)
unaware (adj.): non conscient(e) (de), ignorant(e) (de)
uncharted (adj.): inexploré(e)
underprivileged (adj.): défavorisé(e)
undertake (v.): entreprendre
undervalued (adj.): sous-estimé(e)
unhealthy (adj.): en mauvaise santé
uninhabitable (adj.): inhabitable
unite (v.): s'unir
unplug (v.): débrancher
unsanitary (adj.): peu hygiénique
upcycle (v.): donner une nouvelle vie à
user (n.): utilisateur(trice)

V

vacation (US): vacances
value (n.): valeur
valued (adj.): estimé(e)
Virtual Reality, VR (n.): réalité virtuelle

W

wage (n.): salaire
warn (v.): prévenir, alerter
warning (n.): alerte, alarme, avertissement
waterfall (n.): cascade
wear out (v.): s'user
weight gain / loss (n.): prise / perte de poids
weightlessness (n.): apesanteur
wonderful (adj.): merveilleux(se)
work etiquette (n.): règles de travail, protocole
work in shifts (v.): travailler par équipes
work longer hours (exp.): faire des heures supplémentaires, augmenter son temps de travail
work of art (n.): œuvre d'art
work station (n.): poste de travail
worker (n.): travailleur(se), salarié(e), employé(e)
working conditions (n.): conditions de travail
working days (n.): jours de travail
workplace (n.): lieu de travail
workweek (n.): semaine de travail
worth (n.): valeur

Z

zero gravity (n.): apesanteur

CRÉDITS ICONOGRAPHIQUES

Couv. Wharariki Beach, Puponga (Archway Islands), Nouvelle-Zélande ; **p. 8** Theo Wargo/WireImage/Getty Images ; **p. 9** PBS Newshour Weekend/Creative News Group ; **p. 10** Emka74/Shutterstock ; **p. 11** Charlie Neibergall/AP/SIPA ; **p. 12** www.statista.com/chart/17692/teenagers-favorite-clothing-and-footwear-brands ; **p. 13** Getty Images ; Niki Bern, 2013 ; **p. 14** Frank Leonhardt/dpa Picture-Alliance via AFP ; Vans-X-MOMA via Bestimage ; **p. 15** Whitten Sabbatini/The New York Times-REDUX/REA ; **p. 16** Boclips/TED ; **p. 17** Doug Mills/The New York Times-REDUX-REA ; **p. 18** Sotheby's via Bestimage ; **p. 19** John Iacono/Sports Illustrated via Getty Images ; **p. 21** Alamy/Randy Duchaine/Photo12 ; **p. 22** Jon Arnold Images/Hemis.fr ; **p. 23** Tourismireland.com ; **p. 24** Clodagh Kilcoyne/Getty Images ; Charles McQuillan/Getty Images ; **p. 25** Maia Kennedy/Alamy Live News/Photo12 ; **p. 26** Mecky/Getty Images ; **p. 27** Edwin Remsberg/Getty Images ; **p. 28** Photoshot/Aurimages ; Enda Bowe/British Broadcasting Corporation (BBC)/Hulu Originals/Element Pictures/Collection Christophel ; **p. 29** Kamil Zihnioglu/AP/SIPA ; **p. 30** Nicola K photos/Alamy/Photo12 ; **p. 33** Paul McErlane/Getty Images ; **p. 34** Interfoto/Alamy Banque d'images ; **p. 35** www.youtube.com/c/CharlotteHanRethinking ; **p. 36** Alamy/Sue Cunningham Photographic/Photo12 ; **p. 37** Rene Johnston/Toronto Star via Getty Images ; **p. 38** Angie Yeoh/Shutterstock ; **p. 39** David Simonds ; Julie Clopper/Getty Images ; **p. 40** Mrinal Pal/Shutterstock ; **p. 42** Stefani Reynolds-CNP/Newscom/SIPA ; **p. 43** Mindspace ; **p. 44** www.statista.com/chart/4279/the-gender-pay-gap-in-developed-nations-visualised ; Javier Larrea/Agefotostock ; **p. 45** Understanding Gender at Work: How to Use, Lose and Expose Blind Spots for Career Success Copyright © 2017 Delee Fromm/CTV ; **p. 46** UN Women ; **p. 47** AP/Sipa ; Office of the Prime Minister Justin Trudeau ; **p. 48** Focus Features/Kobal/REX/Shutterstock/Aurimages ; Pan Media Agency/FilmMagic/Getty Images ; **p. 49** Eric Thayer/REUTERS ; **p. 50** ABC Australian Broadcasting ; **p. 51** Matthew McDermott/Polaris/Starface ; **p. 53** Andrew Kelly/Reuters ; **p. 54** Getty Images ; **p. 55** BBC Studios ; **p. 56** The Riveter Dallas/DR ; Buffer & AngelList ; Buffer & AngelList ; **p. 57** Pavel Ilyukhin/Shutterstock ; **p. 58** M Swiet Productions/Getty Images ; **p. 59** Amanda Peterson Beadle, 24 Mai 2012 Thinkprogress.com ; Bryce Covert/Adam Peck, 30/07/2014, thinkprogress.com ; **p. 60** Dilbert © 2010 Scott Adams, Inc. Used by permission of Andrews McMeel Syndication. All rights reserved. ; Growth Engineering Ltd/Gallup ans Oswald, Proto & Sgroi ; **p. 61** Getty Images ; **p. 62** Alamy/PF (usna)/Photo12 ; **p. 63** Moe Zoyari/REDUX-REA ; **p. 65** J.D. Crowe/Cagle Cartoons ; **p. 66** UNICEF/UN055381/Manpreet Romana ; **p. 67** Gates Notes, LLC ; **p. 68** Andrea Bruce/NOOR ; Water.org ; **p. 69** Plan C Studios/Viacom18/BBQ_DFY/Aurimages ; **p. 70** CBS News/Veritone ; **p. 71** Wateraid World Toilet Day ; Martinera ; **p. 72** Alamy/Guillem Lopez/Photo12 ; **p. 73** Jack Jeffries/Who Gives A Crap ; **p. 75** Alamy/Ulrich Doering/Photo12 ; **p. 76** Pablo Monsalve/VIEWpress via Getty Images ; **p. 77** Focus Features/Kobal/REX/Shutterstock/Aurimages ; **p. 78** "Strange Fruit" © 2019 by Lloyd G. Wade @www.lloydgwade.com ; **p. 79** © Michael D'Antuono ArtandResponse.com ; **p. 80** Kadir Nelson/Rolling Stone ; Hyoung Chang/MediaNews Group/The Denver Post via Getty Images ; Luisa Ricciarini/Leemage/Bridgeman ; **p. 81** Vanessa Carvalho/ZUMA Press/ZUMA/REA ; Dave Whamond/CagleCartoons.com ; © 2020 Scott Stantis all rights reserved. Distributed by Tribune Content Agency ; **p. 82** Marvel/Walt Disney Studios Motion Pictures/Courtesy Everett Collection/Aurimages ; Everett Collection/Aurimages ; **p. 83** Erik Pendzich/REX/SIPA ; **p. 84** Morning Consult ; **p. 85** Ben & Jerry's ; **p. 87** Nicole Wandera/the omicollective ; **p. 88** SeventyFour/Shutterstock ; **p. 89** Regine Mahaux/Getty Images ; **p. 90** Brand, J. E., Jervis, J., Huggins, P. M., & Wilson, T. W. (2019). Digital Australia 2020. Eveleigh, NSW: IGEA. www.igea.net ; **p. 91** Fuse/Getty Image ; **p. 92** Getty Images ; **p. 94** Amblin Entertainment/Warner Bros/BBQ_DFY/Aurimages ; David Fisher/Shutterstok/SIPA ; **p. 96** : HstrongART/Shutterstock ; **p. 97** MR. Cole_Photographer/Getty Images ; U.S. Air Force photo by Sean M. Worrell ; **p. 98** Alvarez/Getty Images ; www.statista.com/chart/22392/global-revenue-of-selected-entertainment-industry-sectors ; **p. 101** Alamy/News/Photo12 ; **p. 102** Minh Uong ; **p. 103** © 2020 Common Sense Media. All rights reserved. Common Sense Education is a registered trademark of Common Sense Media ; **p. 104** PLEA Community Services Society of BC ; **p. 105** Bloomicon/Shutterstock ; Alamy/CJG -Technology/Photo12 ; **p. 106** Alexandra Popova/Shutterstock ; **p. 107** Ferrari/Starface ; **p. 109** Suzanne Kreiter/The Boston Globe via Getty Images ; McLittle Stock/Shutterstock ; **p. 111** Nick Sirotich ; **p. 112** Cory Disbrow/Getty Images ; **p. 113** PinPep/Cover Images/SIPA ; **p. 114** Walt Disney Pictures/Fairview Entertainment/ChristopheL ; **p. 115** Ron English American Depress: oil on canvas, 2007 ; **p. 116** Prod DB/Disney/DR ; **p. 117** Jesse Grant/Getty Images for Disney ; Walt Disney Studios Motion Pictures/© Marvel courtesy Everett Collection/Aurimages ; **p. 118** Dina Goldstein ; **p. 119** Matthew Baker/Getty Images ; Lucie Lang/Shutterstock ; **p. 120** Michael Loccisano/Getty Images ; **p. 122** Kathy Hutchins/Shutterstock ; **p. 125** Ward Sutton ; **p. 126** Red Production Company/BBC/Collection ChristopheL ; **p. 127** NHS ; Oli Scarff/AFP ; **p. 128** David Bukach/ABC/3AD/EnterMedia Contents/Shore Z Productions/Sony Pictures Television/Collection ChristopheL ; Adam Taylor/Fox/Courtesy Everett Collection/Aurimages ; Michael George/The New York Times-REDUX/REA ; **p. 129** Ron Tom/ABC/courtesy Everett Collection/Aurimages ; **p. 130** By permission of Steve Benson and Creators Syndicate, Inc. ; Steve Breen, The San Diego Union Tribune, © 2020 ; **p. 131** Stuart Martin/University Hospital Southampton/AFP ; We Fight Together/David Watkins ; **p. 132** Media Wales Ltd/Rob Browne ; **p. 133** Lipinksi Dominic/PA Photos/ABACA ; **p. 134** Chris Dorney/Shutterstock ; **p. 135** MDVIP ; **p. 137** Adam Zyglis ; **p. 138** Jacobs Stock Photography Ltd/Getty Images ; **p. 142** Collection Christophel © BBC One/Heyday Television/NBC Universal International Studios ; www.statista.com/chart/19256/the-most-surveilled-cities-in-the-world ; **p. 143** Photo by Anita Lasocka for www.no-cctv.org.uk ; **p. 144** ymgerman/Shutterstock ; Brian McFadden ; **p. 146** Alamy/Jacky Chapman/Photo12 ; **p. 147** UNESCO Bangkok ; Shalini Kantayya/7th Empire Media ; **p. 149** Alamy/Andriy Popov/Photo12 ; **p. 150-151** NASA ; **p. 152** Corbis/Getty Images ; **p. 153** Cathleen Allison/AP/SIPA ; **p. 154** Maciej Frolow/Getty Images ; Allan Sanders ; **p. 155** NASA ; **p. 156** NASA/JPL ; Steven Hobbs/Stocktrek Images/Getty Images ; **p. 157** NASA's Centennial Challenges/Images/AI. SpaceFactory ; **p. 158** Adrian Mann ; **p. 159** Pictures Ltd./Corbis via Getty Images ; Jonathan Newton/The Washington Post via Getty Images ; Loren Elliott/Getty Images ; **p. 161** Jon Carter/www.cartoonstock.com ; **p. 162** Per-Anders Pettersson/Getty Images ; **p. 163** © The Economist Newspaper Limited, London, 11th September 2018 ; **p. 164** Per-Anders Pettersson/Getty Images ; Alamy/Universal Images Group North America LLCDeAgostini/Photo12 ; **p. 165** Schalk van Zuydam/AP/SIPA ; **p. 166** Brendan Boughen/Cartoon Stock ; Temilade Adelaja/Reuters ; **p. 167** Alamy/Andrew McConnell/Photo12 ; **p. 168** Terry Mosher/Aislin ; **p. 169** MG Motor UK ; BBC Studios ; **p. 170**-171 Amnesty International ; **p. 173** Benjamin Lowy/Getty Images Reportage ; **p. 174** Alamy/Parkerphotography/Photo12 ; **p. 175** Institute for Food, Nutrition and Health, Working together to find solutions across the food system, University of Reading ; **p. 176** foodfoundation.org.uk ; **p. 177** image BROKER/Jochen Tack/Photo12 ; Health Matters ; Whole systems approach to obesity/Public Health England ; **p. 178** https://eatthemtodefeatthem.com/ ; Alamy/Colin McPherson/Photo12 ; **p. 179** Darren Fletcher/The Sun/News Licensing/ABACAPRESS.COM ; **p. 181** ShareAction/mistermunro.co.uk ; Alamy/Ashley Cooper/Photo12 ; **p. 182** Alamy/opturadesign/Photo12 ; www.thegoodmoodfood.com.au ; **p. 183** Public Health England in association with the Welsh Government, Food Standards Scotland and the Food Standards Agency in Northern Ireland © Crown copyright 2016 ; **p. 185** Alamy/Alex Segre/Photo12 ; **p. 186** Randriver/Getty Images ; **p. 187** National Congress of American Indians ; **p. 188** Alamy/Pacific Press Media Production Corp./Photo12 ; **p. 189** Nina Riggio ; **p. 190** Artwork by Jared Yazzie for Amplifier.org ; Photo courtesy of Amplifier featuring artwork by Shepard Fairey ; **p. 191** Carolyn Kaster/AP/SIPA ; **p. 192** EPA-EFE/Richard Wainwright ; **p. 193** BJ Warnick/Newscom/Alamy ; Glen Le Lievre ; **p. 194** TEDxFargo ; **p. 195** Photographer Wade Lewis and model Shantell Miskin ; Richard Lautens/Toronto Star via Getty Images ; **p. 196** C-SPAN ; **p. 197** Government of Canada ; **p. 199** Monte Wolverton/CagleCartoons.com

CRÉDITS TEXTES

p. 10 © Grailed.com, D.R. ; **p. 11** Kamala Harris, *what her sneakers mean*, Priya Elan, 3 September 2020 © Guardian News & Media Ltd 2021 ; **p. 12** November 12, 2019 © Stitch Fashion, D.R. ; **p. 13** Excerpt from *So Yesterday* by Scott Westerfeld, copyright © 2004 by Scott D. Westerfeld. Used by permission of Razorbill, an imprint of Penguin Young Readers Group, a division of Penguin Random House LLC. All rights reserved ; **p. 17** Stephen Yu, May 28, 2020 © Farfetech, D.R. ; **p. 18** Air Jordan 1 History Lesson, Nick Engvall, sneakerhistory.com ; **p. 19** May 18, 2020, © Reuters, D.R. ; Luke Denne, May 18, 2020 © Nbcnews.com ; **p. 26** www.tourismireland.com ; **p. 27** Paris Donnatella Callan © Ireland Before You ; **p. 28** Meredith Carey April 29, 2020 © Conde Nast Traveler ; **p. 29** Cristina Abellan Matamoros & Wolfgang Spindler, 20/03/2020 © Euronews ; **p. 30** April 10, 2018 © Founder Institute ; **p. 31** Jonathan Keane, What Apple's landmark court win against the EU means for Ireland, Published September 1, 2020 © CNBC Europe, www.cnbc.com ; **p. 36** Daniel Loeschen, June 28, 2019 © Mixer Direct, D.R. ; **p. 37** © SuccessStory.com, D.R. ; **p. 38** How Airbnb took over the world, Harriet Sherwood, 5 May 2019 © Guardian News & Media Ltd 2021 ; **p. 39** © www.ad-lister.co.uk, D.R. ; **p. 40** Leo Saini, October 20, 2019 © Medium, D.R. ; **p. 46** In New Zealand, we are starting to value women's work fairly. It's time for the world to follow, Julie Anne Genter, 8 March 2020, © Guardian News & Media Ltd 2021 ; **p. 51** Aria Bendix, December 12, 2020 © Business Insider, D.R. ; **p. 56** Euan Black, April 15, 2020 © The New Daily, D.R. ; **p. 57** Fancy working in paradise? Here's how you can live the dream, Shane Hickey, 23 August 2020, © Guardian News & Media Ltd 2021 ; **p. 58** Louise Hall, Monday 9 November 2020 © The Independent ; **p. 59** www.pewresearch.org ; **p. 60** Rachel Hill © HireHive.com ; **p. 61** Why having friends at work is so crucial for your success, Zameena Mejia, March 30, 2018, © cnbc.com ; **p. 62** © Feminists for life of America, D.R. ; **p. 68** James Estrin, September 4, 2018, © New York Times ; **p. 69** Akshay Kumar, November 13, 2017 © Guardian News & Media Ltd 2021 ; **p. 70** Closing the Water Access Gap in the United States: A National Action Plan Closing the Water Access Gap in the United States © DigDeep/US Water Alliance, 2020 ; **p. 72-73** © UNICEF ; **p. 78** "Strange Fruit", Paroles et musique : Lewis Allan © 1957 Edward B. Marks Music Co. ; **p. 82** © La Grande Afrique, February 24, 2018, D.R. ; **p. 83** Brooklyn White, June 20, 2018, hellogiggles.com ; Kelly Richman-Abdou and Sara Barnes, February 17, 2021, © My Modern MET, D.R. ; **p. 84** Eugene Y. Chan, August 21, 2020 © The Conversation, D.R. ; **p. 85** Becks Collins © The Marketing Society, D.R. ; **p. 91** Seb Joseph, December 7, 2020 © Digiday.com, D.R. ; **p. 92** 'Geek philanthropy': the gamers raising millions through marathon live streams, Patrick Lum, 28 February 2019 © Guardian News & Media Ltd 2021 ; **p. 93** AOC played Among Us and achieved what most politicians fail at: acting normal, Joshua Riveran, 22 October 2020 © Guardian News & Media Ltd 2021 ; **p. 94** Excerpt from *Ready Player One* by Ernest Cline, copyright © 2011 by Dark All Day, Inc. Used by permission of Crown Books, an imprint of Random House, a division of Penguin Random House LLC. All right reserved, D.R. ; **p. 95** © weebly.com, D.R. ; **p. 96** Hal Koss, February 3, 2020. Updated: May 19, 2020 © Builtin, D.R. ; **p. 99** Seb Joseph, December 1, 2020 © Digiday.com, D.R. ; **p. 104** © (consulted in March 2021) BulliesOut. All rights reserved ; **p. 105** © Watauga High School, D.R. ; **p. 106** Sean Herman, Oct. 30, 2020 © Forbes/Forbes Technology Council, D.R. ; **p. 107** Zamira Rahim, December 25, 2020, © Courtesy CNN ; Louise Matsakis, 02/15/2019 © wired.com ; **p. 108-109** Doug Bailey, August 14, 2017 © The Boston Globe, D.R. ; **p. 115** Aaron Schnoor, March 17, 2020 © BetterMarketing/Medium, D.R. ; **p. 121** (Couverture et texte) THE RIDE OF A LIFETIME: LESSONS LEARNED FROM 15 YEARS AS CEO OF THE WALT DISNEY COMPANY by Robert Iger, copyright © 2019 by Robert Iger. Used by permission of Random House, an imprint and division of Penguin Random House LLC. All rights reserved. ; **p. 123** (Graphique et texte) This article was published in Publication "Working for the Mouse", A survey of Disneyland Resort Employees. Peter Dreier/Daniel Flaming/Lucero Herrera/Martha Matsuoka/Jane Carlen/Patrick Burns, ISBN: 1021393202452, © Elsevier (2018) ; **p. 129** Lily Martis, March, 2020 © Monster, D.R. ; **p. 133** Ankur Sharma, MD, MPH, June 7, 2020, ©KevinMD.com, D.R. ; **p. 134** Profit over people, cost over care: America's broken healthcare exposed by virus, Amanda Holpuch, 16 April, 2020 © Guardian News & Media Ltd 202 ; **p. 140** From 1984 by Copyright © Eric Blair 1949 Copyright © The estate of the late Sonia Brownell Orwell 1987. Published by Martin Secker & Warburg Ltd 1994, 1950, 1987, Penguin Books 1954, 1989, 2008. Reproduced by permission of Penguin Books Ltd. © ; **p. 141** © 1951 by the Fortnightly Publishing Company, renewed 1979 by Ray Bradbury ; **p. 143** Ivana Davidovic © BBC News, 18 November 2019, www.bbc.com/news/business-50348861 ; **p. 145** Reproduced by permission of Australian Broadcasting Corporation, Library Sales, Nadia Daly © 2020 ABC ; **p. 146** It's not just A-levels, algorithms have a nightmarish new power over our lives, Arwa Mahdawi, 19 August, 2020 © Guardian News & Media Ltd 2021 ; **p. 152** © history.nasa.gov, D.R. ; **p. 153** Apollo 11 site should be granted heritage status, says space agency boss, Ian Sample, 19 July 2019 © Guardian News & Media Ltd 2021 ; **p. 155** Reprinted/adapted by permission from Springer Nature © 2019, Springer Nature Limited ; **p. 157** © 2017 by Olivia Koski, Jana Grcevich, and Guerilla Science, LLC. Used by permission of Penguin Books, an imprint of Penguin Publishing Group, a division of Penguin Random House LLC. All rights reserved ; **p. 159** Jasper Jolly, February 6, 2021 © Guardian News & Media Ltd 2021 ; **p. 164-165** Aimee Pearcy, October 24, 2019, © OneZero/Medium ; **p. 165** © CBS News. December 17, 2019 ; **p. 167** © World Economic Forum (weforum.org) ; **p. 168** Justine Calma, Dell pledges to make greener computers over the next decade, November 12, 2019 © The Verge.com ; **p. 176** Regina Keith, October 23, 2020, © The Conversation, D.R. ; **p. 177** Cancer Research UK, www.cancerresearchuk.org, Last reviewed 25 January 2021 ; **p. 179** UK to ban all online junk food advertising to tackle obesity, Mark Sweney, 10 November 2020 © Guardian News & Media Ltd 2021 ; **p. 180** © Supermarket Perimeter, July 2020. www.nxtbook.com/sosland/sp/2020_07_01/index.php#/p/14 ; **p. 182** March 11, 2020 © HelloTech, D.R. ; **p. 188** Will Peischel, July 6, 2020 © Mother Jones ; **p. 189** Their greed is gonna kill us: Indian Country fights against more fracking, Cody Nelson in Santa Fe, New Mexico, 10 June 2020 © Guardian News & Media Ltd 2021 ; **p. 191** I'll be fierce for all of us: Deb Haaland on climate, Native rights and Biden, Nina Lakhani, 27 December 2020 © Guardian News & Media Ltd 2021 ; **p. 192** © BBC News, 9 December 2020 ; **p. 194** Chelsey Burnside, 19 Nov. 2020 © Local Love.ca ; **p. 195** Indigenous fashion is the future. It's time for First Nations people to reclaim it, Guardian Australia, 19 November 2020, © Guardian News & Media Ltd 2021 ; **p. 196** Gregory Scruggs, May 1, 2019 © Thomson Reuters Foundation, D.R. ; **p. 197** Edited on 2011, Update on 2017, © Courtesy of the Canadian Encyclopedia, Historica Canada, www.thecanadianencyclopedia.ca.

Malgré nos efforts, nous n'avons pu joindre certains ayants droit. Des droits usuels leur sont réservés en comptabilité.